Love in a Time of Hate

Love in a Time of Hate

Liberation Psychology in Latin America

NANCY CARO HOLLANDER

RUTGERS UNIVERSITY PRESS
New Brunswick, New Jersey

Library of Congress Cataloging-in-Publication Data

Hollander, Nancy Caro, 1939–
    Love in a time of hate : liberation psychology in Latin America /
Nancy Caro Hollander.
      p. cm.
    Includes bibliographical references and index.
    ISBN 0-8135-2425-3 (alk. paper). — ISBN 0-8135-2426-1 (pbk. :
alk. paper)
    1. Refugees, Political—Mental health—Latin America. 2. Victims
of state-sponsored terrorism—Mental health—Latin America.
3. Political persecution—Latin America—Psychological aspects.
4. Psychologists—Latin America—Psychology. 5. Psychoanalysis—
Latin America—Psychology. I. Title.
RC451.4.P57H65   1997
616.85'21—dc21   97-9639
                                                                CIP

British Cataloging-in-Publication information available

Manufactured in the United States of America

To Mimi
siempre presente

It is memory, both conscious and subconscious, which to a large extent constructs our present reality, and it is out of memory that identity and myth are mediated. . . .

Traumatic memory . . . sadly and unnecessarily all too often is "relived" in isolation. This reliving can be relentless and seems brought on in part by a desire to find or attach meaning to events which by virtue of their horrific nature, are at a certain level "unspeakable." Each voice is but a fragment, each of you a momentary witness. Together we constitute a "chorus," an incomplete one, but a chorus nevertheless.

—FRANZISKA ROSENTHAL LOUW, *on the wall of a temporary artistic exhibition at Ellis Island:* Passages: Jewish Women's Immigration and Family History, *April 1995.*

Contents

Acknowledgments

My DEEPEST GRATITUDE goes to Mimi Langer, whose comradeship I will treasure always. She was a brilliant psychoanalyst, with an astute understanding of people that gave her commitment to progressive political struggles a uniquely compassionate and practical sensibility. I thank her for having included me in her family of friends, for her dedication to telling her part of this story, and for paying close attention to the personal as well as the political in all that she did. I owe a profound debt, as well, to the other protagonists of this book, who in courageously revealing intimate details of their personal feelings as well as their intellectual perceptions about complex and difficult subject matters, helped to bring life and vitality to the story that unfolds in these pages. A very special thanks to Juan Carlos and Silvia for constant friendship and solidarity, for warm hospitality during my many trips to Buenos Aires, for our 3 A.M. animated (and often hilarious) discussions of psychoanalysis, Peronism, *el movimiento*, and the contemporary global crisis, all of which were delicious intellectual feasts. Thanks also to Yamila and Roman for their gracious tolerance of my invasion of their living space and for being the very best of the next generation. To Julia, whose integrity and honesty I admire and whose friendship I value, a grateful thanks for our warm and fascinating discussions in Buenos Aires, Los Angeles, and San Francisco.

I am also extremely grateful for the collaboration of many other Latin American mental-health compañeros; they are too numerous to mention, but special thanks go to Nacho Maldonado, Silvia Berman, Gilberta Royer de Garcia Reinoso, Miguel and Mirta Matrajt, Armando Bauleo, and Marta de Brasi, as well as to Alicia Stolkiner, Patricia Escalante, and the other members of the Internationalist Team of Mental Health Workers, Mexico-Nicaragua. And for filling in important pieces of the puzzle, additional thanks to Graciela Fernández Meijide, Laura Conti, Marcelo and Elizabeth Biancheti, Janine Puget, Maria L. Polento, Antonio Barutia, Hernán Kesselman, and Edmundo

Zimmerman. To Ana, Martin, Tomás, and (especially) Veronica Langer, my appreciation for candid discussions about their experiences as the children of Mimi Langer and for helping me to know their mother better.

On this side of the border, I am grateful for the love and support of my family and friends, which sustained me during the exhilarating moments as well as the self-doubt and mini-crises of writing this book. I am deeply appreciative to my husband, Steve, for his intelligence and his commitment to the values of this project, his enduring love through the years, our critical discussions—often in the wee hours—about psychoanalysis and social change, and his unfailing technological expertise, which rescued me when through my own ineptitude my computer threatened to eradicate entire chapters of this book. I am eternally indebted to my son, Rafa, in more ways than I can say, but especially for his comforting presence during the past several years when we kept each other company—he doing his homework and I writing this book—and when, because of his talent at sports, he liberated me from my study to enjoy the exciting and happy experience of being a "soccer mom."

To my intellectual and political sister, Susan Gutwill, I am profoundly grateful for our years of scholarly work together, which has helped me hone my psychoanalytic, political, and feminist understanding, for her careful and helpful readings of the various drafts of this book, and for our deeply personal commitment to one another, which sustains us through the long-distance challenges of a bicoastal friendship. To Stephanie Solomon, my heartfelt appreciation for our close, chosen family bonds, for her many intellectual gifts—including an incisive social and feminist consciousness, which makes her a dynamite jazz singer—and for her enthusiastic support of my work. To my friends Karra Bikson, Lisa Aronson, Marvin and Kathy Traeger, Ken Cloake and Joan Goldsmith, Diane Fletcher-Hoppe, Beth Farb, Herb Schreier, and Judy Stacey, I am indebted for important excursions into Marxism, neoliberalism, psychoanalysis, Buddhism, and postmodernism, which sharpened my analytic skills, cushioned the otherwise lonely task of writing, and reconfirmed our visions of a humane world. To my colleague Latin Americanist Marjorie Bray, my gratitude for contributing her astute editorial skills during the writing of the several final drafts of the manuscript and for helping to make the text accessible to readers with little background in Latin American studies or psychoanalysis. To my editors at Rutgers University Press, I owe thanks, first to Karen Reeds for her encouragement of this project and of my shift from academic discourse to a "reader-friendly" narrative style that is more evocative and experience-near, and second to Leslie Mitchner for her enthusiastic and creative contributions in the book's final stages. To my copyeditor, Pamela Fischer, my appreciation for her intelligent and discerning attention to detail in the editing of the final manuscript.

This book germinated for over a decade, but the preparation for it began long before. I would like to thank my friends and colleagues in Latin America who helped me learn about the warmth and passion of their cultures. Special gratitude goes to Juanita and Daniel Pereyra, Carlos Perez, Inez Hercovich, Gabriella Cristeller, Angela Pazarin, Lili Massafero, and Omar Cabezas, who brought me directly in touch with popular culture, peoples' struggles, and feminism in their countries. North of the border, I owe an immeasurable debt to my compañeros in Lucha Films, with whom I learned to transmit through the dramatic medium of film the beauty and tragedy that is Latin America. I also thank Blase and Teresa Bonpane and other friends in the Office of the Americas; our shared community activism since the early 1980s related to Central America and the Caribbean has deepened my understanding of the social turmoil and the U.S. role in the region. My gratitude, as well, to free-speech Pacifica radio (KPFK-FM in Los Angeles), where for fifteen years I produced and hosted a biweekly radio program that required my continual interaction with political activists, academics, and psychoanalysts from Latin America, which gave me the opportunity to keep my finger on the pulse of social and political developments throughout the continent. Finally, I thank my teachers, supervisors, and fellow candidates at the Psychoanalytic Center of California, who have imparted to me their serious and respectful commitment to the craft of psychoanalysis.

Love in a Time of Hate

Introduction

Elaborating Liberation Psychology

I feel
in my bones
the bones
of those
who once were.
In me,
they are
skeletons,
we are
what I am,
I am
those who were
yesterday.

—MAURICIO ROSENCOF, "On Suffering, Song, and White
Horses," in Saúl Sosnowski and Louise B. Popkin, eds.,
Repression, Exile, and Democracy (1993)

THE WORLD'S ATTENTION has been focused for several years on the civil strife
that has torn societies apart from Bosnia to Rwanda. We have watched in horror the destructive impulses unleashed in ethnic cleansing and tribal hatreds
that caused the rape, torture, and murder of hundreds of thousands of men,
women, and children. We have also witnessed the daunting task of bringing
to justice those guilty of crimes against humanity. How do we understand the
human capacity to inflict and endure such violence? How do we comprehend
its toll on the human spirit? Is it possible to live through the trauma of extreme violation of human rights and sustain hope and faith in human goodness and our capacity to build loving and creative social bonds?

This book addresses these questions within the context of another kind
of war, one that has been less visible to most of us in the United States. This
story takes place in Latin America and describes the psychological impact on
people who are forced to live in the culture of fear imposed by terrorist states.
It is told through the lives of ten politically progressive Argentine, Chilean,

I

and Uruguayan psychoanalysts and psychologists who, along with millions of their compatriots, were victims of the brutal military dictatorships that ruled their countries during the 1970s and 1980s. These military regimes unleashed a war of ideological cleansing aimed at silencing all critical discourse and political dissent among their own citizens. The protagonists of this book and their families survived the gross violation of human rights during the era of state terror. But today they live in its legacy with other Latin Americans whose cultures are being corroded by the social violence that accompanies the ever-increasing gap between the privileged elites and the disenfranchised majority.

The story unfolds through the individual experiences of these ten women and men, whose professional training and social sensibilities enable them to illuminate various aspects of the psychology of political repression. They help us understand the nature of the psychological tools used by authoritarian states to achieve political domination over their citizens as well as the psychological defenses people mobilize in their efforts to adapt to the rules of a repressive society. In sharing their lives with us, these ten women and men also help us appreciate the psychology of courage that enables individuals to stand up for what they believe and to join with others in challenging repressive governments. Their personal experiences and astute psychological observations show us how human beings can transcend the devastation of traumatic loss to find joy in even the smallest triumphs within the struggle for social justice. Perhaps their insights will help us understand more about our own psychological responses to the growing social violence here in the United States, itself a manifestation of deteriorating economic conditions and political disenchantment.

One of the themes in our protagonists' discourse is the psychological difficulty human beings experience when dealing with the reality of violence. Many of us are inclined to deny its existence or its impact on us. This theme emerges in the book in the context of my analysis of the political struggles in contemporary Latin America between those who wish to forget—deny—what took place during the years of military dictatorship and those who assert the need to recognize and remember the truth of what occurred, no matter how disturbing, in the hope that understanding it will prevent its recurrence. I have personally experienced the tension between these two positions in the process of writing this book, aspects of which have been painful to detail. In this regard, I have been reminded of a game my son, Rafael, and I would play when he was a child of two and a half, practicing the developmental achievement of distinguishing between reality and fantasy. It would begin with his telling me a fanciful account of something that had occurred during his day. He would enthusiastically weave his tale, always a fascinating mixture of reasonable-sounding and fantastic elements. When he finished, I would play my role by looking very surprised and asking, "Rafa, did that *really* happen?" To which he would cock his head, shake his finger, and impishly respond, "Naaaah, Mama, that not happen," triumphant in his knowledge that most of his story was the product of imagination, not reality. I have often wished that many of the events described in these pages had existed only in the realm of fantasy and that, like my child with me, I could declare to the reader that they really did not happen. I daresay we would all be relieved.

But, alas, this is not the case. In fact, I recognize that at such moments, like millions of Latin Americans, I engage in the wish to disavow a traumatic reality because it seems too difficult to face. But, like other millions of Latin Americans, I am more committed to the opposite desire, which is to acknowledge the truth and to bear witness to its devastating reality, in the hope that doing so may contribute to the struggle against its repetition. Admittedly, this is a continuous challenge given that the violation of human rights continues in similar and different ways throughout Latin America and in many other parts of the world today. To my son, who is now twelve years old, and to all his generation, we owe our efforts to help them know the truth in a way that empowers them to change the world for the better.

How did I come to write this particular version of the story of Latin American political repression and the struggle against it? Although its genesis is undoubtedly a complex one, I trace its specific antecedents to a pivotal—and decentering—experience I had in the summer of 1981, when, as a professor of Latin American history and women's studies, I went to Madrid on a research project, the consequences of which were unforeseen.

Madrid, Spain: July 1981

I sat in the cool interior of El Portalon, a café-bar in the heart of old Madrid during a sweltering, late mid-summer afternoon. The walls were covered with dramatically colorful Latin American solidarity posters exalting peoples' struggles and condemning military dictatorships in the Americas. In the background played the music of the Latin American New Song movement, a soulful denunciation of the forces that wound the human spirit and its rousing affirmation of the capacity to battle against them. The bar had been the inspiration of my good friend Juanita Pereyra, who, she'd happily announced to me by phone a year earlier, had come upon "the perfect solution" to surviving financially in exile far from her Argentine homeland while providing the Latin American refugee community with a gathering place to keep alive a sense of continuity with the political culture left behind.

I had come to Madrid in the summer of 1981 to research an article I hoped would contribute to the growing feminist literature on class and gender determinants of female political activism. To this end, I was to interview Argentine women who had been members of the radical organizations that had mobilized a mass movement in the early 1970s to demand a redistribution of power and wealth in their country. These women had been forced into exile following the bloody military coup in 1976 that had unleashed a violent war against the Argentine civilian population. My research would be a sequel to the history of Argentine women I had written when I lived in Buenos Aires between 1969 and 1974. It would also take up several themes addressed in the documentary film *Communiqué from Argentina* which a group of colleagues and I had made in the mid-seventies. The film, which portrays the complexities of Argentine radical politics through the life of a prominent female activist from the Peronist left, had been completed in late 1976, shortly after the coup. By that time, the film's protagonist was exiled in Madrid and the censorship policies of the military government prevented its release in Argentina. Because of their commitment to social change, some of the women who appear in the film were among the tens of thousands who disappeared or were murdered by the military. Other colleagues and friends I had known for years in Argentina suffered the same fate. Thus I came to this meeting in Madrid with research interests that were deeply affected by the fact that, like many Argentines, I had lost people I cared about to the soldiers' machine guns and the torturers' weapons.

El Portalon had not yet opened for the evening when the women began to trickle in slowly. They congregated at tables to chat together, as each waited her turn to talk with me. Some of them I had known in Argentina years before, others in Madrid during past visits, and still others I was meeting for the first time. They ranged in age from their mid-twenties to their late forties, their strikingly attractive Mediterranean features and fashionably informal dress revealing nothing to the casual observer of the horrendous circumstances of their recent pasts. Enthusiastically, I set about to begin my research. I initiated the first two or three interviews with a brief summary of my purpose for meeting with them, explaining that I was investigating issues that were of concern to feminist scholars and activists in many countries: What, I wondered, was their point of view about the role of women in revolutionary struggles? Could they tell me about how, as radicals interested in fashioning a new social order in Latin America, they conceptualized the relative weight of feminist concerns as against the more general political problems of class exploitation and underdevelopment? Could they talk about their own experience with the contradictions between their organizations' formal endorsement of a feminist agenda and the sexist attitudes and behavior of their male compañeros?

Each woman attempted, with difficulty as I realized later, to begin responding to the questions I posed. But each one's narrative eventually led us far afield. As I think back, I cannot recall the moment at which I began to shift my attention from my original interest to new ones that emerged from the women's testimonials. I do remember how I began to feel as I listened to them speak about what were, from their point of view, the salient themes to address: the horrific events that had turned their lives upside down during their final weeks and months in Argentina and the profound emotional and social rupture forced exile had meant to them.

As the sun set and the evening sky began to dim El Portalon's interior, I became aware that eventually, as I met with each woman, I did not even raise my original questions. I simply followed as one after another led me through a personal chronicle of the horrendous fate that had befallen her in the aftermath of the coup, when each had become a target of the military junta. Some of the women had been political activists, others had not, a fact that seemed to make little difference with regard to the violence they suffered at the hands of military and paramilitary forces. As I listened to their narratives, I began to lose my equanimity; I could not think of what to ask or say, or how to process what I was being told. Why, I puzzled vaguely, did all this seem so new? And what was I feeling so confused about? After all, by now I was quite familiar with the contours of the military's assault on the civilian population, which purposefully cast a repressive net over political activists and apolitical citizens alike.

I think I knew at the time that it was important to these women to tell their stories, to testify before a witness about the egregious violations they had suffered. How else could they have stood talking about it? Some spoke haltingly, staring directly into my eyes; several talked rapidly, as if there were not enough time to tell all; and others spoke in hushed tones, looking away as if to hide from the impact of their terrible words. Some fidgeted incessantly, others chain smoked, and a few seemed to go limp as their words came. One woman told of having to abandon her children to relatives as she frantically scrambled to elude the military forces stalking her from house to house; another revealed how, as she walked along the wide avenues of Buenos Aires, she was kidnapped by hooded men leaping out at her from one of the infamous unmarked Ford Falcons used by the right-wing death squads, only to be left for dead on a remote country road after being tortured and raped in one of the government's clandestine concentration camps; another spoke of having been sought by military forces who, bursting into her home without a warrant and finding only her younger brother, kidnapped him instead, torturing and killing him for no reason in particular; yet another told of being forced to watch while prison guards tortured her elderly parents in order to secure information she did not have; and one reported how, when her pregnant daughter suddenly vanished, clearly the victim of a military or death-squad action, her endless searches for her daughter and grandchild had yielded nothing but a gaping hole in her heart; many told of having narrowly escaped similar fates before they were forced to flee into the uncertainty and dislocation of exile. The stories went on like this for hours.

The more I heard, the more shocked, enraged, and saddened I felt by their pain and suffering. I also felt baffled by a dimension of their experience that I could not understand enough to interpret. I began to see that in spite of my initial impression there were marked differences among them, barely visible beneath the uniform surface of their good looks and the apparent ease of their social interactions. Some had managed to regroup once in exile and to get help from friends and support networks to obtain lodging and work, although their employment was usually in unskilled and underpaid positions, such as washing floors or selling trinkets in the streets. Only a lucky minority of the professionals secured work in their fields immediately. Some were fortunate to have access to extended family networks that provided a refuge in exile; others were without kin but had their own children with them. Still others were alone. Although some had managed to preserve their marriages, whether or not their spouses were with them in Madrid, the majority seemed to have suffered a cleavage in their primary relationships, which they tended to view as the personal fall-out of the political disaster that had gripped them so brutally in its vise. Some were admired by the others for their stoicism and unflappability and for their capacity to provide a loving and dependable home for their children. Several were cause for deep concern because of their emotional instability or their penchant to seek an elusive solace in alcohol or in multiple liaisons with men who could be counted on merely to leave them.

Only in retrospect would I think through the sources of the shock I felt in the presence of these women and why their devastation seemed so irresistibly contagious. It felt qualitatively different from experiences I had earlier while living in Argentina, when people I knew were directly affected by the acts of repression perpetrated by prior military governments. In the past, the military had gunned down striking workers, jailed members of the political opposition without due process, and refused to make public the identities of political prisoners who had been executed while in prison. But these human rights violations had taken place within the context of an increasingly organized opposition, whose growing political weight made people optimistic that together they could succeed in fundamentally altering the unjust aspects of Argentine society. General strikes, university occupations, mass mobilizations—each represented a growing victory over a series of governments that, even as they rattled their sabers, were increasingly on the defensive. But, just a few short years later, the mass movement was smashed, and following the

1976 coup, the military junta's ruthlessness knew no boundaries. This military government intended to wipe out all signs of opposition. The atrocities committed annihilated not only people but also any sense of their collective empowerment to make a better future. Now there was only loss, and these women's lives were part of the mass experience of the demolition of the hope for change. This, indeed, was a different historical moment, and I too was feeling this loss cast in hopelessness.

There was more. I realized I could not depend on my social science training or my radical political theory or my feminist analysis to assess these women as individual survivors of a collective tragedy. I could not account for their capacity to endure the brutalities they had been subjected to without going mad. Nor could I explain the variation in their success or failure to cope psychologically with severe disruption. I could not interpret why some were able to retain enough optimism to build a decent life in exile for themselves and their children or why others were beaten down, incapable of fixing the damage inside so as to go on in any constructive fashion with their lives. Although they all clung to their social connections with one another, only some retained an involvement in the exile community's political or human rights struggles. Moreover, their individual responses seemed not to depend solely on the severity of their victimization at the hands of the repressive forces in Argentina. But what other forces were at work to determine their psychological states? What did this group of women and their reactions to military dictatorship tell me about the global impact of political repression on a society? What could I learn about the psychological and social resilience of a people living under authoritarian rule? What about the generation struck down or the one fated to grow up under the harsh constraints of the Generals' rule? Under what conditions would people retain or lose the capacity to fight back? What about the future of democracy, of social justice? What of the possibility of organizing resistance to the massive onslaught against human rights? What would make possible the reparation of so much human suffering?

These were questions of a different order than those that had motivated the meeting that evening in El Portalon. It would take me several years to begin to answer them and to understand their importance in relation to the other concerns that had guided my previous academic and political endeavors. I remember realizing that in order to fully understand the human response to social phenomena such as exploitative class relations, imperialism, or revolution, I would have to learn more about the human psyche. I would have to explore psychology in order to better comprehend the subjective meanings of the profound social, economic, and political crises facing millions of people throughout Latin America.

On my return to Los Angeles, I wrote my paper on gender and political activism for the Latin American Studies Association conference, although my efforts were confounded by the nagging questions raised in my meeting with the women in Madrid. Some months later, I spent the evening with an Argentine sociologist friend visiting from his Mexico City exile. In the midst of our animated discussion about Argentine politics, he suddenly asked me a fortuitous question that would dramatically shift the course of my life toward the goal that I had set for myself in Madrid but had done little to actualize in the subsequent months. "Nancy, I have to ask you something," my friend said, interrupting our heated debate about the ideological significance of Peronism in Argentine history. "Don't you know Marie Langer? You two would really get on, you're interested in so many of the same things, and you share such similar points of view about politics, feminism—even about Eva Perón! Haven't you seen Langer's new book, which describes her life as a politically radical psychoanalyst in Argentina?"

Entering the Psychic Matrix

A fateful question indeed. And when my friend sent me *Memoria, historia y diálogo psicoanalítico*, published in Mexico in 1981, I was transfixed by the woman who emerged from its pages. Langer's life encompassed some of the pivotal historical developments of the twentieth century. A prominent Latin American psychoanalyst, her professional practice was informed by her feminism and political radicalism. As I read her book, the contours of Langer's extraordinary life became apparent. An Austrian Jew born in 1910, she grew up in the exciting, politicized culture of Vienna, which was governed by an elected Marxist party, the Social Democrats. After graduating from medical school in the mid-1930s, she attended Freud's Psychoanalytic Institute until her antifascist convictions prompted her to join an International Medical Brigade bound for the Spanish Civil War. After the fall of the Spanish Republic, Langer emigrated to Buenos Aires, where in 1942 she was one of the six founders of the prestigious Argentine Psychoanalytic Association.

During the next several decades, Langer worked tirelessly to develop psychoanalysis in Latin America, and from the late 1960s on, when Argentina was ruled by a series of military governments, she became a prominent figure in the human rights movement among mental-health professionals in the Southern Cone. She called for a psychoanalysis whose theory would embrace a Marxist conceptualization of class society in order to shed light on the inevitable psychological suffering that was the product of a social order composed of inherently exploitative relations. Her outspoken denunciation of the human rights violations of repressive governments in Argentina provoked the infamous right-wing death squad, the Argentine Anticommunist Alliance

(Triple A), to include her name on its death list in 1974, thus forcing her into exile for the second time in her life.

Langer joined the Argentine exile community in Mexico City. She resumed a private practice, taught and supervised at the National Autonomous University of Mexico, and actively participated in the human rights movement among refugees from the Southern Cone living in exile in Mexico. She provided psychological treatment in the refugee communities to survivors from military-run Argentina, Chile, Uruguay, and Central America.

Even before I finished her book, I knew I wanted to write Langer's biography. Her life, I told myself, would be the perfect vehicle for me to explore the intersection of the many fascinating aspects of Latin American culture that I had always found so compelling. I would also be able to address the intersection of Marxism and feminism, which was increasingly reflected in the theory and practice of social transformation throughout Latin America. And because Langer was a psychoanalyst, here was my opportunity to explore more deeply the psychological domain of human experience precisely in the political context that had stimulated my interest in Madrid. But, aside from all these reasoned motives, I felt excited by the idea of meeting and working with a woman whose values and passions I shared and whom I already deeply admired.

My first contact with Langer was to show me that in addition to what I had learned about her through her book she had a warmth and informality that were endearing. I wrote to her in an extremely formal Spanish, attempting to indicate linguistically the respectful distance appropriate to an initial contact with a prominent individual. I introduced myself and proposed my idea for a biographical project. When I subsequently telephoned her and began with a stiff, "*Buenos días, Doctora Langer . . .* ," she quickly interrupted me and, in a friendly, Viennese-accented Spanish, said, "Nancy, how nice to receive your letter. But, my dear, don't you remember? I met you at the screening of your film in the Argentine Center in Mexico City several years ago. Ah . . . ," she continued, "but how could you recall everyone who spoke with you that night? What an exciting evening that was, no? How your film captured so much of the history we lived through. Well, how nice to hear from you, my dear, and what is this about writing my biography?"

I was completely disarmed and quickly realized that I was already considered a friend and colleague. In fact, the *doctora* was quite willing to entertain my proposal. As we chatted about it, she exuberantly told me that shortly after her book was published, she became the co-coordinator of the Internationalist Team of Mental Health Workers, Mexico-Nicaragua, whose purpose was to help the Sandinistas develop Nicaragua's first national system of mental-health care. The twelve members of the team—psychoanalysts, psychiatrists, and psychologists from Argentina, Chile, and Mexico—were all residing in

Mexico City. "Imagine," she said excitedly, "the first country undergoing radical social transformation that has enlisted a psychoanalytically informed model of mental health to help create its health care system. It's the first time in history, so you can see I'm very passionate about this. Suddenly this unhappy exile has turned into a victorious adventure for me!"

In more ways than I could have imagined, my relationship with Marie Langer would profoundly enrich my life. In subsequent years, I was a frequent visitor to Mexico City, where I observed her professional work and human rights activism. I taped sixty hours of interviews with her and many more with family members and colleagues. Her home was in the old colonial section of Mexico City, nestled behind massive walls that shut out the hustle and pollution of the city's noisy, congested streets. We would sit in front of the enormous window in the living room looking out onto the verdant gardens, and she would curl up in the same corner of the couch and smile, "O.K., compañera, where do we begin today?" Her physical presence belied her seventy-odd years. She was slim and tan, with a shock of white hair and startling blue eyes that alternated between penetrating directness and sidelong coquettish glances. Often dressed in jeans and a Latin American peasant shirt, she gesticulated dramatically as she spoke and puffed on her omnipresent cigarette. Her discourse was punctuated by frequent coughing, and I would gently chide her for smoking excessively. In one of our first discussions about radical politics and psychology, she told me, "Listen, I'll tell you what Marxism and psychoanalysis have in common: if you've once understood the concept of surplus value [the part of the value produced by the worker's labor that is not paid for by the capitalist but expropriated in the form of profit] and thus the exploitation of one class by another, you can never forget it; in the same way, if you've understood the concept of the unconscious, even if only through the analysis of a dream or a 'Freudian slip,' you can't forget that either. Marx and Freud, each in his own way, delved below the mere appearance of things, and in so doing exposed the latent reality that directs our lives."

Over several years, I came to know Marie's two daughters and their families, also living in Mexico, as well as the exile community of mental-health professionals from Argentina, Chile, and Uruguay. Whenever I could, I participated in the weekly meetings of the Internationalist Team that took place every Monday night in Marie's home for the purposes of organizing the overall strategy of the work in Nicaragua. The members of the Team traveled to Nicaragua in twos and threes on a rotational basis for ten days out of each month, and the work had to be coordinated so as to provide continuity to their training efforts in hospitals, clinics, and universities. I realized how profoundly Marie affected those around her, how her charismatic strength and charm, which I had first gleaned from reading her book, drew people to her like a magnet.

The most fascinating part of this research experience was my trip to Nicaragua with Marie and her colleague Ignacio Maldonado; there I was able to participate directly in the creative work of the Internationalist Team and to witness the response she sparked in the appreciative physicians, teachers, social workers, and psychologists she taught and supervised. During this trip I adopted the habit of calling her "Mimi," a nickname she claimed she did not relish but by which most everyone who knew and loved her affectionately called her.

I eagerly absorbed the psychological education that was an inevitable by-product of this involvement with politically committed Latin American psychoanalysts, although ultimately I sought my own formal training. My understanding of individual and group psychology deepened, informing my analysis of state-organized political repression and the psychic trauma that is its outcome. Mimi and I were both absorbed in the solidarity movement with Central American refugees, she in Mexico and I in Los Angeles, and I struggled to balance my involvement with this community and my work on her biography. Meanwhile my husband and I were in the early months of first-time parenthood, and all else subsided as I happily gave into the somnolent and sublime love affair with my infant. As my maternal experience unfolded, I came to know *en carne propia* (through personal experience) the unique intensity of the maternal bond, a lesson that would permit me to understand more profoundly the incredibly courageous women I would meet in the various mothers and grandmothers organizations from Argentina and Central America—those women who tenaciously confront military governments with the demand that the repressive forces return their disappeared children alive.

In the mid-eighties, Mimi and I agreed that I should take the time to translate her seminal book on women for English-speaking readers. Neither of us realized what a daunting task this would be, and for the next several years I disappeared behind a computer and a multitude of Spanish-English dictionaries. After seemingly endless drafts, I finally emerged with a respectable translation of *Motherhood and Sexuality*, to which I added a lengthy biographical essay that contextualized Mimi's contributions to feminist and psychoanalytic literature on female psychology.[1]

Mimi would never have the pleasure of seeing the book's publication. In the midst of my struggles with translating, the horrifying news arrived that she was suffering from inoperable cancer. I visited her twice more in Mexico during the next year, after which she returned to Argentina, her adopted homeland, once again under democratic rule. There she spent the last months of her life. We spoke frequently by telephone, conversations in which she oscillated between lucid observations about the social issues that had brought sense of meaning and dignity to her life and saddened admissions of her deteriorating emotional and physical strength. I felt I could hear her very life slipping away through the tenuous transcontinental connection. Her death, which came in December 1987 at the age of seventy-seven, was a profound blow to all of us who had known her well and whose personal, professional, and political lives had been deeply affected by her. Public commemorations were held in Buenos Aires, Managua, and Mexico City, where the mass media covered the events, as they too paid homage to one of Latin America's most important psychoanalysts and spokespersons for justice and human rights.

Writing a biography of an individual who is living is difficult in and of itself, but suffering her death in the midst of the project is unsettling indeed. I felt that my voice had been lost and so, too, my ability to proceed. This reaction crystallized an issue that had lain dormant, surfacing only in articles I had written about her: my struggle to create a separate identity from my subject. The fact was that I admired her and believed she deserved to be recognized internationally for her contributions to the development of a socially engaged psychoanalysis. But my admiration was potentially a liability, and as I confronted my obligation to find my own perspective and narrative voice, I wrestled, as well, with the point of writing the book. After all, Mimi and I had always seen it not so much as a study of her personality or the intimate details of family and personal relationships but as a vehicle for telling a larger story. We both wanted to use her life to speak about the tumultuous political conditions of Latin America and of the movement of mental-health professionals committed to a psychology that recognizes in practice the political context of individual human suffering. This dilemma would be resolved in an unexpected manner.

Weaving the Common Thread

I began to travel to Buenos Aires to interview Mimi's two sons and their families as well as colleagues with whom she had worked during her four decades in Argentina. As I spent more time in Latin America, my relationships with other politically progressive Argentine psychoanalysts and with their counterparts in Uruguay and Chile strengthened and deepened. All of them had known Mimi, and most felt their lives to have been deeply affected by her. Moreover, as I developed closer ties with those who had remained in Argentina during military rule, I was able to explore in depth their personal experiences and ideas about the psychological effects of living in state terror. My involvement with the Grandmothers of the Plaza de Mayo and the mental-health professionals who aided them in their struggles to locate their disappeared children and grandchildren deepened my understanding of the relationship between political activism and mental health. Over time, I established close bonds with individuals who represent three generations of psychoanalysts and psychologists, all of whom are dedicated to the integration of a Marxist sociology and a psychoanalytic psychology in order to analyze the different axes of crisis in their societies. Their professional practice in different ways and in a variety of settings is devoted to helping people develop a critical consciousness not only about their unconscious minds but also about the social forces responsible for their psychological pain. In the politically polarized societies of Latin America, engagement rather than neutrality defines their lives and work.

I eventually came to realize that the story I needed to tell was not an individual history but a collective one and that Mimi Langer should be joined on the written page as she had been in life by those who struggled with her against social violence and on behalf of a more decent and humane society. Thus I decided on a chorus of voices to speak to North Americans about oppression and resistance in Latin America. This is, after all, a history of a shared social practice.

The process of choosing among all of the individuals whose lives embody the substance of my study was a difficult one indeed. I was forced, perhaps by my own writing limitations but also by the necesssity of containing an inherently unwieldy task, to select in addition to Mimi Langer nine people whose stories highlight the themes of the book. I had known all of them for years, having spoken with each on numerous occasions about their experiences and many of the issues related to this study. In October 1994, I traveled to Buenos Aires, Montevideo, and Santiago in order to gather the precise information I would need for writing this book. I spent long hours taping discussions with each of my protagonists and returned home with an alarming amount of recorded material and more of their authored books and articles to add to my already crowded bookshelves and desk. Once again I disappeared behind my computer, this time to transcribe the hours of taped interviews with my subjects. As I transcribed, I had the chance to relive the discussions, to see in my mind's eye the various physical environments in which we had spoken together, to recall individual facial expressions and gestures as they recounted painful or joyous experiences and offered insights and analyses of a host of relevant topics. I saw the wisdom of my decision to write about a group experience. Together with Mimi these individuals provide a rich panorama of the perspectives and practice that constitute what I call "liberation psychology." These stories are infused with fear, victory, loss, bereavement, joy, achievement, and survival. They represent many of the collective experiences of the citizens of Argentina, Chile, and Uruguay, whose lives were profoundly disrupted by the violence of state terror.

The Argentines include Juan Carlos Volnovich, a child psychoanalyst whose progressive political activism forced him, his wife, Silvia, and their two small children into exile for eight years. Unlike other analysts who went to Paris, Madrid, Mexico City, or Rome, Juan Carlos and Silvia chose Havana, where, in spite of the behaviorist orientation of Cuban psychiatry, they developed successful, psychoanalytically based practices. During their time in exile, Juan Carlos's psychiatrist brother, Jorge, was disappeared by the Argentine military junta, and they waged a successful international campaign to save his life. When Juan Carlos returned with his family from exile, he became actively engaged with the Grandmothers of the Plaza de Mayo and their efforts to locate their disappeared grandchildren and to keep alive the human rights struggle in postdictatorship Argentina.

Julia Braun is an Argentine psychoanalyst who, along with her psychoanalyst husband and fifteen-year-old son, made the agonizing decision to remain in Argentina during the dictatorship in order to search for their seventeen-year-old son, who was disappeared by the military. She braved the potential retribution of the dictatorship to become active in a working-class community whose impoverished families suffered from the daily violence of poverty as well as the state's organized political repression. Julia provided therapeutic aid to the many families that suffered from the disappearance of loved ones by the military and paramilitary forces. She has written extensively about the special mourning required by this specific kind of psychic trauma.

Eduardo "Tato" Pavlovsky, a psychoanalytically trained Argentine playwright and actor whose works are internationally renowned, was responsible for the introduction of psychodrama as a method of group psychotherapeutic treatment of children and adults. Tato was driven into exile by the military junta because of his progressive political activism from the late 1960s on. He spent only a few years in exile in Madrid before his wish to be in his homeland overcame his fears of its ruthless government, and he returned to Argentina three years before the fall of the dictatorship. Courageously, he has written and directed several highly acclaimed theatrical works that explore the psychological complexities of torture and other aspects of political repression. He continues, as well, to lead groups in psychodrama aimed at helping people who work in community, educational, and human rights organizations to understand themselves and their impact on others more profoundly.

Diana Kordon, Dario Lagos, and Lucila Edelman are psychoanalytically trained Argentine psychologists who, along with those already mentioned, were engaged in the movement of progressive mental-health workers in the late 1960s and early 1970s. Following the coup in 1976, in spite of the fact that the military turned their wrath on psychoanalysts and psychologists because of their identification with popular struggles and human rights movements, these three were committed to staying in their country in order to oppose the military junta. Thus they remained in Buenos Aires during the years of intense, state-organized violence, living in continuous fear for their own and their children's safety. They ultimately designed a unique experiment in which they functioned as a psychological team to provide emotional and political support to the Mothers of the Plaza de Mayo. They continue in this specific role, although their team also both researches the various manifestations of social violence that have gripped Argentina since its return to constitutional government and provides therapeutic attention to its victims.

The Uruguayan experience is depicted by Marcelo Viñar and his wife, Maren Ulriksen de Viñar, a Chilean by birth, two psychoanalysts who, from the late 1960s on, were active in that country's progressive political life as it, too, slid into a devastating militarization of civil society. As the uniquely democratic institutions and progressive social welfare tradition of Uruguay gave way by the early 1970s to economic and political crisis, Marcelo was jailed in one of Montevideo's political prisons for several months, and Maren waged a campaign for his freedom. They ultimately sought exile in Paris, where they worked clinically within the exile community. They also studied and wrote about the psychological effects of political repression and exile. With the restoration of democratic government in Uruguay, they returned to their country, where they have lectured and written about the psychological impact of torture, exile, and repatriation.

The Chilean experience with state terror is portrayed through Elizabeth Lira, a psychologist who witnessed the military coup in September 1973 that overturned the Popular Unity government of Salvador Allende, the first democratically elected socialist president in the Americas. She survived the aftermath of the military assault on the Chilean people and ultimately began to work with the progressive Church to help survivors of torture and individuals and families whose loved ones were disappeared by the repressive state. Like all the others in this story, Elizabeth risked her personal safety to denounce the excesses of the military junta that ruled her country for eighteen years. She has helped organize international conferences on the psychological impact of political repression and has authored numerous books and articles on the psychosocial dynamics of the culture of fear. Since the eighties, she has traveled frequently to El Salvador in order to work with her counterparts there, helping to keep alive the tradition of Ignacio Martin-Baró, a Jesuit priest and Central America's most important social psychologist, who was assassinated by U.S.-trained Salvadoran soldiers in 1989.

About Liberation Psychology

This book is as much about the genesis of a distinctive form of psychology as it is about the people who practice it in order to free themselves and their patients from the terrors of dictatorship and social violence. I use the term *liberation psychology* to capture the unique characteristics of the work of Marie Langer and her colleagues. Their efforts to address the emotional and social sources of human suffering are reminiscent of *liberation theology*, a movement born in the ferment of the early 1960s within the Catholic Church that addressed the spiritual and material sources of oppression in Latin America.

The Church's longstanding identification with the wealthy and powerful of society had produced a growing alienation among baptized Catholics, only 20 percent of whom from the early sixties on were regularly attending mass. Protestant evangelism was on the rise, and Catholic student groups and young radical priests were joining guerrilla organizations because, as Camilo Torres, a Colombian priest who joined the National Liberation Army, claimed, "The Catholic who is not a revolutionary is living in mortal sin."[2] In response to the crisis, Pope John XXIII organized in 1962 the Second Vatican Council, which over the next four years brought together bishops from all over the world to chart a new, more socially progressive direction for the Catholic Church. In 1967, Pope Paul VI issued the encyclical *Popularum Progressio*, in which he criticized imperialism, neocolonialism, and the dehumanizing waste of capitalism manifested in the massive poverty it produced.[3] A year later, Latin American bishops met in Medellín, Colombia, where a new liberation theology was born that committed the Church to "a preferential option for the poor," the defense of human rights, and the struggle against the injustices of Latin America's economic dependence on the industrialized world.

Liberation theology combined the Christian idea that man is alienated from God and his fellow beings with the Marxist idea that the economic and social structures in which human beings live are a fundamental source of alienation. A group of bishops even asked the Church to condemn capitalism and to ally itself with socialists struggling for radical changes in society. Although liberation theology was the first manifestation of a new Christianity that aligned itself with social revolution, the movement Christians for Socialism also emerged and rejected the role of the institutionalized Church as the defender of the faith. There soon appeared throughout the continent thousands of Christian Base Communities, grass-roots groups of working-class or peasant Catholics who, armed with bibles, both reinterpreted Christian faith to link it with progressive politics and embraced an ethic of social action. These sectors of Christianity supported progressive movements when they came to power, such as the Popular Unity government in Chile (1970–1973) and the

Sandinista government in Nicaragua (1979–1990). The Sandinista Revolution, in fact, established the only government in Latin America that included priests in cabinet posts, reflecting the celebrated slogan of that country's popular Church: "Between revolution and religion, there's no contradiction."

As I became more familiar with the theory and practice of the politically progressive psychoanalysts and psychologists in the Southern Cone, it seemed to me that they represented within the mental-health profession a movement similar to that of liberation theology. From their point of view, there was essentially no contradiction between Freud and Marx. Indeed, they sought a convergence between a psychoanalytic theory of the unconscious roots of mental anguish and a Marxist theory of the economic origins of social violence and exploitative class relations as the basis for a praxis bent on combating both. The individuals whose stories are told in this book have striven to understand the interrelationship between alienated personal existence and alienated social relations, between individual anomie and social oppression, and between individual mental health and collective empowerment. Their "preferential option for the poor" took them from their bourgeois and middle-class private practices into the public hospitals and community clinics of the popular classes. Their critique of the concept of psychotherapeutic neutrality—as well as their rejection of the possibility of political neutrality—grew out of their own experience in the polarized social conditions of their countries and prompted them to put their professional skills at the service of those engaged in the radical transformation of society.

My inclination to call their ideology and praxis liberation psychology was supported when I became familiar some years later with the work of Martín-Baró, who independently chose this term to describe psychology in Central America. Martín-Baró argued that Central America, a region enmeshed in military repression, civil wars, and liberation struggles, demanded a new psychology—which he called liberation psychology—that would free itself of old individualistic models and become an ally in the emancipatory struggles of the popular classes.[4]

Certainly the protagonists of this book agree with Martín-Baró's call to psychologists to challenge the social context of people's psychological suffering. But today they are equally interested in reassessing their own political activism and in understanding why revolutionary movements have failed in their goal to alter oppressive social institutions. In their exploration of the meaning of emancipatory struggle in the current period, these progressive psychoanalysts and psychologists are interested in understanding the problematic nature of the revolutionary leadership and strategies of the 1960s and 1970s, whose mistakes may very well have contributed to the triumph of the system they wished to change.

I have organized the chapters in this book so as to address the various psychological and sociological questions I consider central to an analysis of the culture of fear and its legacy in the social violence that plagues Latin America today. I also explore the psychological factors that contribute to the human capacity to struggle against political repression and to sustain hope in the possibility of fighting on behalf of peace and social justice. My biggest challenge was to organize the innumerable hours of rich material contained in my interviews so that it would unfold in an intelligible fashion to illustrate the major themes of the book. In what has often felt like the construction of a massive jigsaw puzzle, I have woven throughout the chapters the narratives of the protagonists of this story so that their vivid firsthand experiences and thoughtful observations bring alive the book's subject. Their responses to the finished product reassure me that I have faithfully represented them in my depiction of this history. I am most grateful for their generosity of spirit in sharing with me so candidly their personal stories. In our ever more perplexing and unpredictable world, their passionate embrace of life—with all its contradictions—permits them to keep up the good fight.

Chapter 1

History and Memory

Historical memory . . . has to do with recovering not only the sense of one's own identity and the pride of belonging to a people but also a reliance on a tradition and a culture, and above all, with rescuing those aspects of identity which served yesterday, and will serve today, for liberation.

—IGNACIO MARTÍN-BARÓ, *Writings for a Liberation Psychology* (1994)

IN LATIN AMERICA, when people are asked about their personal lives or those of their families or about their city, a labor union, a theater, a café, a school, a political party, or just about anything, they usually begin at the beginning—several generations back. History and histories are deeply encoded in Latin Americans' consciousness, and their tendency to recount their personal stories with a vital sense of the events and forces in the past that helped to give birth to them is often disconcerting to North Americans, who are known for mobility and lack of attachment to place or to the history of place.

Latin Americans are also likely to contextualize specific aspects of their life experience and that of their families—when their family immigrated to Latin America or when they moved to such-and-such neighborhood or when they joined a specific union or political party or when they had their children—within the general historical referents of their country. They tend, as well, to link the personal side of their lives to the dominant political conflicts of their own or their parents' generation or to think about their individual economic fates as part of the general economic history and destiny of their country. Thus, an apparently simple question stimulates an elaborate tale that goes far beyond the straightforward response expected. Such exchanges can be exasperating, but, with a little patience on the part of the listener, they illuminate not only the meaning of the particular answer but also a way of thinking that highlights the importance of memory (*memoria*) and the impact of the past on the present.

So it went in my discussions with the participants in this project. When I began our taped interviews by asking them to give me a brief biographical sketch, they enthusiastically launched into a surprisingly detailed account of their familial past. They knew the names and professions of their great-great-great-grandparents and could even recount individual experiences, conflicts, and aspirations of some of these distant generations. They situated their recollections of family histories via historical landmarks—for example, "My great-grandmother came to Argentina shortly after the extermination of the Indians on the pampas in the 1870s" or "My father was a child when his family immigrated as part of the famous attempt by the international Jewish colonization Association to found farm colonies for the Jews in rural Argentina—you know, the famous 'Jewish cowboys' [*gauchos judios*] of the 1880s" or "My childhood was deeply affected because I grew up in the 1940s and 1950s, during the Perón years, when all my classmates but me hated Evita" or "I learned early on in my household about how my country's dependence on copper was producing the labor strikes that brought the country to a halt."

So I will proceed, as did our ten protagonists, by invoking the historical frame and the important role memory plays in one's perspective on the present. The history of Latin America provides a way to understand our protagonists' perceptions, sentiments, choices, and commitments, the roots of which—they are the first to say—are in the distant and recent past. In fact, the social fabric created as far back as the European conquest of America and its peoples some five centuries ago had woven deeply within it the contradictions leading ultimately to both state terror and liberation psychology in contemporary Latin America.

A Continent in Pain

In Latin America, a wide spectrum of people share a particular perspective on the historical roots of today's deep-seated social antagonisms, one that I have learned well from my colleagues and compañeros in the region. It is articulated in academic lectures and in politicians' speeches, depicted in artists' colorful murals, and written in the rhythmic verses of poetry. It can be heard in union meetings and university student debates, as well as on street corners when people argue about current events. It emerges in the dialogue of the protagonists of this book. When elaborated as historical narrative, this perspective on the fundamental contradictions in Latin American societies discloses a unique economic and societal panorama.

Today, Latin Americans face severe economic problems and inequities that are the result of fundamental patterns that began centuries ago. Ironically, Latin America, like other areas on the periphery of the world capitalist economy, has been cursed from the beginning by its extraordinary wealth. One powerful nation after another from the center has exploited its prolific natural and human resources for its own ends. The "open veins" of the continent have spilled forth their gold, silver, wheat, bananas, sugar, coffee, cotton, copper, rubber, hides, and petroleum to enrich and develop other continents in what Eduardo Galeano calls "five hundred years of pillage."[1] The debilitating pattern of external control over economic life began in the colonial period, when mercantilist Spain and Portugal exercised the right of conquest to appropriate their colonies' wealth in their own interest. Since the nineteenth century, the nominally independent nations of Latin America have continued to be dominated by outside forces through the informal, neocolonial patterns established by first British and then U.S. commercial, financial, strategic, and military interests. These colonial and neocolonial patterns have daunted attempts to develop independent nationally based economic structures in Latin America.[2] Important colonial institutions, such as the Church and the military, have retained their political influence well into the present era, and a pattern both of reliance on a charismatic individual for governance and of the perpetuation of such an individual or a political party in power for years or decades has proved difficult to eradicate.

The region has been characterized by stark class and racial divisions since the colonial period, when a privileged alliance of European-descended landowners, Church officials, and merchant elites established their rule over the darker-skinned popular classes of Indian and African ancestry. Following independence in the mid-1800s, these social relations were maintained as successful financial and manufacturing entrepreneurs linked their ambitions along with their fortunes to the interests of the traditional landholding elite. From the beginning, the upper classes made large investments in raw materials that were exported abroad. The handsome profits gleaned from international trade enabled them to develop a lavish lifestyle that rivaled that of their wealthy European counterparts. While benefiting them as a class, the export-oriented economy inhibited industrialization and the establishment of a local infrastructure, leaving their countries far behind Europe and the United States. From the late nineteenth century on, the expanding middle sectors, including European immigrants who came seeking their fortunes in the "New World," rarely challenged the existing class structure but instead generally reinforced it through their identification with the values of the elites and their wish to emulate their lifestyle.

Throughout the continent, the social order has rested on extreme exploitation of the masses of peasants and rural and urban workers, who have occupied the lowest rungs on the socioeconomic ladder and have generally been excluded from economic well-being and political power. Social relations have also been dominated by patriarchal traditions, which in Latin American culture have been manifested in bipolar conceptions of gender: masculinity (*machismo*) has been associated with exaggerated aggressiveness among men and an arrogant and sexually aggressive attitude toward women, while femininity has been identified as moral superiority, as embodied in the cult of the Virgin Mother, who represents the ideal of nurturing motherhood and chastity. Such gender stereotypes, alongside the legal subordination of women, have succeeded in making invisible women's significant contributions to society in their roles as wives, mothers, laborers, entrepreneurs, professionals, and political activists.[3]

From colonial days on, outside forces have influenced Latin American national politics, which have been marked by strong divisions between those sectors allied with foreign interests and those opposed to them. Since the late nineteenth century, for example, governments have often come to power because of support from U.S. dollars, arms, or military forces, irrespective of citizens' preferences. Governments have fallen as well simply because of their association with Uncle Sam. For millions of people, "Yankee go home" has been a battle cry protesting the heavy-handed manipulation of Latin American political life in order to assure a privileged position for U.S. economic interests.[4] In fact, the first great social revolution of the twentieth century, which broke out in Mexico in 1910, was in part a violent response to the grip U.S. investors held on the Mexican economy.

Many Latin Americans remember the Great Depression and the Second World War as the historical moment of their prime opportunity to challenge the flagrantly interventionist policies of the United States. Governments were elected or took power that instituted nationalist economic policies to facilitate industrialization controlled by Latin American investors. Cultural life was another arena in which Latin Americans expressed growing nationalist sentiments. Artists, musicians, writers, and filmmakers criticized their countries' long-standing dependence on cultural modes that were steadily imported, along with capital and technology, from Europe and the United States. Now they found inspiration in the history of indigenous and black resistance struggles and modes of artistic expression.

Most of the protagonists of this book grew up in the tumultuous post–World War II period, influenced by the nationalist cultural movements and learning about politics in the context of the growing tensions between the United States and their countries. They recall the U.S. attempts to reassert predominance throughout the Western Hemisphere and U.S. confrontations with Latin American nationalists who strove to maintain their countries' fragile independence from their northern neighbor. Although U.S. leaders understood the nationalist nature of the threats to their investment and trading designs, they used Cold War anticommunist ideology to justify their aggressive attacks on reform efforts in Latin America. The U.S. media conveyed to the public that its government's aggressive political and military actions in the region were necessary to defend democracy and freedom in the face of Soviet totalitarian expansion, which threatened the "American way of life."[5] The United States labeled as a "communist threat" not only the Marxist left but any reformist or nationalist party or movement that sought to control Latin American resources for Latin Americans.

As the United States indulged in repeated interventions in the internal affairs of its southern neighbors, our protagonists joined a host of Latin American critics who became ever more radical in their denunciation of the United States as an imperialist power. Their claims seemed to be confirmed in 1954, when the U.S. State Department and the CIA organized a military coup to oust the democratically elected reformist government of Guatemala after it nationalized unused United Fruit holdings as part of its land-reform program.[6] Denunciations became even louder in 1961, when the United States trained and armed Cuban mercenaries for the Bay of Pigs invasion of Cuba to overturn the revolutionary government that two years earlier had successfully overthrown the U.S.-backed military dictatorship of Fulgencio Batista.[7] The Cuban Revolution was depicted in the United States as the extension of the Soviet Union's empire, which was bent on eroding free enterprise and democracy in Cuba. But to millions of Latin Americans, it meant a social transformation that sought to end the economic inequities and human rights violations of neocolonialism and military rule and to redistribute wealth and opportunity for the Cuban people. Fidel Castro and Che Guevara embodied resistance to U.S. expansionism and the exercise of the principle of national self-determination.

Throughout the 1960s, U.S.-sponsored political and military programs suppressed local demands for reform; U.S. policymakers and ideologues insisted that they were saving the hemisphere for democracy, even when they had to do so violently and without the people's consent. Both the State Department and advocates from the private sector argued that when U.S. corporations earned high profits from their investments and trade, Latin Americans also benefited and that U.S. and Latin American interests were in harmony, not contradiction. In fact, they believed that Latin American development required the continual flow southward of U.S. capital, technology, and the cultural values associated with the Protestant work ethic.[8] Moreover, they contended that capitalism and democracy were inextricably linked and any other economic system would inevitably lead to undemocratic government. They ignored the fact that authoritarian government in Latin America was often the result of intensified class struggle under capitalism.

Progressive Latin Americans, however, were not blind to the relationship

between the rise in foreign capitalist investment, on the one hand, and political authoritarianism and the impoverishment of ever-increasing numbers
of people, on the other. Like the protagonists of this book, these Latin Americans were much more likely to entertain an alternative view associated with
the Marxist left that has been a part of Latin American intellectual and political traditions since the late nineteenth century. Marxism has offered a compelling mode of analysis to explain the stark contradictions of Latin American
society and has been a central element in the continent's legitimate political
discourse, intellectual treatises, labor struggles, and party politics. Marxist ideas
were readily accepted in a continent that since the late eighteenth century
embraced revolutionary ideas for achieving political and social change. The
notion that humanity should and could move toward goals of social justice
through revolution had been reflected in the thought and action of Latin
American independence heroes from Simón Bolívar to José Martí.

Marx's concept of liberation, by which he meant the right both to be free
from control by powerful interests that impose poverty and ignorance and to
live unsubjugated in community with others, has found resonance among Latin
American thinkers and activists since the mid-nineteenth century. They have
shared with Marx the optimistic conviction that the exploitative class relations of capitalist society were destined to change and that the popular classes
would restructure the system's competitive and repressive institutions and cultural values to free themselves from fear, superstition, poverty, aggression, and
enslavement. Marxism has appeared in different forms: as an economic analysis
of the laws of capital, which reveals a system characterized by inevitable crises and an increasing rate of exploitation of the working classes by the owners of the means of production; as a humanistic analysis of society based on
an idealistic and visionary concern with the liberation of humanity; and as
an analysis of imperialism in the tradition of Lenin, which has explained U.S.
military and economic intervention throughout the Americas.

Marxist and non-Marxist socialist activism has not been monolithic but
has been characterized by a variety of political parties and movements that
have developed diverse strategies and tactics to challenge the hegemonic structures and ideology of Latin American capitalism. The left has been an important sector within the labor movement in every country and has been a
significant player in electoral politics as well. It has contributed to the theory
and practice of the women's rights movement in many nations since the turn
of the century. It has played an important role in the rise of welfare states in
various countries, which, while inefficient and unable to spark development,
have saved significant sectors of the population from uncontrolled exploitation and exclusion. Through their ongoing struggles against authoritarian governments, many sectors of the left have also put their weight behind the

democratic process. Indeed, in recent years, where constitutional governments have replaced dictatorships, they have done so in part because of the pressure from the left. Grass-roots struggles in rural and urban areas alike have often been organized to elect left candidates because of the belief that they will improve living and working conditions for the majority.[9]

By the mid-1960s, Marxist explanations of Latin American poverty and injustice were influenced by a new intellectual orientation known as dependency theory, which added an important focus to the debates about the causes of underdevelopment. Writers in this tradition strove to demonstrate the fallacies in the U.S. assumption that Latin America would develop only with the importation of capital, technology, and cultural values from the United States. They postulated that, far from representing the solution to Latin American social ills, capitalism was actually the cause of underdevelopment, which was the inevitable result of the continent's role within the world capitalist system.[10] In fact, they maintained, capitalism had condemned Latin America through international capitalist investment and trade patterns that increased economic growth in the metropolitan centers (the United States and Europe) through the appropriation of the economic surplus of the satellites (Latin America, Africa, and Asia). Continuing investments from the metropolis might increase industrialization in the periphery, but in the process capital, profits, and natural resources would be drained back to the metropolis. Dependent capitalism in the peripheral nations would not be able to compete and would be left underdeveloped. A skewed division of wealth internationally would be accentuated, mirrored in the growing gap between the standards of living of the working classes in the metropolis and those on the periphery and between the wealthy and the popular classes on the periphery.

The proliferation of ideas associated with dependency theory was reflected in shifts within the left from strategies to reform aspects of capitalism to an emphasis on the need for the revolutionary alteration of the system itself, which was reinforced by the example of the Cuban Revolution. The militant left's influence grew throughout the continent as workers, peasants, students, and women looked for radical and immediate solutions to the contradictions inherent in the prevailing model of economic growth. They were tired of a system that allocated the lion's share of aggregate industrial and agricultural wealth to foreigners and a small domestic elite and that condemned the middle and popular classes to a desperate—and losing—battle to enjoy a decent part of the wealth their labor produced.

Argentina, Uruguay, and Chile all manifested the general social, economic, and political patterns described above. In spite of their different political histories, by the late 1960s each country was imprisoned in the contradictions attendant on an export-oriented economy dominated by foreign capital and vulnerable to the oscillations of the international market. Each country experienced an economic crisis that provoked significant sectors of the middle and working classes to demand redistributive policies from governments unwilling or unable to respond. And each country came to a point where it appeared that social revolution would succeed in challenging the existing order. This profound social polarization ultimately led to military coups in all three countries—June 1973 in Uruguay, September 1973 in Chile, and March 1976 in Argentina. The era of state terror was ushered in by authoritarian dictatorships with similar ideologies and strategies, whose assault against the civilian population was unprecedented in the Southern Cone.[11] Although our story emerges from this broad tapestry, it also contains the specific textures of the unique traditions of each of the three nations. The stories of three of our protagonists and their own personal, professional, and political experiences reveal the background they share as well as their ties to the specific history of each of their nations in the Southern Cone.

Uruguay: Sheep and the Welfare State

Marcelo Viñar is a big bear of a man, with a deep, gravelly voice and twinkling eyes. He has a magnetic and robust appeal; when serious, he speaks slowly and reflectively, making his way carefully through his words. Although there is sometimes a vague sadness about him, he often chuckles as he speaks ironically about life, politics, and the human condition.

Marcelo and his Chilean wife and colleague, Maren Ulriksen de Viñar, have been talking into my tape recorder for seven hours straight in their Montevideo home. They have responded candidly to my difficult questions about their lives first under military rule and then in exile. Our only interruptions have been Maren's periodic searches for their articles and books on trauma and survival and Marcelo's preparations of a typical *asado gaucho*, an elaborate grill of the delicious beef grown on the pampas. We need to take a break, and while Maren grabs a quick nap, Marcelo and I walk through their genteel, middle-class neighborhood to see Montevideo's newest shopping mall.

The mall, he tells me, has been fashioned out of a prison, where the Uruguayan military dictatorship had tortured its political opponents. For years, the victims' screams had pierced the silence of the late night hours, reminding neighbors of the price of speaking out. Today, the turrets and cells of the prison have been integrated into the fanciful architecture of the mall's boutiques and shops, whose bright lights and lively music beckon the public to a fantasyland of consumerism. "You must see it with your own eyes," Marcelo insists and then muses, "I can't tell which is worse, the before or after of this terrible place."

I am struck speechless by the sight of the people from all social classes who are crowding through the (prison/mall) archway, hurrying to spend their hard-earned money. It is a shocking sight, a visual symbol of forgetting and remembering all at once. The huge complex is an enduring monument to its past function, the annihilation of citizens' civil rights. At the same time, it declares the triumph of an economic system that puts into debt and dependency governments and individuals alike. As we wander around the complex, trying to figure out how the fashionable architect decided which parts of the prison to leave intact, I wonder whether this hybrid structure is meant as a warning: submit to the system, or the mall will easily be reconverted into a prison.

As we turn to walk back toward Marcelo's house, the sudden sound of music from a loudspeaker coming closer and closer interrupts our somber thoughts. We turn to see a pickup truck drive slowly by. It is covered with progressive political slogans for an upcoming election and loaded with young people yelling political greetings, waving, and throwing leaflets to the people on the sidewalks. Marcelo's face slowly lights up. Proudly gesturing with his chin at these activists, he smiles, "You see, it is the next generation coming back to life." Marcelo is optimistic that these resilient youths will overcome the legacy of silence from the years of military rule and bring this pastoral country back toward its traditional embrace of political pluralism. Our day of discussions has revealed his pride in his country's generally pacifist and conciliatory history and his acute awareness of its profound effect on his own psychological and political formation.

Marcelo captures the reputation of Uruguay when he says that it is "a very bucolic and peaceful country, the Switzerland of America."[12] Indeed, Uruguay is distinct in Latin America for its longstanding tradition of progressive government. Originally intended to be a buffer zone in the ongoing territorial disputes between Argentina and Brazil, Uruguay became a small independent republic in 1828. Its fertile pampas spawned a landowning elite whose two main political parties managed to create a stable pattern of governance, which by the latter nineteenth century was reinforced by economic prosperity. Material progress resulted from advances in stockbreeding, fencing, the refrigerated ship, and railroad construction, which yielded increasing exports of wool, mutton, hides, and beef.

The relative homogeneity of Uruguay's population was due to its small number of indigenous peoples and a steady migration of Europeans from the latter days of the Spanish Empire on. In the nineteenth century, Italians and Spaniards formed the majority of immigrants who came to "make it in America" (*hacer América*). But others came as well, including Marcelo Viñar's grandparents, who immigrated from Russia and Rumania at the turn of the

century, arriving first in Argentina as part of the plan to establish rural Jewish colonies, but ultimately settling in Uruguay in the small provincial town
of Paisandú. As Marcelo is quick to point out, "It's true that I am the grandson of the famous Jewish cowboys [gauchos judios], but my family soon came
to this country and became part of the European immigrant communities that
would have a great impact on Uruguayan culture and society. So, you see, my
roots are within the mainstream of my country's development."

By the turn of the twentieth century, an enlightened middle class emerged
from among the European immigrants, producing an outstanding statesman
whose progressive influence on Uruguayan politics would be felt until his death
in 1929. José Batlle, the articulate newspaper editor who twice became president, emphasized the expansion of education, the restriction of foreign economic interests, and the enactment of a broad social welfare program. Asserting
the state's obligation to narrow the gap between rich and poor, Batlle's advanced legislation guaranteed workers the right to unionize, a minimum wage,
an eight-hour day, pensions, accident insurance, and paid holidays. Marcelo
recalls that as a young man his father, "who at the age of fifteen had rebel-
liously left home to seek his fortune in Argentina, decided to return to Uruguay because of the progressive political culture that had been created by
Batlle." He adds proudly, "Until the Cuban Revolution, Uruguay was the most
advanced country in the Western Hemisphere with respect to workers' rights,
education, and basic services such as medical care."

In the 1930s, the government endorsed an industrialization plan that, by
1952, increased by fourfold the number of industrial firms in the country. This
industrial expansion brought many of Uruguay's young people from the rural
areas to Montevideo and other cities in search for economic opportunities.
During this period the government invested in cultural activities and scientific endeavors, including, as Marcelo points out, psychiatry and child psychiatry, which received a lot of support in the early 1950s. Even the Uruguayan
Psychoanalytic Association, which was established in 1955, received subsidies from the government for aspects of its activities.

But by the late fifties declining world prices for its agricultural exports—
especially wool—plummeted Uruguay into a crisis. Falling state revenues began to restrict the elaborate welfare benefits, which deeply affected the living
standards of the middle and working classes. Bad times provoked a dramatic
emigration, and in less than a decade Uruguay lost nearly 20 percent of its
economically active population, which sought opportunities abroad. National
debates addressed the cause of the crisis. On the one side, conservative land-
holders, bankers, and industrialists blamed the critical economic conditions
on excessive welfare statism and demanded privatization as the solution. On
the other side, the progressive middle and working classes pointed to the fact

that the value of the private sector's exports had dropped by half in recent years, demonstrating how Uruguay's status as a dependent capitalist country made it vulnerable to the fluctuations in world demand for its primary products. Any economic improvement under the present system was next to impossible, they insisted. In fact, for increasing numbers of Uruguayans, including Marcelo, the revolution that had just taken place in Cuba seemed a beacon, shining its light in the direction of agrarian reform and nationalization of industry as strategies for treating the ailing political economy of their country.

These tumultuous political debates and others about underdevelopment and social justice were the backdrop for Marcelo's education at the National University in Montevideo. He credits his social consciousness to his experience in the university community during the 1950s and 1960s, first as an undergraduate and later as a medical student. "The university provided an environment that encouraged a social sensibility, a radical questioning of how to alter society so as to improve it. Politics were always for me associated with education, intellectual curiosity and exploration. The university offered the opportunity to study to make oneself better, and the emphasis was on morality and ethics. I felt that it was necessary to understand the world in order to change it and that becoming a competent professional was part of preparing to be a good revolutionary."

In 1965, Marcelo graduated from medical school and began to study psychoanalysis. In the same year he met and married Maren, a beautiful young Chilean who was a fifth-year student at the University of Chile Medical School. Maren fascinated Marcelo. She came from a very different background than he, the product of fourth-generation Danish immigrants on her father's side and on her mother's the Catholic oligarchy, whose origins could be traced to the eighteenth-century landowning aristocracy. Since childhood she had learned the value of fighting for humanitarian principles—an ethics gleaned from her father's anti-Nazi activities in Santiago's German community and her family's involvement in the solidarity movement with the Spanish Republic. Maren had first learned about torture as a little girl when a young Spanish refugee staying with her family cried constantly for her brother, a political prisoner who had been brutally tortured by Franco's fascists. Maren's wish to study medicine seemed to her a logical outcome of growing up in a family that taught her about the many cultures within Chile and how professionally trained people could help to improve the conditions of the poor and contribute to the struggle for social justice.

"I met Maren and began my psychoanalytic treatment in the same year," says Marcelo, "and I don't know which changed my life more profoundly." Typically, Maren's version is the "more romantic one," as she puts it, illustrated by the vivid details of their first encounter at an international conference on medical psychology in Brazil in 1959. Together they were introduced to the Argentine founders of psychoanalysis, which was for both a thrilling experience. They were especially drawn to Marie Langer, "who was a true teacher and whose thought opened up a whole new world for us to identify with. Mimi was so smart and sensitive, so easy to admire and to get close to. We named her the godmother of our relationship."

In the late 1960s, while Marcelo was still a candidate in training at the Uruguayan Psychoanalytic Association, Uruguay's economic crisis was exacerbated by the government's agreement to freeze wages and prices in order to receive loans from the International Monetary Fund. In response to this further tightening of their belts, workers declared some seven thousand strikes, which paralyzed the country, and the president introduced "emergency security measures" to censor the press, ban strikes, and repress leftists. Many people were accused of hiding "subversives" or supporting strike actions and were rounded up and thrown in jail.

Under such conditions, the left attracted increasing numbers of people, especially intellectuals, students, white-collar professionals, service employees, and peasants and workers. Marcelo and Maren, both of whom were respected psychoanalysts by then, participated in the political mobilization. "This period was so exciting because it was a collective process," recalls Maren. "And Marcelo was an important part of it. As a professor in the medical school, for example, he led the shift in orientation of the entire approach to medical education. One fundamental thing they changed was to get the students out of a purely biological introduction into medicine to one that focused on the totality of the human system, including psychological and social aspects as well as physiology. They linked students' training to outreach in the community in order to encourage a social consciousness about the various determinants of the health of individuals, families, and groups. This philosophy reflected the opening of the university in general to the fundamental problems of people, which was indicated in the slogan 'Students and Workers United and Moving Forward.'" Marcelo recalls nostalgically, "It was a great period, when the Physicians' Union and the Central Confederation of Workers would meet together on campus to discuss the social priorities in education. There was such engagement and expectation of change."

The traditional left—activists in the unions and on the campuses—was composed of the Socialist and Communist Parties, which were legal and worked within the established political system. But by the mid-sixties, an armed urban guerrilla organization, called the National Liberation Movement (Tupamaros), was attracting mainly middle-class youths impressed by the Cuban Revolution and the Christian radicalism of liberation theology. The Tupamaros raided business, government, and foreign-embassy offices to capture documents that exposed widespread corruption. In true Robin-Hood tradition, they kidnapped high officials and carried out bank robberies, using the money to distribute basic necessities to poor communities. Like their counterparts emerging throughout the continent, the Tupamaros had popular appeal, although, as Marcelo stresses, "in general, the working class continued to support the strategy of the Central Confederation of Workers, which represented the traditional left, interested in the electoral strategy for change." As the state began to come down full force against the Tupamaros, even those who had initially supported them began to have second thoughts. For many, the Tupamaros became identified with government-sponsored repression which was escalating at an alarming rate. And, indeed, increasingly the military, police, and right-wing death squads were turning Uruguay's model democracy into an urban battlefield.

In 1971, the Broad Front (Frente Amplio), a new coalition of the Christian Democrats, Socialists, and Communists, with conditional support from the Tupamaros, was organized to challenge the two dominant political parties in the upcoming national election. With less campaign money and media access than their opposition, the Frente made a respectable showing, but ultrarightist cattle rancher Juan María Bordaberry won the presidency in what was viewed by many as a victory shrouded in fraud.

The Uruguayan military stood in the wings, primed by their Brazilian counterparts who had engineered a repressive military coup in their country in 1964. As conditions deteriorated and workers launched general strikes and mass mobilizations to protest the militarization of society, the Congress responded by voting a "State of Internal War" in April 1972, granting the military unlimited powers. Many people were arrested, usually accused of supporting or sympathizing with the Tupamaros. During this period, Marcelo was among the thousands taken away in the middle of the night and imprisoned, in his case for several months. Maren helped to organize an international campaign of support for him, which ultimately secured his release. The months in prison were a brutal personal experience that taught him much about the psychological effects of political repression.

By early 1973, the military declared the Tupamaros totally destroyed, but public protest continued, and military and police repression mounted. President Bordaberry cooperated with the military as they moved closer to a coup, while thousands of Uruguayans with means fled into exile. In June 1973, the military, counseled by the Brazilian generals, made their de facto rule official, dismissing the Congress, banning left organizations, closing the National University, and instituting press censorship. Thus was inaugurated a reign of terror that would strangle the tiny nation for the next decade through an all-out offensive to erase its tradition of liberal democracy. The Viñars would be among those forced into exile, where as part of the refugee community in Paris they would observe, treat, and write about the individual and social repercussions of state terror.

Chile: Copper, Democracy, and Socialism

Elizabeth Lira and I sit in her study, an improvised second floor of her modest home in a working-class section on the outskirts of Santiago, where she lives with her twenty-five-year-old disabled son and twenty-four-year-old daughter. The study is a treasure chest of books, journals, and unpublished papers the likes of which would excite any historian. Partially in response to my obvious delight, but mainly because it is her life passion to educate about state terror and to repair its profound injustices, Elizabeth eagerly pulls from this shelf and that file cabinet papers that shed light on the past several decades of turbulence in her country. Now she locates a volume of unpublished articles written in the mid-1970s by the participants of a clandestine conference on psychology and political repression, to which Marie Langer had written an introduction. Knowing of my special interest in Mimi, she hands me this prize, smiling at me as I gratefully take it.

An attractive woman who appears much younger than her fifty years, Elizabeth has absentmindedly clipped back the loose strands of her light brown hair to keep from being distracted as she searches for relevant documents. She has donned an old, oversized heavy sweater to warm her short and compact body in the study's cold interior. When she responds to my questions about her life and work as a Chilean psychologist who has dedicated years to the fight against authoritarianism, her gentle manner and lilting voice carry a sense of urgency, and she speaks rapidly, as if there was no time to lose.

We have spent days here in the study, gathering sources and talking. Elizabeth tells me that although this humble community in which she has lived since the late 1960s is politically conservative, she has always felt respected by her neighbors in spite of her openly progressive politics. Just several blocks away, she tells me, is the community of La Victoria, one of the most militant neighborhoods on the outskirts of Santiago. Because of its combative history, La Victoria became a specific target of the military when it launched its coup on September 11, 1973. The walls of the homes and small shops in La Victoria still bear the bullet holes that are visual reminders of the brutal repression of its inhabitants by soldiers and police. "We could hear and see the helicopters overhead and tanks forcing their way through the improvised barricades the neighbors had erected." Elizabeth tells me. "We knew what was in store for La Victoria's families, who refused to give up the loss of their elected socialist government without a fight."

Such visual signs of the military regime are ubiquitous, a subtle part of everyday life. For example, Elizabeth shows me how her street deadends some ten blocks away in a partially constructed towering edifice, whose open-air floors seem to ascend to the clouds. Planned as a hospital that would serve the local community, it is a monument to the sudden termination of the social programs of the Popular Unity (Unidad Popular, or UP) government when the military junta withdrew the funds needed for its completion. This skeleton of a building is an eerie reminder of what the poor lost in the military's assault on Chilean democracy in 1973.

When Elizabeth speaks of the days, weeks, and months following the bloody military coup that overthrew the elected UP government, she describes the sense of chaos, unpredictability, and terror into which she was plunged. A political activist left alone with two small children after her husband was forced into hiding, she struggled to maintain her equilibrium while she evaluated the media's distorted claims and interpreted the (often coded) information arriving from comrades in order to calculate how best to protect her family. For security reasons, contact with others had to be measured, and except for the infrequent visits from fellow militants from around the country passing through Santiago on their way into exile she was all too often alone. Twenty-one years later, however, amidst the frightening recollections, Elizabeth is able to relate with a wry humor the details of tragi-comic incidents that make us both laugh.

Elizabeth tells me that the most progressive Chileans could not have imagined the extreme violence that would encompass their country once the military usurped power from their elected representatives. Alongside Uruguay, Chile had one of the strongest traditions of democratic rule in Latin America. Others would have bet their lives on the will of the people to fight in the streets to defend their democratic government. "Too many who wanted social change overestimated the level of commitment of the grass roots, the workers and peasants, to stand firm in defense of the Popular Unity government when things began to get rough and it was clear that the right wing was organizing a coup. They didn't understand the impact of the brilliant ideological and economic war waged against the UP, which demoralized and devastated even its supporters." For Elizabeth, who defines herself as politically cautious by nature, neither the coup nor the peoples' reluctance to challenge the soldiers was surprising.

Even though the popular classes in Chile have a long history of fighting for their rights, Elizabeth believes she has learned an important lesson from her years of work with peasant communities in the countryside. "I have always encountered class-conscious peasants, people who are willing to fight the large *hacendados* [landowners] for the land that was once theirs or to fight an unjust system for the right to education and decent wages. . . . But we need to remember the power of the dominant class, especially the tenacious power of its ideology, which has been internalized by the very classes whose inter-ests would be served by overturning the wealthy and their value system." She says that any strategy for change in Chile should be based on a dispassionate assessment of what is possible and that it is important to learn from history. Chile's history does, indeed, reveal both the militancy of the popular classes and the ability of the elite to maintain itself in power.

Chile is a long and narrow land with the Pacific Ocean on its coastal western shores and its neighbor Argentina on its mountainous eastern bor-der.[13] After the Spanish conquest of the area, the region was a center of agri-culture and mining. Although European diseases wiped out much of the indigenous population, mixing between the two groups made for a relatively homogenous citizenry, although most Chileans prefer to think of themselves as essentially of European lineage and tradition.

Chile developed into a highly urban society whose history nonetheless has been dominated by its mineral wealth. In the nineteenth century, world demand for first silver, then nitrates, and finally copper created a new sector of wealthy mine owners and merchants. They became part of the ruling elite traditionally composed of a landowning aristocracy that often merged their interests through intermarriage. A working class also arose, essentially native-born and first unionized in the nitrate fields of the north.

In the early twentieth century, copper production underwent a techno-logical revolution requiring great amounts of capital, which resulted in the absorption of the mines by foreign interests. By 1920, the industry was con-trolled by three companies, two of which were owned by Anaconda and the third by Kennecott, both U.S. corporations. The export-oriented ruling class fashioned an elite parliamentary democracy that functioned with relative sta-bility. However, even by the turn of the century the Chilean working class had manifested a significant leftist orientation in its militant struggles for better wages and working conditions. Workers became so combative that by the mid-1920s the elite and its middle-class allies were developing social welfare leg-islation as a preemptive strategy to head off more extensive organizing by independent radical unions.

In the midst of a crisis provoked by the Great Depression, Chileans voted into power a popular front representing a broad spectrum of parties, includ-ing the Democrats, Radicals, Socialists, and Communists. Its relatively mod-erate reformist program for creating a larger role for the government in economic matters riled the elites, who, after regaining political leadership in the postwar period, orchestrated a witch hunt against the left. "Even though the left got about 20 percent of the vote, a terrible persecution against the

Communist and Socialist Parties was legitimized," Elizabeth says. "People were fired from their jobs; members of the Communist Party were put in prison. . . . But a few short years later, in 1953, a broad workers' confederation [Central Unico de Trabajadores] was formed, which in my mind was the birth, the beginning of an alliance that would ultimately bring Allende to power in 1970."

These political developments took place when Elizabeth was a small child. Indeed, throughout her childhood during the immediate postwar years, her country was engaged in a full-scale social conflict, with violent strikes waged throughout the country. Economic conditions deteriorated during the 1950s, and the high cost of basic necessities, including utilities and transportation, stimulated popular protest. Riots broke out in Santiago and other cities, prompting the government to declare a state of siege. Elizabeth's middle-class family, "impoverished with so many mouths to feed—I was the oldest of eleven children," managed to offset the economic woes typical of their struggling counterparts when her father was hired by a religious group from the United States to be the caretaker of a large rural mansion whose owner was a prominent associate of the powerful statesman Andres Bello. This arrangement enabled her family to survive economically, and for Elizabeth it was a pivotal experience that taught her "to learn to love the countryside, where we lived until I was thirteen years old."

During the 1960s, Elizabeth's family lived in San Bernardo, a small town fifteen kilometers south of Santiago, where she attended the local Catholic school. By this time, Chilean political life was undergoing a readjustment, and the Marxist left, including the Socialist and Communist Parties, was once again a legitimate player in electoral politics. Elizabeth recalls that her household was rather typical of Chilean homes, in that politics were hotly debated and "everyone—including my numerous siblings and I—had a strong opinion, whether or not we knew what was really going on!" Though not an activist, her father was inclined first toward conservative Catholic politics and then the reform-oriented Christian Democrats. In the late sixties, this political party divided, and a leftist tendency emerged that would later draw Elizabeth into political activism.

In 1960, Elizabeth graduated from high school, and in the following year she entered the Catholic University in Santiago to study psychology, a major she chose because of her interest in philosophy. Her social awakening, however, came as a result of her relationship with "a group of people unaffiliated with the university who were studying in Chile from all over Latin America and exploring the major issues facing our countries." In 1964, she participated with other university students in a summer project that took them to the countryside to work with poor peasant families. "I went to a small town in the Cordillera [the Andes mountain range to the east of Santiago] and there encountered a host of problems that affected the lives of the rural poor. There were many different illnesses, no main road, massive amounts of insects, things that really impressed us students from the city. It seemed to me the only way to resolve these dramatic problems was through a profound political change, altering things at the root. . . . I met lots of other young people, students studying law, the social sciences, agronomy, and so forth, all interested in what to do to improve the conditions of the popular classes. At this point I realized that the discipline of psychology was isolated from the social issues of the day, and I abandoned it in favor of the social sciences."

The issue of extreme poverty in the country, as well as Chile's dependence on copper, its primary export commodity, which was completely in the hands of U.S. corporations, became important aspects of the heated 1964 presidential election. Christian Democratic Eduardo Frei, who was favored by the United States and by the Chilean right, mounted an electoral campaign for a "Revolution in Liberty"—over 50 percent of which was paid for by the CIA—to head off the popular FRAP (a Socialist-Communist alliance) candidate, Allende. Ignoring the local roots of Chilean Marxism, candidate Frei launched an anticommunist campaign in which he branded FRAP an extension of Moscow. Although he won the election, Frei's subsequent policies did not attract enough faithful followers to his strategy of moderate reform to weather the next election.

A new political formation emerged in the late sixties, a break-off from the Christian Democrats called the Movement of Unified Action (MAPU), which was close to the left and attracted many students and professionals to its more radical reformist impulse. Elizabeth, now married and the mother of a small child, joined MAPU in 1970. She remembers this period as exciting, one in which people were interested in all kinds of political questions and involved in many different social projects. "Chile wasn't as polarized as it would later become. The cultural environment was open and included voices of the left in all domains. It was natural to go to a meeting at the university and hear the poet Pablo Neruda or the New Song composer Violeta Parra or listen to any number of leftist leaders. We would go to a demonstration to hear the poet Nicolás Guillén speak about the Cuban Revolution or to listen to an ex–political prisoner or a writer from Spain speak about Franco and the Spanish Civil War." This increasingly politicized environment developed as Frei's reformist politics proved incapable of addressing the major ills of Chile's economy. In the 1970 elections, despite frantic U.S. covert action, the people of Chile elected Allende, the candidate of the Communist and Socialist coalition called Popular Unity, as their new president.

Throughout the world, people interested in strategies for social change looked to Chile to see whether it was possible to use the ballot box to vote in socialism. With the judiciary and parliament still controlled by representatives of the bourgeoisie, Allende set about the difficult task of implementing substantive reforms. Although his initial strategy was to freeze prices and raise wages to produce a short-term redistribution of income, he soon began to carry out the economically nationalist policies promised in his electoral campaign. He extended the modest nationalization of copper firms begun under Frei to the entire copper industry, a move that was popular even among the opposition. But as Allende carried out more nationalizations—especially of U.S. firms—the U.S. government was quick to react, mounting an international "invisible blockade" against Chile. While preventing all loans and lines of credit from going to the country, the United States simultaneously increased aid to the Chilean armed forces. Meanwhile, pushed by militant workers and impatient peasants, Allende continued to extend the state's role in the economy, nationalizing more firms and initiating a land-reform program. His government also supported the efforts of hundreds of thousands of people who took part in community-based construction, health-care, educational, and cultural projects throughout the country.

This was a euphoric period for Chileans like Elizabeth, who remembers that "it was like an enormous fiesta. We were so enthusiastic. It felt like we were creating something big, something important. Many people came from all over Latin America, and we were especially pleased that North Americans came to participate, to demonstrate solidarity. There was a cultural explosion, with films coming from all over the world, book exhibits from other countries, artisan fairs, cultural conferences, all free. The center of Santiago was filled with people from the popular classes. I'd never seen the city belong to its inhabitants like that. Of course, our excitement was matched by the terror growing among the wealthy, who had the sensation that the poor were invading their space and taking over."

Clearly this mobilization of the popular classes along with sympathetic students and cultural and professional sectors made the UP's redistributive policies even more frightening to the elite and its entrepreneurial middle-class allies, whose antipathy was reinforced by U.S. dollars and propaganda in a massive anti-UP campaign. Even though the ideological and strategic differences among the political parties of the UP coalition often compromised the effectiveness of their response to the intensification of a climate of crisis in the country, their popularity grew. When the mid-term parliamentary and municipal elections indicated an increase of support for UP candidates, rather than the usual decline in popularity of incumbent parties, the right-wing sectors of the military won the go-ahead to abandon the long-time respect for the democratic process in Chile in favor of a coup to oust the UP.

A strategy of economic destabilization was carried out during 1972 and

1973. The combination of a U.S.-backed international boycott of Chilean products and credit sources, a right-wing media campaign blaming increasing economic difficulties on the UP, and a series of (CIA-backed and -financed) strikes by entrepreneurial sectors, including truckers and doctors, threatened total chaos. Elizabeth remembers how the open environment of increased liberties and economic opportunities shifted to one of grinding difficulty. "Basic necessities became more scarce, and every day people were forced to wait in long lines in the hopes of obtaining an ever-declining supply of foodstuffs, heating oil, diapers, and other essential goods," she recalls. "All the while storekeepers were hoarding supplies to sell to the rich on the black market." As the economic situation worsened, a right-wing propaganda war blamed the UP government and claimed the crisis would only extend under its rule, in this way successfully reducing the potential opposition to the military coup that would overthrow a democratically elected government.[14]

The stage was set, and on September 11, 1973, the military attacked the presidential palace, which resulted in the death of President Allende. A military junta declared itself the new government and began a draconian attack on the Chilean population. Civilian politicians, including ex-President Frei, supported the coup in the belief that the democratic tradition of Chile would prevail and that they would inherit the reins of government. But the military defied tradition by holding onto power for the next eighteen years and by instituting a repressive culture of fear. The impact of state terror on the Chilean people would bring Elizabeth Lira back to psychology. Her participation in the human rights movement would prompt her to develop an understanding of social trauma and to explore ways to help the victims of political repression to deal with its psychological sequelae.

Argentina: Beef and Populism

As always, Buenos Aires is teeming with life, its colorful streets jammed with people, kiosks, flower stands, automobiles, motorcycles, and buses in a kind of nonstop visual dance that never ceases to excite the senses. It is especially beautiful on this early fall day, for the trees that line the streets have not yet lost their leaves, and the sun crisply lights up the multicolored buildings. Like Rome and Paris, cosmopolitan Buenos Aires has a magical attraction and is a wondrous surprise spread out along the wide, silver-hued La Plata River, whose waters empty into the South Atlantic. I think about how thrilled I am to be back in this intense environment as I walk along the narrow sidewalk with Juan Carlos Volnovich. I struggle to keep up as his six-foot, two-inch frame moves ahead at a rapid clip. He is talking excitedly as he guides me to one of the neighborhood's hundreds of charming restaurants. As we are seated, I note the fresh white tablecloth and wine glasses, which remind me that the noon-time meal in this Latin capital is always an elaborate and tasty ritual. With a tango hauntingly playing in the background, we continue our discussion about the conference Juan Carlos has helped to organize for the Grandmothers of the Plaza de Mayo, and whose sessions we have been attending for three days and nights.

The conference has featured public presentations by legal and mental-health professionals from Argentina, the United States, and Europe; since the late 1970s these professionals have aided the Grandmothers in their efforts to locate their grandchildren who were disappeared by the military junta during their seven-year-long Dirty War (the name given to the military's illegal detentions, torture, and murder of tens of thousands of Argentine citizens, a terrorist strategy chosen to eliminate all actual and potential opposition to the established order). The conference participants include Argentine colleagues in both fields, as well as the general public. "This is so important," Juan Carlos tells me in his typically animated fashion. "The Grandmothers are among the few voices still urging us to deal with the legacy of the Dirty War. And look how many people are attending these sessions. The press coverage is fantastic, don't you think?" I am to present a paper in the afternoon's plenary session about the psychological impact of social violence in the United States. Having read it, Juan Carlos assures me that it will stimulate much concern among the participants, who need to think about the new manifestations of violence in Argentine society since the end of military rule. "We must understand the nature of this historical moment in order to intervene appropriately," he says. This is what is so engaging about Juan Carlos, his enthusiasm, his passion, his sense of being in the middle of significant events and of participating in movements that will make a difference in peoples' lives.

He is also very funny. As we recount an especially dramatic session of the previous afternoon, his ability to capture the humor and irony of an incident that was simultaneously disturbing has us both giggling irrepressibly. The session had been planned as an open dialogue with the audience to follow presentations by some of Buenos Aires's most prestigious psychoanalysts, who are also well known as outspoken human rights advocates. They had just finished brilliantly analyzing the significance of various aspects of the Grandmothers' struggle. A young university student in the audience rose and addressed them. She told them that they did not understand the plight of her generation. "Look," she said, "you speak of 'the struggle.' But you have no idea what it is like for us. We grew up without heroes; we have no Che or Fidel; we've known only a society run by the military, and now its gruesome aftermath . . . a decadent society, with the torturers walking among us. We have no hope. Now there is just this New World Order, which isn't so new after all. It provides us with little more than the hope of surviving. There are fewer and fewer jobs, with less and less meaning. And yet there seems to be an endless supply of the latest consumer goods, which is all many people think about. What are the alternatives for those of us who know something is wrong? What does human rights mean in this so-called democratic society filled with corruption at every level?"

When the young woman finished, there was a dead silence. She had caught the usually articulate speakers off guard, and they were unable to muster a response. The session ended there, in the silence. Though Juan Carlos had felt a chill at this young woman's remarks, in retrospect he cannot help being amused at the discomfort of his colleagues. He knows that in his own generation's wish to find continuity with the meaning that past political struggles had given their lives, they often forget that the younger generation is bereft of their certainty about what to fight for and what to fight against.

But, then, nothing has ever been crystal clear in Argentine politics. And Juan Carlos is the first to acknowledge that his generation of political activists, including the mental-health professionals among them, often had recourse to the psychological defense of denial in order to endure the contradictions of their political culture and revolutionary struggles. These contradictions are perhaps the legacy of a society whose self-image has been a conflicted one. Argentina is, after all, a little piece of Europe in the third world, a sophisticated first-world culture bound up with a neocolonial economy and revolutionary agenda. The roots of this conflict lie of course in the distant past.

From the beginning, Argentina's fate was locked to that of Europe.[15] Lacking precious metals and a numerous, settled indigenous population, it was a backwater of the Spanish Empire until the eighteenth century, when Buenos Aires became an important port for trade with Europe. After independence in the 1820s, Argentine politics was dominated by a wealthy rancher, Juan Manuel de Rosas, who built a powerful government machine that represented the interests of the landowning elite. However, Rosas's xenophobic hatred of foreign powers and his charismatic appeal to the rough-hewn gauchos on the large estates and the artisans and workers in the cities made him powerful enemies who overthrew him in the early 1850s.

The European-identified intellectuals, who had lived in exile during Rosas's regime, returned to govern the country. To them and the rest of the elite class, Rosas represented the barbarism of the gaucho who had destroyed the civilized (European) culture of Buenos Aires. Desperately antagonistic to the Indians and mestizos (people of mixed European and Indian descent) and to their cultures, these intellectuals set about to develop political structures, an educational system, and cultural values that emulated those of Europe and the United States.

In the 1870s, the Argentine government launched the "Indian Wars," exterminating or subduing indigenous populations and enabling the expansion of the landed oligarchy into the fertile territories to the south and west of Buenos Aires. Then, based on its ability to supply agricultural goods—grain and meat—needed by the North Atlantic industrial world, the Argentine economy expanded at a remarkable rate. However, although Argentina had an important resource—the pampas—it lacked capital and labor, both of which came from Europe. The British supplied the capital for investment in docks, packing houses, and public utilities, and British firms handled shipping, insurance, and banking. Labor was also supplied by Europe, as millions of workers streamed into Argentina, primarily from Italy and Spain. So many immigrants came seeking their fortunes that by 1914 approximately 30 percent of the population was foreign-born, a demographic situation that produced a distinctly European culture and a consuming preoccupation among Argentines with the question of what was their authentic national identity.

The European immigrants affected the language, culture, and politics of Argentina. In the working-class neighborhoods of Buenos Aires, a colorful dialect, *lumfardo*, was born, while the tango emerged from the immigrant poor as an expression of the angst of geographical dislocation and the anomie of urban life. The union movement from the 1870s on was influenced by European anarchist and socialist exiles, who were militant organizers for workers' rights. By the turn of the century, organized labor emerged as an important force in Argentine politics, with the anarchists fighting for better wages and working conditions and vocally protesting against the elite's European-oriented, laissez-faire model of progress.

Many immigrants came to Argentina with artisan and professional skills that enabled them to achieve middle-class status in one generation. Such was the case with the forebearers of Juan Carlos Volnovich, who, like most Argentine psychoanalysts and psychologists, traces his roots to an immigrant past. In the late nineteenth century, Juan Carlos's paternal grandparents, Romanian and Polish Jews, came to Buenos Aires, where his grandfather made a relatively good income as a tailor. Although neither grandparent ever learned to speak or write Spanish, clinging instead to their native Yiddish, their four sons achieved significant upward mobility in one generation. Two of them became doctors, and the other two were successful businessmen. "My mother's history was very different," Juan Carlos recalls. "She belonged to an aristocratic family, one with a good deal of intellectual accomplishments." His maternal great-grandparents, Viennese Jews, had immigrated to Buenos Aires, and soon prospered in business. Although Juan Carlos's grandfather was born in Argentina, he was sent to Europe to be educated. He returned with an engineering degree, but his additional training at the University of Buenos Aires in other fields brought him much status in the intellectual community of the city. He founded Jewish schools throughout the country and ultimately became the director of the Research Institute of the prestigious Jewish center, Asociación Mutual Israelita Argentina, in Buenos Aires.

Like Juan Carlos's family, immigrants who were part of the middle class contributed to the mainly European-oriented artistic and intellectual life of Buenos Aires. This middle class also took on the elite-dominated electoral arena and fought successfully to extend voting rights to all adult males, encouraging political participation among the middle and working classes. But even though the middle-class Radical Party won the election of 1916 with support from the workers, its president proved himself no more a friend of labor than his elite predecessors. In 1919, for example, economic difficulties produced a series of militant strikes throughout the country, and thousands of demonstrating workers were shot and killed by a right-wing paramilitary movement before the Radical government forcibly ended the strikes and repressed the anarchist leadership. The government could not eliminate organized labor, however, for the Socialist Party, which emphasized political action through participation at the ballot box, and the Communist Party, which stressed militant labor organizing, gained a voice in the union movement.

A military coup in 1930 returned government to the elite, which was forced to support policies fostering industrialization during the thirties and early forties. New factories sprouted up around Buenos Aires, and with immigration from abroad cut off, mestizos from the interior migrated to the capital city looking for work to fill the increased demand for labor. These migrants—called *cabecitas negras* (black heads or greasers) by the racist oligarchy and middle class—became the grateful supporters of Juan Domingo Perón, an army officer who in the early forties became the secretary of labor and social welfare. In that position, Perón strengthened the unions, backed extensive labor legislation, and thus was responsible for raising the dignity and improving the standard of living of the increasingly mestizo working class. When he ran for president in 1946, Perón was supported by a coalition of the new nationalist industrial class and the working class. He handily won against his opposition, an alliance of forces ranging from the traditional right and its U.S. supporters, which feared his economic nationalism, to the traditional Marxist left, which mistakenly saw him as an American variant of European fascism.[16]

From 1946 until 1955, Perón, with his charismatic wife, Evita, at his side until her death from cancer in 1952 at the age of thirty-three, built a populist movement based on the principles of national sovereignty and social justice. His nationalization of U.S. and British investments in strategic sectors of the economy impressed Argentine industrialists interested in the economic autonomy of their country. His elaborate social welfare programs, which expanded workers' rights and privileges, appealed to the popular classes. His anti-European nationalism, redistributive politics, and populist appeals to the poor and working population alienated not only the elite but the intellectuals as well because of their marked preference for European culture and values over the country's indigenous cultural roots. Class and ethnic tensions were made more acrimonious by Perón's use of strong-arm tactics where necessary to secure implementation of his policies.

Although Juan Carlos's family was not particularly political, he says of himself that his "childhood was marked by Peronism." Juan Carlos was born in November 1941, and when he was a few months old, his parents moved from Buenos Aires to a small Jewish colony of two thousand inhabitants in the territory of La Pampa, where his father acquired much prestige as the town's only physician. They remained there throughout the war and the following seven years. Paralyzed by polio at the age of one, Juan Carlos spent the first five years of his life in and out of hospitals with his attentive mother at his side. Although he recovered, except for a faint hint of a limp, his mother decided that "since I would not be able to excel physically, I would have to be very intelligent." He recalls being taught to read at an early age; as a child of five, he was moved to tears when he read a book his grandfather wrote about the tragedy of millions of European Jews killed at the hands of the Nazis, called *The Survivors Speak*. "A kind of 'Schindler's List,' it was filled with testimonies and photographs of concentration camp survivors."

Like all Jews in Argentina, young Juan Carlos was aware of the Holocaust. But, unlike most Jews in the country, he was infatuated with the Peróns. He remembers with a mischievous smile that when he started elementary school, he "fell in love with Evita," whose engaging photograph was in every classroom and whose book, *The Reason for My Life*, was required reading. "It was Perón's power as a leader and Evita's charismatic beauty, her lavish dresses, her impassioned speeches for the downtrodden that awakened my fantasies as a boy. I guess now I would say that my Oedipus complex was lived out with Perón and Evita, but most especially with her!"

In 1952, Juan Carlos's family moved back to Buenos Aires, where he entered secondary school. Within several years, a series of economic crises was destabilizing the alliance that had supported Perón, thus emboldening the restive military. The generals' anti-Peronist sentiments, shared by the landowning elite, the Church, and the middle class, were now being reflected within the industrial bourgeoisie as well because its pro-Peronist politics had been eviscerated by its growing alliance with foreign capital interests now penetrating the floundering economy. The working class remained solidly Peronist, although now isolated and not sufficiently strong to maintain their adored leader in power. In 1954, Perón was overthrown in a coup that sent him into exile in Madrid, where he continued to influence the direction of Argentine political life for the next eighteen years. Until 1972, inept civilian and repressive military regimes took turns attempting to guide Argentina's rollercoaster economy and to eliminate Peronism as a legitimate political force.

Juan Carlos entered medical school several years after the coup, at the precocious age of sixteen. Like many middle-class intellectuals, he partook of the boom in cultural life that followed Perón's ouster. Students, professionals, and intellectuals joined the film clubs, philosophical societies, and literary groups that multiplied during this period and flooded Buenos Aires with the latest in European art, literature, and cinema. Psychoanalysis was an important element in every aspect of cultural expression. Slowly, by the early sixties, the first signs of a new radical politics, influenced by the Cuban Revolution and liberation theology, began to make themselves felt among Argentines seeking a way of understanding their society, which seemed to be in endless turmoil politically and increasing difficulty economically.

In 1962, Juan Carlos met Silvia Werthein, a university student majoring in psychology. "She opened up a whole new world to me," he says, "and lifted me out of the narrow parameters of my medical studies and preoccupation with music and the arts. All at once, through Silvia, politics and psychology entered my life. The second time we saw each other, we fell in love, and we've been together ever since." Silvia introduced Juan Carlos to radical politics through her personal connection to the Cuban Revolution. In 1960, her physician brother, Leonardo, had written to fellow Argentine Che Guevara, who invited him to come to Cuba to work as a physician in the rural zones where the Revolution was building clinics and hospitals for the peasantry and rural workers. Later, Leonardo became the director of epidemiology in the young Revolution's Ministry of Health. In 1960, Silvia had also gone to Cuba to take part in the celebrated literacy campaign for some months. "Cuba came to mean hope," Juan Carlos recalls. "When the Bay of Pigs failed, my previous cynicism about the impossibility of anything new happening in Latin America under the nose of the United States changed to one of optimism—maybe we can do something, I thought." So during the sixties, Juan Carlos and Silvia felt a growing identification with revolutionary movements. "A Latin American revolution," he explains, "not a variant of the Soviet Union, but a revolution secured through an armed struggle that could put the 'salt of the earth' in power. We didn't join any of the leftist parties that were either reinvigorating themselves or sprouting up anew, like so many other young people we knew. Instead, we read Camus, Sartre, de Beauvoir, and applauded revolutionaries like Che Guevara in Bolivia and the priest Camilo Torres in Colombia." Meanwhile, through Silvia, Juan Carlos also came to know the world of psychoanalysis, which he would ultimately choose as his profession.

By the late sixties, Argentina was drawn into a cauldron of intensifying contradictions. As U.S. multinational corporations fairly gobbled up the country's industrial and commercial sectors, nationalistic sentiment intensified, lending fuel to the fire of increasing class confrontation in response to declining wages, soaring prices, and rising unemployment. Middle-class aspirations were choked off by the combination of stagnation and hyperinflation, and many professionals, entrepreneurs, and intellectuals did an about-face with respect to Peronism. Juan Carlos and Silvia were among the middle class who came to believe that the Peronist movement was the vehicle through which much-needed radical social change would occur in Argentina. They found their niche within the movement being led by the new, combative, grass-roots Peronist labor unions and revolutionary Peronist organizations, which had become radicalized over the years as their attempts to win economic and social reforms met with tenacious resistance from politicians bent on preserving the status quo.

The revolutionary armed Peronist groups ultimately coalesced into one organization called the Montoneros, which drew popular support from militant workers and youth. Like tens of thousands of young professionals, Juan Carlos and Silvia identified with the Montoneros as the political vanguard in Argentina. Even the ivory tower of psychoanalysis was penetrated by the effervescent social upheavals. By the late sixties, Juan Carlos, now a candidate in training at the Argentine Psychoanalytic Association, was involved with other politically progressive analysts and candidates in attempting to link the psychoanalytic enterprise to the national agenda for radical change. Especially significant to him was his supervisor, Marie Langer, whose own radical politics he would come to know and admire and whose political path would often cross his own in subsequent years.

In 1972, in the first national elections since 1966, a Peronist coalition won, placing a progressive, mild-mannered doctor in the presidency and ushering in a short-lived period of free expression and political mobilization popularly referred to as "The Euphoria." Political prisoners were freed, mass demonstrations were organized to articulate support for a more open society and implementation of social reforms, and people from every social sector were organized to work on community-improvement projects in the most economically and socially deprived neighborhoods. During this period, Juan Carlos participated with other politically progressive psychoanalysts and psychologists in a variety of community-based projects to bring psychoanalysis to the popular classes. He and his colleagues wrote articles and books analyzing the dynamics of authoritarian society and postulated ways of understanding the relationship between oppressive class relations and psychic pain.[17]

Some months after the election, Perón returned from exile with his wife, Isabel, whom he had met in 1954 when she was a nightclub dancer in Panama. In an unprecedented development, extraordinary elections took place shortly afterward, and Perón and "Isabelita" were elected president and vice president with an astounding 62 percent of the vote. But, as the military had hoped, old man Perón now identified himself with the conservative factions of his movement and turned on the revolutionary forces whose efforts had brought him back to Argentina from his eighteen-year exile. When Perón died in 1974, his incompetent wife assumed the presidency, guiding the country into economic disaster, political corruption, and increasing repression of the Peronist and Marxist left by right-wing death squads, such as the Argentine Anticommunist Alliance (Triple A).

Life in Argentina became a nightmare for many citizens. Juan Carlos continued his political activism in legal community-based groups allied with the Montoneros, mainly providing desperately needed psychological intervention for the children of political activists. Like thousands of professionals, he and Silvia lived a double life, maintaining their private practices to support themselves, protecting their family as best they could, and continuing their work in a radical movement that was falling under the heavy weight of government-organized paramilitary repression. "It was terrifying," Juan Carlos remembers with a frown. "Our young son and daughter could never tell anyone where we lived. It was an environment that induced complete paranoia. We constantly thought about leaving Argentina but always concluded that we owed it to our country to stay."

Anyone associated with radical politics felt endangered by the increasingly open presence of right-wing death squads. Already during the prior year and a half there had been a steady emigration as people fled the growing violence. Marie Langer and other colleagues of Juan Carlos, whose names had appeared on the death list of the Triple A, had long ago been forced to leave the country. But the chaotic and frightening economic and political conditions were affecting more than political activists. Indeed, they were wearing down the entire society. Hyperinflation was making each family's struggle to obtain food and other basic necessities more and more unpredictable, while the incompetent and decadent rule of Isabel and her advisors was each day less defensible.

These uncertain conditions caused intolerable anxiety in the population at large, so that many, especially among the middle class, welcomed the inevitable military coup when it happened on March 24, 1976. Accustomed to the generals' occupation of the presidential palace, they told themselves they were once again simply trading democracy for longed-for law and order. They could not guess what lay in store for them: the Dirty War. Under the guise of eliminating the armed left opposition (which in reality had already been vanquished), the military carried out an unparalleled assault on civil society. Its aim was to eliminate all vestiges of progressive thought and organization, even if it meant the killing of a good percentage of several generations of Argentine citizens.

Juan Carlos and Silvia remained in Argentina for nine months following the coup. With their political comrades dead, arrested, or in exile, they "felt like orphans." Although still reluctant to leave, a twist of fate propelled them from this nightmare, and in December 1976 they and their two children tearfully left their country. They would spend the years of the Dirty War in exile in Cuba, where Juan Carlos would have a unique opportunity to practice psychoanalysis and treat children from Argentina, Chile, and Uruguay whose parents had been disappeared or killed by these countries' terrorist states.

MARCELO AND MAREN VIÑAR, Elizabeth Lira, and Juan Carlos Volnovich all knew one another, as well as the other protagonists of our story whom we shall presently encounter, during the tumultuous period when they came of age professionally and politically. Their relationships deepened as they met over the subsequent years to work together or to share their observations of and experiences in the maelstrom of state terror and its aftermath. But we are getting ahead of our story. For there is a bit more history and *memoria* to discover about liberation psychology. What, indeed, was the nature of the movement within psychoanalysis that emerged in the explosive sixties to postulate that Marx and Freud were the two pillars of a revolutionary enterprise of social and psychic emancipation?

And why was it that on seizing power in March 1976 the Argentine military, like its counterparts in Uruguay and Chile, declared its Dirty War not only on its armed revolutionary enemy but on all manifestations of progressive thought? As the junta tightened its noose around every institution that threatened its authoritarian rule, a significant target was the mental-health community. "Civilians are also warriors," the generals asserted, "ideas a different form of weapon."[18] The School of Psychology at the National University was closed, entire staffs at community mental health clinics were summarily fired, and books by well-known psychological theorists were added to the public bonfires of banned reading materials. The junta marked psychoanalysts and psychologists as fair game in their onslaught against civil society, declaring that "Marx and Freud are the two main enemies of Western Christian Civilization."[19]

Chapter 2

Freud and Marx:
Politics of Convergence

Behind what appears to us as reality, Freud and Marx both discovered the actual forces that govern us: Freud, the unconscious; and Marx, class struggle.

—MARIE LANGER, *Cuestionamos I* (1971)

"IT BEGAN EARLY one morning in late December . . . it was 1974," Mimi Langer tells me. She is answering my question about why she left Argentina. Even though nine years have passed and her voice is calm, I notice how she lights a cigarette and looks away when she speaks. Her words evoke the scene. She had begun work as usual. Her consultation room in her expansive luxury apartment, situated in the heart of the prosperous Palermo neighborhood of Buenos Aires, felt cozy from the heat of the early sun's rays. But when her first patient arrived, his greeting pierced the tranquillity. "Doctora," his voice was ominously hushed, "I've just discovered that your name is on the Triple A's death list." Somewhat disconcerted, she nonetheless told herself to remain calm, that perhaps his news was only an unfounded rumor. Similar communications from overwrought patients and colleagues throughout the day punctured Mimi's denial and compelled her to take these warnings seriously.

In a hastily arranged family meeting that evening, her daughter Veronica and two sons, Tomás and Martin, insisted that their sixty-four-year-old mother leave the country. "But I was torn," she recalls. "On the one hand, I was truly terrified and wanted to run, and, on the other, I felt guilty at the prospect of abandoning the other mental-health professionals who were active in the movement with me. I knew many of them would also become targets of the paramilitary groups sanctioned by the government." In the end, Mimi acquiesced to her family's demands. She would go to Mexico, she decided, where her older daughter had recently relocated following her marriage to a Mexican writer. "Besides Ana and my professional connections in Mexico City," Mimi told herself, "I know lots of the political refugees in the exile community there."

Suitcases were packed hurriedly, and the details of Mimi's professional and personal life were left unattended in the last minute rush to make the scheduled flight bound for Mexico City. She remembers that as the plane took off, "I stared out of the window and felt the sting of tears pushing through the numb feelings that had helped to move me like a sleepwalker through the past twenty-four hours." The lights of Buenos Aires sparkled as the plane ascended, and she eagerly searched the bright scene below to locate the familiar landmarks of the cosmopolitan city. As the proud South American center of European culture faded from view, Mimi abruptly sat back, feeling as if she were being plummeted into the black hole of an uncharted future. "I looked around at the other passengers, feeling bitter as I wondered how many of them, appearing composed just like me, were also being run out of their country. How many, just like me, were being forced at gun point to follow thousands of professionals and intellectuals before us who had spoken out against the repression? I was scared, and I wondered whether I would ever return. I remember thinking that this was the second time in my life that I was forced to abandon my home to become a political refugee. I also knew that it was the logical outcome of all that had come before."

"Tell me about it," I say. "Ah," she replies, her eyes lighting up, "that takes us back to Vienna, where it all started."

Europe: *The Struggle against Fascism*

"I was born Marie Lisbeth Glas in 1910, the younger of two daughters in a wealthy and progressive Jewish family. What a time it was. . . . I grew up nurtured by privilege, on the one hand, and, on the other, by the exhilarating cultural environment of a city ruled by Europe's only mass-based Social Democratic Party." Indeed, Mimi's youthful mind was formed in a social world permeated by the two most important modes of thought produced by nineteenth-century Europe: Marxism and psychoanalysis. "I remember as a little girl my father telling me about the Russian revolutionary women like Aleksandra Kollontay and Vera Figner. Their exciting lives and professional ambitions made a great impression on me. Later on I would learn about the feminist and socialist ideas that enabled them to go beyond the limiting parameters of respectable bourgeois women like my mother."

A Marxist critique of the exploitative nature of capitalist class relations inspired the politics of the labor movement and leftist parties, including the ruling Social Democrats, who instituted in Vienna progressive programs in education, housing, social security, and health. Mimi speaks enthusiastically about "the workers' universities, sports clubs, and summer camps—some of which I attended—that extended access to education and recreation beyond the privileged classes." The city's cultural renaissance brought provocative themes related to class struggle, sexuality, and the role of women to popular culture, the theater, and the arts. At her exclusive girls' school, the Schwarz-wald Schule, Mimi was introduced to the work of the era's artists, writers, and social scientists, in which psychoanalysis and Marxism were employed to address the subjective and external limits on human productivity and pleasure in contemporary society.

For them, Marx challenged the prevailing bourgeois ideology of equal opportunity for all in capitalism by exposing its exploitative foundation in the capitalist expropriation of the surplus (unpaid) labor of the working class. And Sigmund Freud challenged Enlightenment beliefs in human rationality by uncovering the unconscious mind, whose powerfully irrational and impulse-ridden nature was harnessed to serve civilization at the heavy cost of individual freedom and contentment. In the 1920s, Wilhelm Reich, Otto Fenichel, Siegfried Bernfeld, and Edith Jacobson represented a generation of psychoanalysts whose psychological sensibilities were framed by their commitment to progressive political struggles for justice and equality.

The radical politics of the day embraced the new sexual mores, which challenged the deeply rooted Victorian legacy within Austrian culture. The feminist movement provided new role models for Mimi's generation, encouraging an open expression of sexuality and professional ambitions in women. Mimi describes her adolescence as "a time of excited experimentation with romantic involvements that distracted me from my academic demands. I was really curious about men and sex but resentful that I had to think about marrying 'well.' I remember envying poor women who weren't pressured by their families to fall in love with the 'right man.' I was quite relieved when my family lost their fortune in the Depression, making it impossible to provide me with a dowry. I felt liberated!" When, at the age of nineteen, Mimi decided to go to medical school, she received the enthusiastic support of her father, "for whom I was the son he never had," and reluctant agreement from her mother.

The subsequent direction in her life toward both political activism and psychoanalysis was determined by the rise of Austro-fascism in the early 1930s. During a research semester in Kiel, Germany, in 1932, Mimi experienced "the chilling effect of seeing a mass rally of the National Socialists [Nazis] and the mesmerizing impact of Hitler's speech on the demonstrators. When I returned to Austria, the Nazis began winning regional and municipal elections, and the Austro-fascists threatened the Social Democratic hold on Vienna. I decided to become active in the struggle against fascism. It seemed to me absurd for us to give up without a fight."

Mimi joined the Austrian Communist Party because "I believed that many Jews and the Social Democrats in general were denying the sinister future that

lay in store. I was convinced the Communist Party was the only political movement that recognized the certainty of the Nazis' genocidal plans for the Jews
and leftists." From her feminist viewpoint, it was, as well, the only party at
the time that understood clearly the radical reorganization of society that was
necessary for complete gender equality. In the Communist Party, she quickly
formed relationships with new friends whose similar values and commitment
to the antifascist cause enabled her to "find a new family, comrades who helped
me feel supported and comforted in a threatening world. We could depend
on our mutual dedication to fight the Nazi threat, and we shared a hopeful
vision of a free society." Six weeks after she joined the Communist Party, all
political opposition—including the majority Social Democratic Party—was
declared illegal by Austro-fascism, and Mimi became part of the clandestine
movement with all its attendant dangers.

At the same time, and quite apart from her activism, Mimi pursued her
studies, graduating from medical school in 1935. Her attempt to obtain training in psychiatry was circumvented when Jews were forbidden by the Austro-
fascists to work in the public hospitals that had been part of the Social
Democratic–inspired socialized medical system. Mimi tells me that, ironically,
"Austro-fascism was a decisive factor in my decision to be trained at Freud's
institute." Following an interview with Anna Freud, she was accepted as a
candidate for training in the Vienna Psychoanalytic Institute, where her formal education brought her into contact with luminaries of the psychoanalytic
world, including her professor, Helene Deutsch, and her supervisor, Jeanne
Lampl de Groot.

"Once again, just as in high school, I wasn't a brilliant student—only this
time for political reasons. My mind was elsewhere, on the political battles we
were waging to hold onto civil rights in Austria. I led a double life, split between my psychoanalytic treatment and course work at the institute and my
underground activism in the Communist Party." In charge of antifascist agi-
tation and propaganda for the Party, Mimi proudly asserts that "I can legitimately take credit for organizing the last congress of the Austrian Communist
Party held inside the country before the war, and I did it without exposing
any of the sixty provincial delegates to danger!"

However, this activism had to be hidden from the psychoanalytic community. Indeed, fascism had succeeded in smothering the cross-fertilization
between the theories of progressive politics and of psychoanalysis that had
flourished under Social Democracy in Austria and that in Germany had been
reflected in the innovative practice of Wilhelm Reich, who, for a brief time,
integrated his psychoanalytic theory and clinical work with his political activism in the Communist Party. Now, in the deteriorating political situation,
there was little time for theoretical discussion and an intensifying mutual

suspicion of psychoanalysis by the Communist Party and of leftist politics by psychoanalytic institutions. Under these conditions, "I felt increasingly self-indulgent and guilty about my psychoanalytic treatment and training. With worsening fascist repression and the imprisonment of growing numbers of my rank-and-file comrades, I began to feel that I was studying my umbilical cord while the world was blowing up around me."

The situation became more complicated when, alarmed by the Nazi persecution in Germany of psychoanalysts who were viewed as representatives of a "subversive ideology," and by fascist repression in Austria, the Vienna Psychoanalytic Institute formally declared a position of neutrality with respect to politics. A regulation was passed that prohibited analysts and candidates from participating in clandestine organizations; given the illegality of all opposition parties, this rule essentially forbade individuals related to the institute to participate in the antifascist struggle, in effect requiring that a choice be made between psychoanalysis and political activism. Either analysts had to end the treatment of politically involved patients, thereby ignoring medical ethics, or patients who were political activists had to agree not to speak about politics during their analytic sessions, countermanding the psychoanalytic rule of free association. "This development deeply affected my attitude toward the institute. I believed the administrators had withdrawn from the challenge facing all democratic sectors of Austrian society." It would, in fact, be a pivotal factor in Mimi's struggles later in life and on a faraway continent to bridge the gap between politics and psychoanalysis. But for now she believed psychoanalysts had acted naively or in bad faith, manifesting a severe form of "psychological denial," as if their refusal to respond to the persecution of Jewish analysts in Berlin and to the elimination of all civil rights in Austria could assure the survival of individual analysts or of their profession. "I was enraged, and I devalued psychoanalysis. And I knew that the revolution was more important." When the Spanish Civil War broke out in 1936, like thousands of political progressives, she was drawn to the Spanish Republic, whose progressive social experiment was being consumed in the flames of Franco's fascist onslaught.

Along with Max Langer, a surgeon and her future husband, Mimi joined an International Medical Brigade and spent months on the military front operating on the young Republic's wounded and dying soldiers. Her first contact with Spanish political culture made her marvel at its passion, joy, and comradeship, but months later she felt ground down by the grim reality of war. Working first as Max's anesthesiologist, Mimi eventually performed surgical procedures as well. They both suffered the grueling frustration provoked by the terrible number of amputations they had to perform, with no possibility of prosthesis. At the end of 1937, Max and Mimi were sent to Nice, France, to purchase the equipment they would need to manufacture prosthetic devices. But before they could return, word arrived that the Republic was beyond saving. Thus the couple rejoined Mimi's parents, who had moved to the Sudetenland, Czechoslovakia, to be near her father's relocated business.

This final chapter of Mimi's life in Europe was filled with personal as well as political tragedy. After having suffered a series of miscarriages in Spain, she gave birth to a premature baby girl in Nice, who died after living only a few hours. "I entered into the deepest depression of my life." Shortly following her reunion with her family in what was now called Sudetenland, she realized she was once again pregnant. At the beginning of her second trimester, she began to hemorrhage, and as she was rushed by ambulance to a hospital located in the small town of Reichenberg, she suffered another miscarriage. "I'll never forget what it was like lying in the hospital bed at night, alone, my gown soaked with blood. . . . Through the open window of my room I could hear the terrifying sounds of a passing Nazi demonstration and hundreds of voices yelling, 'Kill the Jews.'"

Mimi pauses for a moment, then collects herself. "You see," she resumes, "these devastating experiences were partly why I later became interested in psychosomatic disturbances in women's reproductive life. At the time I recognized that my miscarriages were a manifestation of a terrible conflict between my wish to have a baby and my fear of bringing a child into a world torn apart by violence and death. Later on, as a psychoanalyst, I would discover that they were symptoms, as well, of deeper conflicts about sexuality and motherhood typical of modern woman."

Latin America: Psychoanalysis in the New World

In 1939, with the growing Nazi threat on the continent, Mimi and Max fled the escalating conflagration. "This opportunity brought me out of my depression. I viewed our departure as an adventure, a chance to start anew." They sailed for Uruguay, where together they endured several difficult and impoverished years. However, they found that in the New World, European immigrants with skill and fortitude could in fact begin again. During the three years in Uruguay, Mimi worked as a cook and a tutor in English and German, and she and Max had the first two of their five children. The couple maintained their political activism by joining the solidarity movement with the Spanish Republic.

Gradually Mimi wended her way back to psychoanalysis. "My reencounter occurred when a German immigrant from the solidarity movement asked me to give a lecture on Marx and Freud as a fund-raiser for the Spanish Republic. I recalled much more of Marxism than of psychoanalytic theory at that moment, but I succeeded by focusing on how both these great thinkers had discovered the latent meaning behind manifest reality." Shortly after, Mimi, Max, and their two children relocated to Buenos Aires, where Max's medical degree was eventually approved by the Argentine authorities and Mimi made her first explorations into the psychoanalytic community of that cosmopolitan city.

By 1942, when the Langers moved to Buenos Aires, psychoanalysis had already been influential for several decades among the city's medical profession and literati. In the twenties, the middle class in general, always avid consumers of the latest intellectual currents from Europe, had been reading the many journals and attending the numerous conferences that were dedicated to exploring a variety of themes in psychoanalysis. And, as in Europe, during the Depression, a significant number of Argentine professionals and academics politically opposed to their country's conservative government had explored the possible intersection between Marxism and psychoanalysis.

Once in Buenos Aires, Mimi dedicated herself to studying all of Freud's works, and this effort, in addition to her training at the Vienna Psychoanalytic Institute, gave her sufficient credentials in those early days to join a group about to launch a training center for psychoanalytic theory and clinical practice in Argentina. In 1942, she became the youngest and the only woman among the six official founders of the Argentine Psychoanalytic Association (APA). She was in formidable company, for her colleagues represented an impressive variety of interdisciplinary, scholarly, and progressive political interests in addition to their medical specializations. Several brought to the task of institution building the benefits of their own training in Europe with prominent individuals in the field and their friendships with outstanding figures in the arts, such as Salvador Dali and Federico García Lorca. In Buenos Aires, the group attracted friends and colleagues whose fascination with psychoanalysis was connected to their passionate and multifaceted interests in philosophy, the arts, and democratic political struggles.[1] The APA developed a full-fledged training program, requiring candidates to complete four years of weekly seminars, a psychoanalytic treatment (four to five sessions weekly) with a training analyst, and three psychoanalytic cases supervised weekly by a training analyst. The APA institute was soon formally recognized by the International Psychoanalytical Association.

The founders of the APA represented a microcosm of Porteño society.[2] They belonged to a generation formed by the dramatic economic and political upheavals of the period. Several, for example, came from families who had, like millions of others, responded to the Depression by migrating from the impoverished interior of the country to Buenos Aires, where they had achieved appreciable upward mobility. Several others, including Mimi, were recent refugees from Europe seeking a safe haven from a world that had come apart before their eyes. For them all, psychoanalysis became the central passion of their lives, something they fervently believed in as a vision of general human liberation as much as a treatment for individual suffering.

To Mimi in particular, psychoanalysis became "a new kind of militancy, one that replaced politics for several decades," during which time she committed her exceptional energies to the creation of the most vital and productive center of psychoanalytic thought and practice in Latin America. "I think my immersion in professional life and my isolation from left politics was partially a defense against my insecurity as an immigrant and my need to find a niche for myself and my family in a new society." It was, as well, a fearfulness about the unfamiliar political culture of Argentina, whose seeming unpredictability provoked a fair amount of anxiety. The decision to keep a low political profile appeared especially advisable during the mid-1940s, when populist President Perón instituted a decade of nationalist antipathy toward British and U.S. economic imperialism and traditional European cultural hegemony over Argentina. Although progressive in the context of Argentine history, Perón's politics threatened the traditions associated with the middle-class European and European-identified psychoanalytic community, as well as their counterparts in the arts and sciences.

However, in spite of the populist spirit of the Peronist government during the forties and fifties, Buenos Aires proved a hospitable cultural environment for the growth of Latin America's most prestigious center of psychoanalytic training. Mimi and the other founding members immersed themselves in the task of constructing their institute, which soon won accolades from colleagues around the world for its contributions to the field. The founders of the APA made great efforts to disseminate psychoanalysis among not only the professional community but the lay public as well. Its journal *Revista de Psicoanálisis,* for example, was sold throughout Buenos Aires in the many bookstores that served an educated clientele interested in the social sciences and the arts.[3]

During this period, Mimi and other immigrant professionals felt it important not to call attention to their leftist leanings or to be active in leftist politics. One had to keep a low profile so that the young psychoanalytic association would not be at risk. Even so, Mimi recalls that "in the APA we never prohibited political activism in an authoritarian way, as had been the case in Vienna, though there was an isolationist climate that discouraged it. Any progressive political activities I engaged in, for example, I did quite apart from my role as an analyst in the APA. I guess you could say that in my public posture I came to renounce Marxism." The fact that the road to the left for politically progressive psychoanalysts had been closed by Stalinism also spurred the replacement of Mimi's political ideology with a psychoanalytic Weltanschauung. Communist psychiatrists in Argentina—as elsewhere throughout the world—were forced by the party to adopt behaviorism as their orientation and to reject psychoanalysis as idealist and a tool of a crumbling social order. "Thus at that time it seemed that my seniors in Vienna had been right: one had to choose between psychoanalysis and Marxism."[4]

The extraordinary impact of psychoanalysis in Buenos Aires may be understood as a simple matter of supply and demand.[5] The culture and institutions of Buenos Aires consumed what the analysts had to give, and by the mid-fifties psychoanalysis enjoyed high visibility. The founding generation and their junior colleagues lectured at hospitals, where they instituted programs for primary prevention, and taught courses at the Medical School and the new Department of Psychology at the University of Buenos Aires. Among the most popular instructors was José Bleger, who in later years would become known in the APA as the "Red Rabbi" because he was the grandson of two rabbis and was himself a Marxist theoretician. Bleger's lectures attracted standing-room-only audiences that included university students as well as the public at large. Juan Carlos Volnovich remembers how he and Silvia would arrive at Bleger's lectures hours early just to get seats and enjoy the festive classroom scene. "When he began to speak, people were everywhere—in the aisles and passageways, sitting on the floor. . . . He explained psychoanalysis in very accessible terms that drew adherents to the field." The presence of Bleger and other analysts from the APA at the university meant that the generation of students awakening to the era's new political activism were equally versed in radical political theory and in psychoanalysis.

Porteños became accustomed to seeing analysts' columns in newspapers, hearing them interviewed on the radio, and buying their publications in bookstores. Private practices burgeoned as the upper-middle and middle classes flocked to psychoanalysis, aware of its prestige in Europe and eager to emulate their counterparts in the metropolis. Being in analysis was an important symbol of upward mobility and status, often within easier financial reach than a new car or a condominium in an upscale neighborhood. And the intelligentsia sought answers on the analyst's couch to the larger existential questions of human angst and the meaning of life. In a fundamental way psychoanalysis was a good fit with prevailing themes in Argentine intellectual life, which, given the extraordinarily high percentage of immigrants and foreign-born in the population, revolved obsessively around the question of who and what Argentines were as a people and a nation. For all these reasons, by the mid-fifties, psychoanalysts were clearly among the Port City's most prestigious professionals.

Mimi's contributions to psychoanalysis were multifold. Her significant impact within the profession was due, in no small part, to her personal charisma as well as her brilliance as an analyst. A complex woman whose serious attitude toward work was complemented by her youthful good looks and charming Viennese-accented Spanish, Mimi attracted a loyal following that gave her voice considerable weight in the internal struggles within the APA. She lent her formidable organizational skills to APA's training program and its relations with other institutions and organizations. Her colleagues were sometimes resentful of her obvious popularity among the candidates, a sentiment that may have found expression when, in response to her "hard-line" critique of any analyst's abuse of transference, they nicknamed her "*la virgen María.*"[6] This appellation never failed to irritate her. "I resented it profoundly," she says indignantly. "I was especially proud of my liberated views about sexuality because of my own upbringing, and I certainly passed them onto my children." Perhaps this nickname reflected the resentment caused by Mimi's independence of spirit, for in controversial matters she tended to follow her own internal voice rather than succumb to pressures exerted by her colleagues. Such was the case regarding her interest in the application of psychoanalytic theory and clinical practice to group treatment. Although opposed by most of her colleagues, who believed psychoanalysis appropriate only for in-depth individual treatment, Mimi's work in group therapy encompassed techniques honed in England and based on Melanie Klein's and Wilford Bion's psychoanalytic studies of group behavior. "It extended my clinical skills and helped me develop a more social application of psychoanalysis beyond the limited parameters of the APA and the social class it catered to."

Although Mimi wrote and lectured on many topics during this period, she was most interested in female psychosexual development and the unconscious conflict women experience in relation to their reproductive lives. "When I reread Freud in the early years in Buenos Aires, I was put off by his phallocentric views on women. It seemed to me he knew nothing of the female experience. I was asked to help translate into Spanish the work of Melanie Klein, whose seminal thinking began the tradition within psychoanalysis known as British object relations. I was very excited because I felt that Klein returned to us women our femininity. Unlike Freud, who viewed the female as a castrated male and female unconscious conflict as a reflection of her envy of men, Klein showed how woman's unconscious conflict is rooted in her anxieties related to her reproductive capacities."

In the early years, Mimi was referred many female patients by the other founding members of the APA, among whom were women who suffered from infertility. Thus she had ample opportunity to test Klein's theories in her clinical practice. She was especially interested in what she viewed as an intensifying conflict among middle-class women between their professional aspirations and their maternal role. As a therapist, she observed their psychological responses to a sociological phenomenon that had occurred since the mid-1930s—namely, an industrial expansion that had resulted in widening work opportunities for women. By 1950, women constituted over a quarter of the country's wage earners and salaried employees. In Buenos Aires alone, almost half of the women between eighteen and twenty-nine worked outside the home. Working-class women increasingly found employment in factories and offices, although they were still also the domestic servants of middle-class women, who were rapidly entering the professional world.

Beginning in the 1930s, Argentine academic and popular cultural pundits had become preoccupied with what they claimed were the catastrophic effects of the entrance of women into the wage labor force, including a declining birth rate, a deterioration in the moral significance of the family, a rise in male unemployment due to "unfair" competition with cheap female labor, and a consequent decline in the dominant position of the father within the family.[7] This view of the threat to society caused by rising opportunities for women was countered in the 1940s and 1950s by Perón and his charismatic wife, Evita, who advocated women's rights, legalized women's suffrage, introduced protective legislation for working women, and encouraged women's political activism within the Peronist women's movement. Although Peronism appealed mainly to working-class women, its progressive politics widened the parameters for all women in the public sphere; these gains, on the one hand, irritated conservatives, who argued for the return of women to their traditional domestic roles, and, on the other, enraged leftists, whose own long history of struggles on behalf of women's rights was being coopted by the Peróns who had the political clout to institute massive reforms on behalf of gender equity. From Mimi's perspective, her middle-class female patients and their conflicts about motherhood and career represented an unconscious response to rising opportunities for Argentine women and to the growing contradictory attitudes and expectations regarding femininity and appropriate female roles in Argentine culture.

When Mimi became aware that a similar social phenomenon was occurring in the United States in the postwar period, she was dismayed to learn that psychoanalysts in the United States responded in a generally conservative way to the changing role of women, offering prescriptive solutions that encouraged women to resolve their role conflicts by returning to the traditional sphere of maternal domesticity. Mimi's own reaction was to posit an alternative perspective based on her radical political and feminist intellectual formation. Contemporary female conflict about sexuality and motherhood, she believed, would best be resolved by institutional reforms that embraced the expansion of the socially acceptable domains of female activity and facilitated their integration with women's maternal role.

In her clinical practice, Mimi focused on the psychosomatic disorders of female reproductive life. She wrote *Motherhood and Sexuality* as her contribution to the psychoanalytic literature about the vicissitudes of contemporary female experience. The book, first published in 1951, was an important departure from the conservative views articulated within psychoanalysis in the post–World War II era. She introduced her study with the argument that until the twentieth century social restrictions had favored the development in women of their maternal functions while fostering repression of sexuality and creativity. As a result, women had frequently suffered symptoms of hysteria and other neurotic disorders. But, she argued, since the turn of the century, unprecedented sexual and social liberties and new economic and social imperatives had created conflicts within women regarding their maternal roles. Consequently, hysteria as the typical female disorder had been replaced by an increase in psychosomatic problems of infertility in women, who suffered a basic conflict with respect to their femininity. Her book elaborated through psychoanalytic theory and clinical examples the unconscious conflicts women suffer at various stages in their reproductive lives.

Motherhood and Sexuality was sold in several editions throughout Latin America to lay as well as professional readers, giving Mimi an international reputation and substantial recognition within the International Psychoanalytical Association. Her prestige as an analyst soared, especially among Porteño middle class women, resulting in a full patient schedule that brought many complaints from APA candidates, who were obliged to wait years before obtaining a training analysis, much less a weekly supervision session, with her.

Indeed, by the early sixties, all the senior psychoanalysts were in great demand. The profession was attractive to an expanding number of candidates who had first been introduced to psychoanalytic theory as part of the cultural flowering that took place following the 1955 ouster of Perón. His exit closed a chapter on populist hostility to highbrow culture, and these young people seemed now to encounter psychoanalysis everywhere. As the sixties wore on and the political right gained ascendancy, psychoanalysis became an increasingly popular professional choice for many who would otherwise have chosen careers in the social sciences; because of being identified with progressive politics and community research, social scientists were targeted for persecution after the military took power once again in 1966. Thus, because psychoanalysis retained its isolation from political and social questions, it became a haven for liberal and left professionals; for them, as for Marie Langer and her generation, it functioned as a substitute for a political ideology.[8]

Psychoanalysis assumed a centrality in the intellectual and popular cultures of Buenos Aires and several other provincial cities of Argentina that was not mirrored in Uruguay or Chile, where it followed two different courses. In Uruguay, the emergence of psychoanalysis as a profession in the mid-1950s was indebted to the help directly offered by the APA in Buenos Aires. The progressive nature of the Uruguayan state since the turn of the century had resulted in an expansive social welfare program that subsidized cultural and scientific activities associated with the university and the private sector as well. Given the stimulating and pluralistic intellectual environment, it is not surprising that physicians began to show an interest in psychoanalysis by the early 1950s. Because there was no psychoanalytic institute in Montevideo, the first generation of physicians who sought training moved to Buenos Aires, where they were admitted to the APA. In order to respond to the growing demand in Uruguay for a formal training center, two British-trained APA analysts, Madelaine and Willy Baranger, moved to Montevideo in 1955 to help found the Uruguayan Psychoanalytic Association (APU). Marcelo Viñar remembers the Barangers as analysts of "very high quality and a seriousness that would leave its mark on the APU. Their tremendous capacity as clinicians and teachers helped to create an institute with profound integrity." Marcelo adds that "the tradition in my country of political pluralism, as well as the deep commitment among scientifically oriented professionals to social questions, also influenced the tenor of the APU." By 1965, when Marcelo, recently graduated from medical school, became a candidate in the APU, he was typical of his generation in his "wish to examine the correlation between psychological and social forces and to understand contemporary human problems as manifested in psychopathological symptoms of the disintegration of the family, abandoned children, and juvenile delinquency—in short, to seek the integration of psychoanalysis and a social project."

Thus, from its inception, psychoanalysis in Uruguay was considered to be more than a methodology for treating mental illness and was identified with social and cultural concerns. Classical psychiatry—which emphasized the physical or chemical treatment of mental or behavioral disorders rather than the psychoanalytic "talking cure"—battled the growing influence of psychoanalysis among mental-health professionals in general. When psychology became a specialization at the university, psychoanalysis won hands down as the major influence in the young field. Perhaps this victory was due not only to the scientific differences between psychiatry and psychoanalysis but also to their tendency to be identified with disparate orientations to the world in general. Marcelo smilingly captures the difference in the kind of people attracted to the two orientations, commenting that a leader of the Physicians' Union once told him that "he did not know which was better, psychoanalysis or classical psychiatry, but he did know that during elections psychoanalysts voted for the progressive candidates and psychiatrists for the conservatives!"

In Chile, psychoanalysis made a somewhat later appearance than in Argentina and Uruguay, where scientific and cultural developments had been more directly affected by trends in Europe. Chile's location on the west coast meant that its major external influence had traditionally been the United States, where psychoanalysis did not occupy such a central position in cultural and academic life. Until the late 1960s, for example, Chilean psychology was dominated by classical psychiatry and behaviorism.

In the late 1950s, the Chilean Psychoanalytic Association (APC) was founded under the auspices of the chair of psychiatry of the University of Chile Medical School. The discipline developed under the tutelage of prominent analyst Ignacio Mate Blanco, who was joined by a small group of young psychoanalysts, including Otto Kernberg, who taught classes at the university. As Maren Viñar recalls, the curiosity of students was awakened by the provocative ideas of psychoanalysis. She was a medical student at the time, and she and a group of classmates would read Freud and spend hours at coffee houses "discussing the unconscious, holistic medicine, and the relationship between Marxism and psychoanalysis." For Maren, whose parents were political radicals and whose father had a copy of the first edition of Freud's *Civilization and Its Discontents*, these discussions were intriguing, not because, as she puts it, she understood anything of psychoanalysis. "Mainly I was reacting to the anonymity of the university hospital, where patients were treated like numbers, . . . a deplorable situation that stimulated my interest in the social and psychological aspects of medicine." Although an autonomous psychoanalytic institute was founded in Santiago in the early sixties, an exodus of the more intellectually vital individuals, including Mate Blanco and Kernberg, from Chile for professional challenges elsewhere, struck a blow to Chilean psychoanalysis from which it took many years to recover.

But Chileans interested in psychoanalysis had the opportunity to learn about it from other sources as well. Such was the case, for example, when in 1959 a group of students that included Maren attended an international meeting on medical psychology in Porto Alegre, Brazil. During the month-long conference the Chileans were exposed to analysts from all over Latin America. It was, however, only in the politically tumultuous late sixties, before the election of the Popular Unity government, that Chilean psychology students began to read Wilhelm Reich and Herbert Marcuse and became aware of the radical currents within psychoanalysis they and other theorists represented. Some Chileans even left the country to study with Marcuse in California and,

on their return, formed discussion groups among Chilean psychologists interested in the radical social philosophy underlying Marcuse's use of psychoanalytic theory.[9]

Argentina: Social Commitment and Psychoanalysis

Mimi says proudly that it was in Argentina that psychoanalysis offered a coherent analysis of the institutional fetters placed on psychological freedom by
the repressive political order and that psychoanalysts actively challenged their
profession to become part of the radical movement for social change. In Argentina the works of Marcuse, as well as those of Reich, Fenichel, and Erich
Fromm—psychoanalysts with socialist convictions and social theorists with a
psychoanalytic critique of bourgeois society—were read in the search for a new
theory and praxis of liberation. Throughout the late sixties and early seventies, a new generation of psychoanalysts would design a politics of engagement,
urging their profession to come down from its ivory tower to address the dramatic social crises facing the country.

The first battles took place within the APA as the younger candidates
critiqued the institute's intellectual stagnation, which they attributed to the
founders' theoretical rigidity and marked lack of interest in exploring new currents within psychoanalysis. They demanded a return to the broader social
questions that had once preoccupied psychoanalysts interested in the relationship between individual and social repression. The candidates also protested
the APA's hierarchical organization, which they argued enabled the founding
members to maintain a tight-knit, elitist control over the administration and
training programs and to prevent the participation of younger, nonvoting faculty and candidates.

Gradually, however, the struggles within the APA became more openly
political as conditions in Argentina worsened following a military coup in
1966. Through the early seventies, a series of military governments implemented politically repressive measures and economic policies that polarized
Argentine society. The national parliament was shut down, choking off legitimate political representation of the country's citizens. One military regime
after another instituted antiworker legislation with the intent of breaking the
strong Peronist union movement that had been organized during the previous two decades. Rising unemployment and dramatic inflationary spirals cut
deep into the standard of living of the working and middle classes. Social welfare legislation was rolled back, threatening access to medical care and retire-
ment pensions for all working people. In addition, the military's antagonism
to free expression brought censorship of the press and the arts, which alienated all sectors interested in the free flow of ideas and open cultural expres-

sion. This explosive situation erupted in the general strikes of 1969, in which major economic sectors of Buenos Aires and provincial cities were brought to a standstill. For the first time in the country's history, a general popular uprising was underway, involving industrial workers as well as middle-class professionals and students, and only the military's occupation of the cities in armored columns backed by air support suppressed the revolts.[10]

THE INSTITUTIONAL DEBATE

The psychoanalytic community was directly affected by these political confrontations throughout the country. Traditional struggles for influence within the APA based on contending factions of training analysts and their analysands or different orientations within the field gave way to a more clearly articulated political battle. "I felt so grateful," remembers Mimi, "that the younger candidates were unabashed about their leftist views. It gave me great encouragement to leave my political silence behind." Indeed, many of the younger candidates had been activist leaders at the university or were members of leftist political parties and movements, and together they denounced the APA's isolation from the crises facing Argentina. Mimi was one of the vocal senior analysts who joined the younger analysts and candidates arguing that legitimate discourse within the APA should include the political questions facing the citizens of their country and that psychoanalysis must embrace a social perspective of psychic suffering. The dissidents accused the APA of becoming a self-enclosed and self-congratulatory safe house for an elite professional sector bound to maintain its privilege and thus its alignment with the ruling class and the existing social order.

The conservative voices within the APA defended its insulation, arguing for the necessity of neutrality in the psychoanalytic enterprise. They claimed that value-free scientific inquiry and clinical treatment demanded that the patient know nothing about the analyst so that the transference to the analyst would facilitate fantasies revealing the nature and etiology of the patient's neurosis. A posture of neutrality on the part of the analyst was required. "We answered with the obvious," Mimi tells me. "We argued that analytic neutrality is an impossibility. Scientific inquiry is, after all, always designed in the context of the ideological frame of the investigator. Besides, everything about the analyst—our language, the location of our offices, our demeanor, how we dress, our fees—represents an identity based on class attitude and affiliation. So how could there ever exist a completely neutral transference on the part of the patient? We insisted that the psychoanalyst is no different from any other individual in society and that the APA's position on neutrality in the face of dramatic social, economic, and political injustices was an instance of ideological as well as psychological denial."[11]

In the face of this open political confrontation, Mimi was ecstatic. For the first time since the painful days in the Vienna Psychoanalytic Institute, she was no longer bound to choose between psychoanalysis and politics. She became more outspoken, emboldened by the younger faculty and candidates, who had entered the APA with the view that psychoanalysis should not be a vehicle for adaptation to an oppressive society but rather an instrument for the development of a critical consciousness. Many of them came to psychoanalytic training with a background in social psychiatry and had received their training at the famous Lanus Hospital, a public institution located in the industrial belt of Buenos Aires that served a poor and working-class population. There they had developed a firsthand understanding of the grinding social and economic realities of working-class family life. Irrespective of their political orientation, they all became acutely conscious of the social components of individual physical and psychological illness.

Juan Carlos Volnovich was among those who gained precious medical and sociological training in Lanus Hospital, and in 1968, in the midst of the emerging struggles in the APA, he applied for psychoanalytic training. By this time he and Silvia, now married, had been to Cuba many times and were enthusiastically supportive of the goals of the Revolution. "Sometimes," he says, "I don't understand the workings of the unconscious," referring to the irony of his interview with Marie Langer as a part of the application process. "She asked me whether I'd already had interviews with other training analysts, and I said, 'Yes, two.' And she replied, 'Poor doctor, how unpleasant to have to tell your life story so many times!' I felt, 'Thank goodness, she understands me,' and during that interview the only thing I talked about was Cuba! I don't know why. When I left I wanted to die. I didn't know Mimi was a leftist then, and I thought, 'You're nuts, how could you talk about Cuba to get into the APA?' I was convinced it was all over for me." Not only was Juan Carlos admitted to the APA, but, in retrospect, he credits that interview with his subsequent good luck in obtaining supervision with Mimi, who was so popular with the candidates that she had a seven-year waiting list!

Juan Carlos was the youngest candidate in the APA, and he finished his classes in a record three years, amid growing tensions in the institute. He was still naive about political theory, but he identified idealistically with the liberation movements throughout Latin America and thus was naturally drawn to the dissident movement within the APA. "There had been José Bleger at the Psychology Department, my experiences at Lanus Hospital, and my connection with Cuba through Silvia. . . . I was 'condemned' to think on the left and in terms of radical change!" Thus he became an ally of those within the APA who postulated that psychoanalytic theory must embrace a Marxist conceptualization of class society and the dominant ideology in order to understand the external factors inhibiting the possibility of individual psychological change.[12]

One of the articulate spokespersons of this position was Eduardo "Tato" Pavlovsky, an analysand of Mimi's who became one of the leaders of the dissidents in the APA. A third-generation Argentine of Russian and Italian background, Tato had come to psychoanalytic training following his graduation from medical school in 1958. It had seemed the appropriate path to follow, given that he came from several generations of medical specialists. Besides, his own experience in psychoanalytic treatment as a love-sick adolescent had deeply impressed him, not only because of its salutary effects on his personal life but because of the psychoanalytic conceptualization of human subjectivity as well. By the time Tato finished his training and became a faculty member of the APA in 1968, he had developed a unique specialty within the field. Early on he had discovered the value of psychodrama, a variant of play therapy, as a method of working with children. After studying with prominent specialists in psychodrama in the United States, he became a pioneer of the method in Argentina. "I consider myself a group therapist and a creator/coordinator of groups, rather than a psychoanalyst in the limited sense of the word," he says. This perspective continued to evolve as Tato found it increasingly difficult to identify with the APA, which he considered to be "a closed world, religious and theological."

In the volatile late sixties, according to Tato, "the historical situation was impacting on our consciousness. I myself had come from a rather reactionary family who raised me in an oligarchic social and cultural environment. There was some tradition, however, of political engagement. My paternal grandfather had suffered persecution under the czar in Russia and had written books about the prerevolutionary climate, especially the phenomenon of nihilism. I always had the impression that there was a family secret because even though you couldn't find a more anticommunist or anti-Semitic family than mine, my grandfather kept a photograph of Lenin on his desk! My father was a middle-class white-collar employee and an avid anti-Peronist. He was imprisoned for a short while in 1952, after which he went into exile in Montevideo and then Asunción, Paraguay. Even though I don't agree with his political ideas, I think I owe a debt to my father for his being a role model, someone willing to act in coherence with his ideals."

Tato's own politicization came slowly, at first through a romantic identification with the Cuban Revolution and then in response to the great social struggles taking place in Argentina. His search for personal meaning led him to become disillusioned with the typical life of a psychoanalyst, "which was reduced to the radius of a single social class. One could live quite well from analyzing only six patients who were wealthy businessmen. This produced in me a sense of unbearable emptiness." Tato's attraction to the theater led him to explore the postwar vanguard movement of Samuel Beckett and Eugène Ionesco and eventually to study with a group of leftist activists who produced an important and innovative theater movement in Buenos Aires. Tall, good-looking, and with a forceful personality, he was a powerful presence on stage. And even though he remained actively engaged in the dissident movement within the APA, he continued to be drawn toward cultural expression because "life in the theater put one much more in touch with the community and with the social context of individual human experience. . . . It provided one with the opportunity to leave behind the bourgeois life style and conscious-ness in which psychoanalysis was steeped."

Tato's increasingly public persona offended many of the conservatives within the APA, who dismissed his involvement as self-indulgent acting out. "From my perspective, the theater helped me a lot with what amounted to an existential crisis. . . . I knew that my profound discontent was healthy." He founded a group of physicians dedicated to studying alternative theater, which made a significant enough impact on Argentine cultural life to be included in the *Hispanic-American Encyclopedia of the History of Argentine Theater*. At the same time, he began to write political plays that brought him fame as a politically conscious and psychologically astute playwright. His *Señor Galindez*, an insightful exploration of the psychology of the torturer, first appeared in the early seventies and became a classic for its intuitive depiction of the type of political repression that would beset Argentina in future years.[13] No won-der, then, that he became one of the principal organizers of the efforts within the APA to bring psychoanalysis and Marxism together as a methodology for challenging existing psychological and social realities.

As tensions within the APA grew, the dissidents realized that similar de-velopments were taking place in the psychoanalytic community in other coun-tries. By 1968, the student and worker protests in many European countries and the antiwar movement in the United States prompted youthful candi-dates in a number of psychoanalytic associations to protest their institutes' isolation from the dramatic questions plaguing society the world over. At two international congresses of the International Psychoanalytical Association, the first in July 1969 in Rome and the second in July 1971 in Vienna, concerned candidates and faculty from many countries held simultaneous counter-congresses to voice their social and political concerns. The Argentines played a pivotal role in these meetings, where the social relevance of psychoanalysis was examined in a host of different languages.

Mimi represented the dissident Argentine presence within the official congress of 1971 in Vienna, where the International Psychoanalytical Asso-ciation was meeting for the first time since the Nazi repression of psychoanalysis and Freud's flight to England more than three decades earlier. In the luxurious Hofburg Imperial Castle and among some of the most prominent psychoanalysts in the world, Mimi presented a highly controversial paper entitled "Psychoanalysis and/or Social Revolution," which was covered extensively by the international press. Mimi says that it was quite fitting that her paper would be presented in Vienna, where she had first been forced to choose between her professional and her political commitments. "It was precisely in Vienna that I would speak not only of psychoanalysis but of Marxism and revolution to boot!" Her paper traced the points of convergence between Marx and Freud, and she asserted the inevitability of the radical transformation of contemporary society. She urged her illustrious colleagues to use their psychoanalytic knowledge to facilitate rather than to oppose the process of change, admonishing them not to follow in the footsteps of the analysts who had left Cuba following the revolution or those who were at that very moment departing from Chile on the heels of the election of Allende. "This time," she declared, "we will renounce neither Marx nor Freud."[14]

And, as if to prove Mimi's point, participants in the counter-congress were establishing Platform, an international organization that would permit dissident analysts and candidates in their own countries to articulate their critiques and develop alternatives to institutionalized psychoanalysis. The Argentines returned to Buenos Aires and under the leadership of two young analysts, Armando Bauleo and Hernán Kesselman, formed Plataforma, which became the organized challenge to the hierarchy of Argentine psychoanalysis. Only three months following the Vienna congress, in response to what the dissidents viewed as the APA's reactionary refusal to respond adequately to the growing political repression perpetrated by the military government, even when it directly affected members of the mental-health community, they concluded that they had no choice but to leave. Another group, called Documento, which had been formed by those opposed to censorship within the APA, reluctantly joined Plataforma in severing its tie to the APA institute.

THE INSTITUTIONAL RUPTURE

Heated discussions and agonizing decisions preceded the rupture. For some, including Mimi, Tato, and Juan Carlos, it was clear that, in order to develop an interdisciplinary and socially relevant psychoanalytic praxis, it was necessary to depart from the APA. For others, however, who agreed with the dissidents' critique, the only legitimate approach was to stay and fight from within the citadel for democratization. As the storm gathered, Mimi felt exhilarated at the chance to take a principled stand. "I was no longer encumbered by family responsibilities. Max had died in 1966, and my grown children were all politically active in their own right. I could now assume the consequences of a radical position. I felt that at last my life would represent coherence with my political convictions. And, best of all, I would now become an activist psychoanalyst and be able to bring my professional skills to the struggle against social and political oppression." All around Mimi, this passionate stance was being expressed. Not only psychoanalysts but musicians, writers, and filmmakers as well were abandoning their citadel—the U.S.- and European-dominated mass media—in the search for an authentically indigenous and critical expression of Latin American reality. Their militancy was captured by Argentine filmmakers Fernando Solanas and Ottavio Getino, producers of the now classic revolutionary film *Hour of the Furnaces*, in their 1969 manifesto announcing the New Latin American Cinema Movement. "The camera is a gun," they wrote, "that shoots twenty-four frames a second." In a similar sense, Mimi believed that psychoanalysis was an explosive weapon in the ideological war against class, ethnic, and gender oppression.

From Tato's perspective, official psychoanalysis was suffocating the creativity and intellectual growth of its members. No longer able to bear the APA hierarchy, which he believed reflected the hierarchical relations of bourgeois society in general, he argued strongly for the rupture. "We did not want to be psychoanalytic practitioners in the narrow sense of the word, insulated and successfully sharing the elite life style of our wealthy patients. Traditional psychoanalysis, which requires a patient to come four times a week and to use the couch is, after all, an economic as well as a scientific model. We were intellectuals, Latin American intellectuals, who wished to utilize our psychoanalytic expertise to understand more profoundly our Latin American reality and to develop new models befitting other social classes. As psychoanalytic intellectuals, our project in the grand scheme of things was to contribute to the popular will to change our society."

It all happened at once for Tato. "So much occurred in just one year: 1971. First, our 'Latin American Manifesto of Psychodrama' in an international congress in Amsterdam in August, where we denounced the North American use of encounter groups as a methodology of adaptation and argued for a group experience that could be an instrument to expose authoritarian structures. Then came Plataforma and *Señor Galindez*." Tato's personal life reflected the tumultuous overturning of custom, as well; his first wife and he separated and he moved into a commune with some ex-APA colleagues to explore "nontraditional forms of family life." At the moment of the rupture, according to Tato, "we did not have it all clearly thought out; we deeply needed to liberate ourselves, and we identified with the Latin American project of social justice and national liberation. We knew we had a psychological tool of colossal importance, but we had only sketchy ideas of how it could be brought together with a political analysis. Each of us would pursue this project in different ways afterward."

Juan Carlos experienced the rupture as a logical extension of his personal relations and his political sensibilities. By this time, he and Silvia had become politically active in the left-Peronist movement. "We lived a completely divided life. On the one hand, we were bourgeois analysts, and, on the other, we were political activists, going poorly dressed to a working-class neighborhood to work in a local community center organized by the Montoneros." Juan Carlos wrote an article critiquing the APA criteria for mental health, which, as he summarized them, were "good work relations, good sexual relations, and good relations with friends." He added another criterion for mental health that he considered to be of fundamental importance: "a sensibility toward social injustice." This stand identified him with those who were deciding to leave the APA, and he was willing to risk his family's financial security in order to be politically consistent. As he humorously recalls, "During the night of the final discussion before the rupture, at one point an enthusiastic training analyst suddenly stopped the heated debate and exclaimed, 'Wait, do you realize what we're doing? You know what this means? It's like burning our Diners' Club card!'" To leave the APA had global consequences in fact: it meant the rejection of membership in a small, elite professional group that enjoyed financial success, social status, and the guarantee of a completely secure future. "We were disposed to do it, to reach for a kind of continuity between our ideals and our practice. I remember that afterward, when a colleague said to several of us that he agreed with our ideas but believed we should stay and fight from within the institute, my friend replied, 'You know what? To be inside the APA is to be outside the country.'"

The split had a dramatic impact on the APA. To some it was a relief that the political activists had left. To others it represented a threat to the vitality of psychoanalysis. Still others were sorry to see some of the best minds in their profession leave the institute but believed in the importance of maintaining a separation between political conviction and professional life.[15] The rupture also had significant repercussions beyond the psychoanalytic community. Juan Carlos was in charge of Plataforma's public relations, and he was inundated with requests for interviews by the press. Newspaper and magazine articles described for the public at large the issues that had prompted the rupture within psychoanalysis, presenting the flurry of debates on the concept of neutrality, which, in the rapidly polarizing conditions of Argentina, was relevant to all citizens.

Plataforma was to last for little more than a year, during which, as Juan Carlos puts it, "we fought like crazy amongst ourselves over different theoretical positions. But we had the good sense to disband the organization before we reproduced the same errors for which we had criticized the APA." Plataforma dissolved, but it had provided the significant function, according to Tato, of creating "a new subjectivity, a new way of thinking, a new consciousness about the possibilities of a noninstitutional psychoanalysis, a socially committed psychoanalysis." Having served its historical purpose, Plataforma disappeared, and its former members joined other political psychoanalysts in a variety of projects permitting them to integrate their professional expertise with their political principles.

In this period of great intellectual productivity, social alternatives to both capitalism and Soviet Stalinism were explored. Mimi recounts how the analysts formed study groups to read Reich, Fromm, Louis Althusser, and other theorists and to apply what they learned to the specific psychosocial situation of repression in Argentina. They elaborated the concept of neutrality. Some dissidents maintained that in contrast to the APA conservatives, who continued to delude themselves about the possibility of clinical and social neutrality, their consciousness of their nonneutrality made possible its elaboration, thus preventing its interference in their patients' treatment. Some argued that denial, not neutrality, motivated an analyst to interpret all aspects of the patient's intense concern and worry about present social conditions as evidence of childhood anxiety emerging in the transference relationship with the analyst. Others argued that only repression could account for a lack of affect on the part of either patient or analyst regarding the experience of living in the midst of military rule. The dissident analysts argued for the importance of being responsive to patients' fears and anxieties about the dramatic social crisis confronting Argentina.

Loss was a theme that permeated their discourse; both patient and analyst experienced losses in many domains as civil society was increasingly threatened by military and paramilitary forces whose repressive brutality indiscriminately targeted individuals engaged in legal public protest as well as members of clandestine organizations. In one case, a student was abducted by the army in the north of Argentina. When it was later discovered he had died under torture, the provincial authorities attempted to investigate the case but were eventually dissuaded by death threats. Such incidents in the early 1970s were an omen of what was to come in the not too distant future.

Mimi edited and published two volumes, called *Cuestionamos* (We Question), in which the contributors analyzed different aspects of the relationship between psychoanalysis and social change.[16] Many themes were explored, including the nature of violence and aggression within repressive societies; the character of mourning in societies where imprisonment, torture, disappearances, and assassinations pervade citizens' daily experience; and the role of reparation in revolutionary struggles. Mimi's paper "Psychoanalysis and/or Social Revolution" appeared in the first volume, and in the second she contributed "Woman: Her Limitations and Potential," a synthesis of her views on the convergence of Marxist, psychoanalytic, and feminist theories in the interpretation of the specific nature of the oppression of women. She also coauthored an article in the same volume that critiqued the complicity of the Brazilian Psychoanalytic Society with the repressive military government that had ruled that country since 1964. She described how a candidate in the Rio Psychoanalytic Society worked with a team of army torturers, teaching them about the psychological responses to torture. "Evidently a training analyst does not know how to stop the psychoanalytic formation of a candidate who is a torturer without bringing inevitable reprisals on himself and the Institute. In all its crudeness this situation captures the relationship between institutionalized Freudianism and the dominant system. Without a doubt, institutional survival can require a very heavy price."

Praxis: Class Struggle and Psychoanalysis

The split within psychoanalysis had occurred as military rule produced an even larger mass movement of opposition to a system that clearly benefited the privileged few at the expense of everyone else. And reflecting the political theory popular throughout Latin America that arose in the ashes of failed reformist strategies to alter existing political and economic structures, many Argentine radicals argued that only an armed struggle would dislodge the ruling class from power. Guerrilla organizations, the two most important of which were the Marxist ERP and the left-Peronist Montoneros, carried out armed attacks against military targets and representatives of foreign capital. This violence was a response to unremitting economic exploitation and the systematic repression of progressive individuals and groups by military and paramilitary forces. The Montoneros had a base within the radicalized Peronist working class, and their romantic appeal to the previously anti-Peronist middle class and students grew rapidly because they were believed to be the uniquely Argentine expression of a mass-based people's struggle against foreign domination and class exploitation. Many of the political psychoanalysts, like Juan Carlos, were sympathetic to the Montoneros and became activists in the legal political organizations allied with them.

Mimi and other dissident analysts had for several years been active in the politically progressive Federation of Argentine Psychiatry (FAP), an organization that criticized the illegal actions of the military government, such as counterinsurgency policies that included the disappearance and murder of political militants and union activists. As members of FAP, they engaged in research and the development of programs that addressed serious social problems, such as alcoholism, manifest in the popular classes. Now that they were no longer members of the medically controlled APA, they sought to democratize psychoanalytic training through the creation of the Organization of Mental Health Workers. For the first time, the traditional status and hierarchical divisions among mental health workers with different specializations were eliminated, and everyone—irrespective of prior training—had access to psychoanalytic classes and supervision. This effort put the Argentine dissidents in the forefront of the demedicalization of psychoanalysis, which would later become an international trend. This professional interest was connected to their larger social commitment. As Mimi puts it, "We believed that a commonly shared professional formation of all mental-health professionals would create a mutually shared sense of professional and political identity. This would increase our solidarity in union struggles and the organized opposition to the military government."

The Organization of Mental Health Workers created the Research and Training Centers (CDIs), the most important of which was in Buenos Aires. The CDI curriculum was divided into three areas of professional preparation: the first two areas elaborated psychoanalytic and Marxist theory, and the third dealt with the relationship between these theories and clinical practice. Mimi recalls fundamental points of convergence between Marx and Freud that were elaborated in the classes. "For example, we taught that both Marx and Freud agreed on the essential irrationality of the prevailing human condition and the idea that humanity is driven by forces it does not understand and therefore cannot control, in spite of its belief to the contrary. We stressed their agreement on the fundamental difference between appearance and reality, by which they meant that what we tell ourselves we do and why are the mere manifest surface below which operate forces we know nothing about. Marx argued that while the French Revolution proclaimed itself on the side of liberty, equality, and fraternity, in actuality, it represented a new historical era and mode of production—capitalism—that was built on compulsion, exploitation, and competition. Marx showed how the wage labor system, with its ideology of individual responsibility, hid [its] essentially exploitative nature . . . and hence the systemic sources of inequity in class relations. We linked Marx's idea that the ruling class could permit no challenge to its domination to Freud's notion of how the superego functions. Freud showed how the superego, which from our point of view is the repository of the prevailing values and attitudes of any social era and its dominant class, relies on defenses such as denial, repression, and displacement to eliminate from the conscious mind thoughts and feelings that challenge its domination."

Mimi continues, "We also tried to show how in both Marx and Freud there is the theme of human alienation. Marx showed how workers produce commodities in a process they don't understand or control. Thus they experience the products as having a life of their own and the process as being characterized by a kind of permanence. In the face of this illusion of permanence it is impossible for one to act as historical agent to change things. Freud dealt with this state of alienation and how it is reproduced through his concept of transference, by which he meant the way we all attribute to present figures in our lives the traits and qualities of significant figures from our early past. Freud showed how patients resist change and become ill because they do not remember their past. The repressed individual does not understand his or her history and is overwhelmed by it, and the neurotic symptom becomes a substitute for the past not remembered. For both Marx and Freud, the inability to comprehend the past condemns one to repeat it. Marx called for revolution, for him an act of revindication through which the working class would reappropriate its power from the exploitative bourgeoisie and go on to develop the social organization that would enable humanity to make its own history. Freud postulated a psychic revindication, a process based on the recovery of all that has been forced out of consciousness, through the psychoanalytic method of overcoming resistance to remembering and knowing. The resolution of the conflict between the rational ego and important components of unconscious life would permit a unity between the different parts of the mind that have been divided against themselves."

Mimi points out that in Argentina the influence of Klein's thought informed psychoanalysts' particular reading of the Marx-Freud dialogue. "We didn't believe that all 'evil' resides only in external reality—that is to say, exclusively within the social and economic institutions of class society. We believed that hate, cruelty, and destructiveness are as much a part of the human psyche as love and creativity. Klein showed us how the child's growing awareness that the parent she or he loves is the same person she or he also hates results in the capacity to feel guilt and its consequent urge to make amends for—to repair—the effects of one's destructive urges. We agreed with Klein that it is the recognition, rather than the disavowal, of the capacity for hatred, envy, greed, and destructiveness that produces the reparative impulse in human beings. So we—unlike Erich Fromm, for example—didn't subscribe to the thesis that all we had to do was change the oppressive structures of capitalism in order to create a sane and decent society. We were convinced that only when the conflict and ambivalence that characterize all human relations are recognized and worked with, rather than denied, could people act out of concern for others and build a just social order."[17]

These theoretical postulates were a part of the core curriculum of the CDI classes. Under the clinical supervision of Mimi and her colleagues, students were also required to fulfill a minimal number of clinical hours by working in hospitals, community clinics, and unions. Although the CDI was a relatively short-lived experiment, Mimi believed it to have accomplished three important tasks before it became a victim of government repression. "It broke the stratification among mental-health professionals and integrated them into one union, demonstrated the possibility of acquiring psychoanalytic training outside the APA at a minimal cost, and showed that psychoanalytic theory and technique could be used with all social classes in a variety of settings." Mimi's political activism in the CDIs and her role as president of the FAP put her in constant danger of being targeted by right-wing paramilitary groups. But she experienced a sense of elation and optimism rather than fear. "At last I could act in concert with my values and beliefs—with my ego ideal—and dedicate myself to the things that really mattered to me. . . . [Now] I could utilize my training as a psychoanalyst in the service of the popular classes."

Many of the political analysts treated patients whose involvement in underground revolutionary activism they often knew nothing about for security reasons. This peculiar situation imposed a problematical limitation on a therapeutic practice whose modus operandi, free association, required that the patient in the analytic setting say as best as possible whatever came to mind. The effectiveness of the therapy was compromised by this situation, but it also protected analysts from knowing things that might endanger them. Juan Carlos encountered this predicament head on when he and other analysts approached the Montoneros to offer their psychological skills to the movement. "We had the messianic idea that this was the historical moment to be accepted as psychoanalysts by the guerrilla movements. But the leadership was not very open to the idea that militants be in psychoanalytic treatment because information might fall into the enemy's hands. And we came to realize that their trust in us depended on our commitment to the organization, which in itself compromised the possibility of neutrality in the treatment. It was such a contradiction." Gradually, however, he began to treat militants, discovering in the actual practice how high the stakes were. "They really needed to talk, and they did so in excess. . . . I ended up knowing too much at times! I thought, 'Oh my god, I have high visibility because of Plataforma. . . . If the police came to my office now . . . '"

Mostly, though, because he was a child analyst, Juan Carlos saw activists' children, who, in response to the growing tension, were beginning to suffer nightmares, learning disorders, insomnia, and psychosomatic illnesses. He and other analysts began to treat people in nontraditional ways, a strategy that would expand in future years when the repression deepened. He would meet a parent and child in a public plaza, for example, neither adult knowing the identity of the other. Sitting on a bench while the child played, the parent would communicate information about the child's difficulties to Juan Carlos while he observed the child's play. In subsequent meetings, arranged in parks and restaurants, he would bring his customary therapeutic materials, including clay, crayons, and toys, and hold informal sessions with the child. "What an ironic situation: . . . for security reasons, neither of us learned each other's names, even though I knew very intimate details about their lives."

Tato chose another route toward political activism, which ultimately exposed him to the same risk of reprisal from a repressive state. He developed a high profile in the cultural world, where his fame was due to his prominence as a playwright and actor and his innovative contributions to psychoanalytic psychodrama. He remained in the public eye as well through the articles he published in the media critical of the authoritarian culture and politics of military-run Argentine.

Both Juan Carlos and Tato recall the excitement they shared about their activities during this period, which permitted them to feel, like Mimi, a euphoric "coherence with their ego ideal." In retrospect, though, both believe that they, like the rest of the left, could sustain their political involvement only by unconsciously denying the risk their activism posed to their personal safety. "It was a kind of omnipotence; I was convinced that nothing could happen to me," recalls Juan Carlos. "My grandfather had written of survivors, and I saw myself in that tradition." Tato was in analysis with Mimi at the time, and when *Señor Galindez* appeared in the theaters, she told him, "Look, Tato, I don't know whether you're conscious of what you've written, but it seems to me they won't forgive you for it." It would take him years to realize that she was correct and that he had been in profound denial about the potential repercussions to his personal safety that would result from his outspoken political stance.

However, the political analysts would enjoy a brief respite before having to deal with such issues, a kind of calm before the storm. The military was on the defensive. Hundreds of thousands of activists were participating in anti-government demonstrations, lending extensive support to strikes and factory occupations and volunteering their labor to improve housing, sanitation, and medical and legal services in the ubiquitous shantytowns where the injustices that resulted from the state's economic and social priorities were the most glaring. New struggles were being articulated as well: in 1972, a feminist movement emerged among middle- and working-class women; small organizations read and translated seminal works of feminist thinkers in the United States and Europe, started consciousness-raising groups to build solidarity among women, and took public positions critical of the repressive military government. One such organization was the Argentine Feminist Union, whose initials in Spanish—UFA—were the same as the expression commonly used by

Argentines when they are exasperated; *ufa* means "enough" or "I've had it up to here."[18]

In fact, millions of Argentines were crying *ufa* to the military. As the signs of mass disaffection with the system became more clear, the military, the elite, and their international allies were prompted to recall Perón from his eighteen-year exile in Madrid in the belief that only he could forestall a revolution in their country. Perón's return was also desired by the left-Peronist mass movement, whose members were convinced that he would facilitate, rather than prevent, radical social transformation. For some months during 1973–1974, following the democratic elections that brought a Peronist-led coalition to power, the progressive forces within the movement dominated the presidency and the congress. This short period provided a political opening for mobilization among many different sectors. The left tendency within the Peronist movement, led by the Montoneros, opened up community centers, called *unidades basicas*, and led workers in the formation of new unions in radical opposition to the old labor bureaucracy. Women activists took part in these various activities, but a special organization for women, called the Agrupación Evita, was also created to deal with the special problems women faced. Influenced by the women's movements in other countries, activists produced a radical analysis of the exploitation of women's labor in the family and of the sexual objectification of women in the mass media. They also made demands for reproductive rights and for day-care centers and other institutions that would support women in the domestic and public spheres.[19]

Within this heady political environment, the challenges were multifold for the political analysts. Mimi and others from FAP entered the most notorious maximum-security prison for political prisoners to investigate and denounce torture and to treat political prisoners who had been jailed during the long years of military rule. Members of FAP and the Organization of Mental Health Workers went to working-class neighborhoods and squatter settlements to volunteer their labor in public-health projects initiated by progressive and left political organizations. They threw themselves with buoyant spirits into radical union and movement activities, seeing themselves as socially conscious citizens who, trained as psychoanalysts, could help people free themselves of the psychological impediments to social engagement. Mimi coauthored articles, including "Psychoanalysis, Class Struggle, and Mental Health," analyzing this valuable experience.[20] "In our therapeutic work, we remained faithful to our psychoanalytic technique of interpreting unconscious conflict. While we refrained from offering advice, suggestions, or didactic interventions, our interpretations of our working-class patients' discourse included a critical perspective of the class and gender determinants of their unconscious pain and rage."

During this period, Tato's political engagement drew him toward traditional Marxist politics rather than the Peronist left, "though I never was a devout anti-Peronist like my father." Moreover, rather than supporting armed struggle, Tato believed electoral politics was an effective strategy for challenging the right wing. "Even though I didn't agree with the guerrilla movement, it produced in me a deep intellectual admiration. At the same time I viewed with trepidation the errors I believed were being made. But I admired these young people, who put their bodies on the line in their total commitment to the cause. I looked up to their courage, their valor. . . . It was such an unequal struggle—they against the armed might of the state. I thought it would lead to unsuspected consequences." Acting in concert with his own assessment of the situation, Tato joined the Socialist Workers Party, a Marxist-Trotskyist party with legal standing, for which he became a candidate in the parliamentary elections in 1971 and again in 1973.

Caught up in the fervor of the times, most of the political analysts, like militants in general, failed to comprehend the short-lived nature of this political opening. Indeed, it even seemed that their country was becoming a sanctuary for the refugees streaming into Argentina from Uruguay and Chile. Many hundreds came in the wake of the right-wing coups, witnesses to the unprecedented reprisals against anyone who had been identified with progressive politics in those two countries.

The situation in Argentina, however, began to clarify by early 1974, when the continuing economic crises and intensifying class confrontations blew the inherently contradictory Peronist coalition apart. The right wing and corrupt sectors within the movement captured the government apparatus and, in league with the elite and its military allies, began to repress the left Peronist and Marxist opposition. Unofficial death squads, often composed of junior army officers, and paramilitary right-wing gangs stepped up their operations, enjoying impunity in their organized violence against the left. The Triple A and other death squads eliminated well-known revolutionaries and others regarded as sympathetic to them. These disappearances and murders were designed not only to kill off the left but to instill terror in the general populace. In anticipation of what would follow on the heels of the military coup in 1976, General Jorge Videla was already warning that "as many people will die in Argentina as is necessary to restore order."[21]

The General's vision of order was translated into a daily atmosphere of ominous threat. Under such conditions, new priorities emerged for the political analysts. The demand grew among victims of political repression for psychotherapy with progressive analysts. People sought psychotherapy as a means of managing anxieties and fears that were more and more the product not only of individual and family histories but of current social reality.

Increasingly, Mimi and her colleagues were called on by the leadership of the Peronist and Marxist left to help activists who had suffered the trauma of torture or to make an assessment about whether particular activists with paranoid tendencies or other psychological disorders endangered comrades by their participation in clandestine activity.

Meanwhile, people were leaving the country, voluntarily seeking a haven from the political storm gathering momentum. Others, including psychoanalysts, left unwillingly in response to certain knowledge that they were no longer safe in Argentina. "When we'd receive a call from a friend who didn't want to talk on the phone but suggested meeting at a café," recalls Juan Carlos, "we knew it would be a good-bye encounter. It was a real blow when Mimi was targeted by the Triple A and left for Mexico. We began to feel abandoned, alone, isolated."

Feeling equally abandoned, alone, and isolated as her plane landed in Mexico, Mimi walked into the airport and a new chapter in her life. Once again a political refugee, she joined thousands of exiled Argentines who faced the challenge of reconstructing their lives far from their country, families, and the political struggle that had given them a sense of personal value and purpose. "It was a crucial turning point in my life, a forced separation from everything familiar, like stepping into an unknown abyss. I felt that I'd had a small taste of the joy of building something important together with thousands of other people who shared my values and principles. Now that was gone, and I had no idea what awaited me."

For our protagonists who remained in Argentina, an equally uncharted future lay in store. They would live through the transition to full-fledged military dictatorship with its unprecedented assault on democracy and human rights. Each would be faced with the excruciating decision of when to leave or how to survive the vicissitudes of the culture of fear that would be perpetrated by the terrorist state.

Chapter 3

The Dynamics of State Terror

First, we are going to kill all of the subversives, then their collaborators, then their sympathizers, then the indifferent, and finally the timid.

—GENERAL IBERICO MANUEL SAINT-JEAN,
governor of Buenos Aires Province (1977)

JULIA BRAUN smiles engagingly as she hands me a cup of espresso and invites me to partake of the delicious pastries before us. We are sitting in the charming, loftlike family room of her new, expansive penthouse, which towers high over the bustle of Buenos Aires. The apartment has a breathtaking, 180-degree view of the city, which in the northeasterly direction features the wide and serene La Plata River with the highrises of Montevideo visible in the distance. The tranquillity of the physical environment, with its casual blend of designer furniture, prized artwork, and roughhewn paintings and statues by Central American artisans, reflects the multiple facets of its owner's persona. Julia is sixty, youthfully attractive and stylish, with a self-contained and gracious sociability. We have known each other for years, but this is the first time that I am hearing the detailed chronology of her life. I am careful to take my cue from her, for we are speaking of difficult things. When she indicates her readiness to continue, I ask her to tell me what it was like to live in Argentina in the years leading up to the coup. "It was the most terrible time of my life," she begins haltingly, "except for later, with the disappearance of Gabriel . . . "

Life in the Transition to State Terror

The metamorphosis of society toward military dictatorship, whether in countries accustomed to democratic institutions, such as Chile and Uruguay, or in ones familiar with the dynamics of military rule, like Argentina, is typically a period of confusion and disorientation. Only with hindsight can one say without a doubt that in such-and-such moment, the signs were incontrovertible.

For a time, the contradictions in external reality, where the apparently reliable continuation of normal, everyday life is ominously punctuated by hints of profound disruption, dovetail with psychic defenses of denial and disavowal. In all three countries, the political analysts lived through agonizing uncertainty about the social drama unfolding before them, responding according to their specific personalities and psychological makeup. Julia believes her particular experience was affected by her lack of active political involvement and the fact that she had not analyzed or written about political repression before she experienced it herself.

When most of her friends in the APA left during the schism in 1971, Julia Braun remained in the institute along with others who agreed with the dissidents' critique but argued that it was better to stay and fight for reform from within. "Maybe I feared that I wouldn't be able to finish my studies, or perhaps I wasn't brave enough. I don't know. And maybe I have tended to stand on the sidelines a bit. But I have always thought that one needs to have a posture of commitment toward society, toward politics, to contribute what one can. One should not pass through life leaving decisions to others."

Julia's sensibilities grew out of her awakening to politics as a young woman during the Perón era. A first-generation Argentine of Hungarian and Polish Jewish parents, she grew up in a modest middle-class neighborhood and attended public schools. Her politicization came in high school through her friendships with students who were interested in culture and politics, some of whom later attended medical school with her during the early 1950s. When many of her friends joined the Communist Youth Federation, Julia did not. "I think out of fear, though I'm not sure of what." But she was a delegate to the medical school's Student Center, a progressive organization whose anti-Peronist sentiments made it the object of government ire. When the center was declared illegal in October 1954, it went underground, and, during a clandestine meeting at Julia's house, the police barged in and arrested everyone.

"I spent four and a half months in prison, but, in comparison with the prisons later on, it was like being in a four-star hotel! There were forty of us university women jailed, and although we were treated decently, the terrible part was that we had no right to a defense and no idea how long we'd be there." The students were finally released, although they never knew why. But this was during the final days of the Perón government, with rumors abounding that the military was preparing for a coup. When the police came for Julia again, this time she was not home, and after that she had to sleep at the homes of relatives and friends. Following the military uprising that toppled Perón from power, she received a letter from the director of penal institutions to the effect that he considered it an honor that she had been in prison for being an anti-Peronist. "That was such a joke, such idiocy! But I believe that this experience must have marked me in some way. I think that in authoritarian governments the prison experience is a warning, a threat. It did not prevent me from being connected to politically active people or continuing to think politically, but in a sense it made me less willing to take bold risks."

In 1957, Julia married a fellow medical student and political comrade, Mariano Dunayevich, whose love she suspects was "imbued with a fair dose of idealization because he visited me in prison and must have viewed me as a kind of heroine." Mariano came from a family of immigrant Jews; he was a grandson of *gauchos judíos* and the son and nephew of respected Porteño physicians. Julia was soon pregnant, and the couple, both struggling young professionals, had their first son, Gabriel, in January 1958. Several years later, in the wake of an epidemic of unknown origins in the province of Buenos Aires, Mariano, a specialist in viruses, was offered a fellowship to study at the Communicable Disease Center at the University of California in Berkeley. When Julia obtained a residency in pediatrics at San Francisco Children's Hospital, they left for the United States, with their parents fairly bursting with pride, "as if we had each won a Nobel Peace Prize!"

They lived in San Francisco for two and a half years, which for Julia represented "from a psychoanalytic point of view, a moment of resignification in my life." During the sixties, the Argentine middle class and intelligentsia attached much significance to going abroad "to perfect oneself," so the experience perforce "had to be the best; we had to be enjoying it to the full; I had to love it, to learn a lot. Only years later could I understand the effort and the suffering it meant to be so far from home, to have my second child, Bernardo, born so far away from my family." Their return to Buenos Aires meant a new disruption and adjustment, which highlighted already-existing problems in Julia's relationship with her husband and in her uncertainty about what she wanted to do with her life. Typical of her culture and class, she sought psychoanalysis to confront these troubling issues. At the same time, she began to work at the renowned Lanus Hospital in the psychopathology department, where she met many young doctors who were interested in psychoanalysis. Intrigued by her personal analytic experience and her work at the hospital, Julia decided to become an analyst. In 1967, she began her training at the APA.

Julia was a third-year candidate, just finishing her training analysis with one of the outspoken political analysts, when the rupture in the institute occurred. Most of her closest friends left the APA, including her analyst. The only thing that tempered her bad feelings about staying was that José Bleger also remained, apparently unwilling to abandon the psychoanalytic home he had helped to create. "I allied myself with him, whom we all deeply admired, and felt in a minimal way justified."

Like so many other leftist intellectuals, Julia and Mariano lived through the turbulent early seventies attracted to Peronism, voting for the progressive Peronists but not participating directly in the movement. Their radical sympathies were clear to their sons, the older of whom became active in his high school student federation, which was one of the student movements influenced by the left Peronists. By 1974, however, the corrupt right-wing Peronist government was targeting for repression the progressive sectors of the movement, from the Montonero guerrillas to the mass-based student and union organizations.

Julia became ever more nervous as she learned that Mimi Langer and others were being chased from the country by the Triple A. She remembers being anxiously preoccupied with her son's situation. Life was dominated by family confrontations as Gabriel became increasingly involved in political activism. "It was such a contradiction. Gabriel would tell us that we were hypocrites, that he was only actualizing the political principles he had learned from us. And he was right. Our position was difficult to defend. I respected his commitment to the values of justice and equality that we had always upheld. He argued that we couldn't teach him one set of values and then ask him to be a traitor to his ideals and his comrades. Like all the young people, he criticized us for our bourgeoisification."

The months went by, and the agony persisted. Julia understood that an important aspect of the struggle with Gabriel was characteristic adolescent rebelliousness toward parental authority with the proclivity to criticize one's parents while simultaneously admiring and identifying with them. "But the stakes were rising precipitously as the real situation became more dangerous." Indeed, by the beginning of 1975, portentous signs of disaster were multiplying. Economic crises produced spiraling inflation, speculation, hoarding, and shortages in basic necessities. Industrial production dropped, unemployment increased, and sales of consumer goods shrank, resulting in demonstrations and strikes that by July culminated in a forty-eight-hour general strike by over seven million workers throughout the country. In response, the congress passed legislation legitimizing repression of the opposition.

Progressive senators, artists, filmmakers, and journalists received telephone calls and letters ordering them to leave the country or face certain assassination. Ads appeared in newspapers signed by the Triple A, giving notice to selected individuals that they were on its death list. Lawyers were warned on threat of death not to defend political prisoners; those who persisted were killed, robbing the jailed of their legal defense. The press was censored: newspapers critical of the government were closed down, and reporters who did not censor themselves were threatened, jailed, or murdered. Police cars appeared suddenly in different neighborhoods of Buenos Aires, simultaneously cordoning off dozens of blocks in each area; anyone traveling by car, by bus, or on foot was stopped, searched, and forced to provide identification. Police carried out house-to-house searches, demanding identification papers from inhabitants, who had to demonstrate their right to be there. Telephones were tapped, mail was opened. Plainclothes police frequented bars and restaurants, observing and listening. More bodies appeared in every city in Argentina riddled with bullets, disfigured by dynamite, burned beyond recognition. In Buenos Aires, a young political activist—pregnant—was kidnapped from a family party and found shot to death the next morning; Silvio Frondizi, the brother of the ex-president and head of a Marxist party, was murdered in front of his family; a worker active in organizing a strike in his factory was missing and later found murdered, his tortured body abandoned in an alley; a leftist Peronist deputy in the congress, Rodolfo Ortega Peña, was shot to death late one night; the executed bodies of three men and two women were found abandoned near a road outside Buenos Aires, each one bearing 140 bullets.

Perpetrated in the final months of Isabel Perón's reactionary government, this repression represented the death rattle of populism. As with everyone they knew, Julia's and Mariano's anxieties intensified. Despite the undeniable danger, Gabriel was more and more politically involved every day, probably active in one of the mass organizations of the Montoneros, although his parents never knew for sure. "We did know, though, that at this point the movement had no chance of winning. Instead, they were heading for total destruction. We saw that the young activists were less and less protected by the leadership from the growing repression, and we were impotent to do anything."

They continued to try, convincing Gabriel and his compañera to participate in weekly family therapy sessions with a progressive and sympathetic analytic colleague. But the chasm between the desperately worried parents and their recalcitrant son remained. Julia and Mariano became more distraught as Gabriel continued his political activism, and they worried constantly when he went for weekends with other students to squatter settlements to help in the construction of houses and in other community projects. As more people began to disappear, Gabriel spoke little about his university-based activities, worried that he might compromise his parents. They sensed his fears, although he never articulated them. In the final days of 1975, when most Argentines assumed that a military coup was imminent, Julia and her husband made a last-ditch effort to protect their son. They suggested that the family leave the country for a time so he could gain some emotional distance to think about what was happening and what he wanted to do. "We respect your ideals," they told him, "so if outside the immediacy of the situation you make a dispassionate assessment and decide that it is the best thing for you to come back, we will honor your wishes." Not surprisingly, Gabriel refused, perhaps sensing their unspoken agenda to try to stop him from returning to Argentina. On January 11, 1976, Gabriel turned eighteen, and his parents hosted a birthday celebration, a festive *asado* for all his friends at their weekend home in Tigre. "It was the last party we ever had for him. I did not know then that it would be our farewell."

Julia lived through the transition to state terror as a politically conscious individual in anguish over the disastrous condition of her country but with an overriding maternal preoccupation about what might happen to her child. For others, like Juan Carlos Volnovich and Tato Pavlovsky, this period brought a daily paradoxical struggle to live their lives as normally as possible while simultaneously acting politically to help prevent the rapid drift toward a catastrophic resolution of the country's political tensions. Like the millions whose lives had been framed by activism, they vacillated between heartrending dread and sublime denial as the noose tightened around them.

As with so many of his political compañeros, Juan Carlos's life became chaotic in the months leading up to the coup. For some time, he had been a psychoanalyst with much prestige in Porteño society, and his patients included foreign diplomats, prominent individuals in the arts, and members of the ruling elite families. The political activists he treated included the radical sons and daughters of the upper and middle classes as well as those from the most humble strata of Argentine society. As conditions in the country deteriorated, more patients sought therapy to help them face the unbearable anxieties of the intense political situation. Juan Carlos also continued to provide psychological interventions for Montonero activists. He witnessed the alarming effects of the state's repressive policies on the decision-making capacities of the Montonero leadership. Just as Julia had feared, the leaders began to demand compromising and perilous commitments from individual activists psychologically unprepared for the experience. As Argentina moved rapidly toward out-and-out fascism, Juan Carlos felt caught in a terrible conflict. Although he worried because of what he saw as the leaders' growing irresponsibility about exposing their young militants to predictable risks, he continued to collaborate because "we still believed we were going to make the revolution and because, especially given my psychoanalytic understanding of people, I accepted the fact that human beings are imperfect. I was not a romantic in that sense. Nothing is ideal, I thought; everything and everybody is characterized by contradictions. How could this not be true, I told myself, of the very revolutionaries with whom we were fighting for a better world. So I stayed."

Security became a primary issue, and everyone Juan Carlos knew moved constantly, sleeping in different locales every night. He, Silvia, and their two little children did the same, and they moved their offices frequently as well. "Sometimes it was very comical because I'd often borrow an office from a colleague and arrive there ten minutes before my patient with no idea about the physical environment. Once, I got to an office that was decorated like one of those two-hour hotel rooms that people rent for sexual rendezvous! But, miraculously, my patients endured this instability, knowing, whether or not they were political activists, that the conditions required such drastic measures."

In retrospect, Juan Carlos realizes that a combination of factors permitted him to bear the enormous tension during this period. One was his unconscious denial that the organized violence of the right-wing state had succeeded in derailing the progressive forces and that they were now in true disarray. "Once the repression reached a certain point, a cogent analysis of what was happening was impossible. At the time, I didn't realize that it was not feasible to analyze the situation, and I continued, like a technocrat, interpreting everything that happened and thinking I could understand it all. I continued to believe nothing could happen to me." However, in spite of their denial, he and Silvia also prepared for the worst, structuring a personal security system to protect their family. They never participated in the same political activities but took turns so as not to expose their children to the risk of losing both parents. And they had an escape plan in place, with passports, visas, open plane tickets, and a plan elaborated for how on a second's notice they and their children could leave the country. But they stayed, keeping alive the hope that somehow the rapid drift toward disaster could be stopped.

Tato, too, refused to leave, although many of his psychoanalytic friends and colleagues in the theater were heading for exile in Uruguay, Brazil, and Spain. Even when a theater that featured *Señor Galindez* was bombed, Tato was resolute. "I think I unconsciously denied the danger because I could not bear giving up so many things—my country, my home, my work. . . . I just told myself, they won't come for me." Meanwhile, he faced anguishing situations in his therapy groups, as individuals who had suffered imprisonment or torture sought psychological help. "Lots of people were dying, and it was impossible to be objective in this period. You couldn't speak only about the Oedipus complex now because we all shared the same fears. The issue of neutrality was dead along with the dying. . . . I tried to be as neutral as possible in order to understand the nature of the more irrational conflicts that a patient might be suffering. But, given the conditions we were living through, sometimes the therapy provided the important function of helping patients with the difficult task of developing a language with which to articulate their experience of terror. In retrospect I realize that often the therapy group provided the only space in which people could put into words the fear, the panic. It was the only space in which to speak. It would be like that for years."

Uruguay's transition to state terror was much like Argentina's. By March 1972, when Juan María Bordaberry became the new Uruguayan president, the

"Switzerland of South America" was enmeshed in an enormous economic and political crisis. Its progressive democracy was being replaced by a military-dominated political system that set about to eliminate the critical voices among organized labor and the middle class. Bordaberry immediately authorized the Law on State Security and Public Order, which permitted the military to increase its role in Uruguayan public life and to launch a full-scale attack on the Tupamaros. The military successfully routed the guerrilla organization by November of that year, a full seven months before they carried out their coup. Although the Tupamaros had already been systematically liquidated, Uruguay continued to undergo a gradual militarization of daily life as soldiers carried out massive searches throughout neighborhoods in Montevideo and large-scale arrests in provincial Uruguayan cities. The military justified their assault on citizens' civil rights as necessary to hunt down individuals associated with the now-destroyed Tupamaros. The media were utilized to sow fear among the population through daily radio and television broadcasts produced by the armed forces that reported on the "progress of the war." The "enemy" in the military's "war" turned out to include thousands of union activists, students, social workers, physicians, lawyers, journalists, and mental-health professionals. The military saw them as constituting a vast network of subversion threatening the status quo.

Many of those targeted by the military, like Marcelo and Maren Viñar, had been identified for years with progressive and leftist values and activities, which had been a legitimate part of Uruguayan pluralistic political culture. Beginning in the tumultuous late sixties, the Viñars and other Uruguayan psychoanalysts, like their Argentine colleagues, had begun to explore the relationship between psychoanalysis and politics. The Viñars participated in one of the first groups organized within the APU to study the intersection between the social and unconscious domains of human experience. The members of this group sought to break out of the fetters of mainstream psychoanalytic theory, which from their perspective had focused too exclusively on the intrapsychic world of the individual. Maren recounts that "in that period it was clear that individual psychological experience was deeply influenced by the social world, and it forced us to move beyond conceptualizing the internal world in a void." She stresses how the themes of social violence and aggression prompted heated theoretical debates over issues about which analysts heatedly disagreed—and still do. "The new political violence that began with the death of students and the repression of strikes forced many of us to see that the external context of psychological life is not calm and stable, that, on the contrary, its dramatic unsettledness disturbs the internal world of the subject."

Maren and Marcelo point out that their involvement in the university, the hospital, and working-class neighborhoods, where they treated families struggling with deprivation and poverty, highlighted the social context of their psychotherapeutic work. In 1970, during a congress in Caracas called Social Reality and Psychoanalysis, the Uruguayan participants formed a study group with Mimi Langer, José Bleger, and other Argentine analysts in order to explore how psychoanalysis could contribute to an understanding of the crisis in their countries. The group met every three months in Montevideo or Buenos Aires to develop new paradigms for an analysis of the role of the unconscious in group behavior. The analysts from both countries felt bound by their mutual commitment to a socially conscious psychoanalysis, although the different cultural contexts in which they lived and worked affected their respective political practice.

When their Argentine colleagues in Plataforma broke from the APA, Maren and Marcelo resisted the parallel pressure to leave the APU. The Uruguayan institute did not mirror the APA's hierarchical structures and closed ideological environment but, like Uruguayan organizations in general, had tended toward a pluralistic openmindedness. So the Viñars remained in the APU but continued to work with the dissident Argentines because they had parallel preoccupations that grew out of the increasingly repressive political environment in both countries. As Marcelo puts it, "We came to see that social repression enters the consultation room, that it is impossible to stay isolated." The Uruguayan group coauthored an article in *Cuestionamos I* in 1971, asking whether therapeutic neutrality was possible within an increasingly politically repressive society. They wrote about a specific situation: a patient of Maren's, a university student, had been shot by the military; should a psychoanalyst, they inquired, participate in the strike organized to protest the murder? "We argued that in this situation no neutral position was possible, that either position—to strike or not to strike—contained a political posture in the face of deepening repression that affected patients and analysts alike. Furthermore, as more of our patients began to be affected by military and police actions, we postulated that when a patient or those close to her are directly affected by political repression and she doesn't speak about it, the analyst's refusal to raise the subject does not reflect therapeutic neutrality but collusion with the patient's denial of reality."

But what Marcelo remembers most is his confusion during this period, the difficulty of evaluating the meaning of events that were relentlessly altering reality as he had always known it. "There was the problem of timing, if you will: how much time it took for an individual to be socialized in a social democratic culture and then how much time it required to recognize that it had changed into a terrorist and terrifying society. The process of political change and the capacity to subjectively absorb and understand this change operate at distinctly different rates. I, for example, was very slow to realize the shift . . . it's as if I continued to believe in democracy when I was living in a country that was already totalitarian. I believe that it is characteristic of the period of transition between democracy and dictatorship that people function by denying reality. During those years we thought, 'I'm not a Tupamaro; I'm part of the democratic left. All I did was collect the dues from three Communist Party members; but the party was legal, they won't put me in jail for that.' Or, 'Five years ago I signed a petition against the Vietnam War, but that wasn't against the law . . . the repression is against the Tupamaros, why would they come for me?' It's exactly as Freud describes, a splitting of the ego, in which one can believe two contradictory things at the same time but not be able to put them together to recognize the obvious truth. Thus two belief systems can coexist without entering into contradiction. This was how reality was characterized at the time. I could not believe that they ever would come after me to take me prisoner, and yet I could believe it."

This state of dissociation that Marcelo describes operated when, in 1971, he was approached by a colleague who requested advice about the medication and hospitalization of a Tupamaro militant who had suffered a psychotic break. Marcelo had known that the patient was a Tupamaro but had told himself there was no problem because he was simply acting under the medical oath, which obliged him to treat anyone needing medical intervention. A year later, he would be imprisoned for this professional decision, which was considered by the military a political rather than a medical act. His crime would come under the purview of "assistance to an association of delinquents." In this regard, Marcelo believes that "it wasn't until I was taken prisoner that my dissociation was challenged. In fact, I think I was helped tremendously by my first interrogations. It was only then that I began to understand that the mentality of my interrogators and my own were as different from one another as Martians and Earthlings. I am grateful to them, actually, because when the military came to get me a second time four years later, I was able to anticipate it and fled the country in time."

In Chile, the transition to state terror took a different course than in Argentina and Uruguay, but Elizabeth Lira's experience was similar to that of her compañeros in the other two countries. She lived through the destabilization of an already-existing leftist government and the creation of the conditions for its elimination. The Chilean military acted in league with President Nixon's 1970 mandate to the CIA to "utilize every appropriate resource" to get rid of Allende. By mid-1972, the international campaign of economic sabotage against Chile and the ongoing ideological attacks of the Chilean bourgeois press, blaming the UP for the ensuing economic difficulties, created a state of continual crisis and foreboding.

"The country was in chaos, but it was clear that it was being orchestrated," remembers Elizabeth. At the height of the economic crisis, she had her second child, Cecelia. "Imagine, there were no diapers! There were terrible shortages of everything—bread, vegetables, cooking oil, meat. . . . The right wing had control of the distribution networks and the wholesale suppliers, and the businessmen were hoarding products to sell on the black market at inflated prices. The people with money had no worry. The rest of us had to stand in long lines, sometimes for five or six hours a day beginning at 5 A.M. And, of course, it was the women who had to do it. Conflicts arose at home because there wasn't enough to eat." Increasingly, daily life became intolerable for millions of people who could not explain to themselves why they had to spend so many hours simply to obtain food. The UP ceased to represent an advantage or source of improvement in their lives. For many, their hope that the poor would one day run the country now seemed to have been a fantasy. The media kept up their threats, insisting that conditions would inevitably deteriorate if the UP continued in power. Consumption was the focus of the propaganda campaign against Allende; through it the media manipulated people's deepening anxiety about the uncertain future. The goal was to diminish popular support for Allende and to neutralize potential resistance to any illegal move to oust him from power.

Worst perhaps was the pervasive sense of confusion. Elizabeth says that "no one could imagine what was coming. I was frightened, though, because I had always felt that the Allende program was very idealistic, with the additional problem that the UP administrators had too little experience to implement the strategy of reforms in a way that could minimize the inevitable social conflict that comes with change." In the midst of the crisis, it was difficult to assess the balance of power. Many of Elizabeth's friends and comrades thought Chile was heading for civil war. Others viewed the huge demonstrations organized by the supporters of the UP as proof of the strength of progressive forces, which they believed could deter the right wing. Elizabeth thinks that the militant left misjudged the situation by overestimating the solidity of their support among the masses. "From my perspective they projected their own unshakable commitment to support Chilean democracy by any means necessary onto the hundreds of thousands who came to the spirited demonstrations they organized. They mistakenly assumed that the progressive forces would stand fast if the country moved into an armed confrontation. They were blinded to the difference for most people between taking part in a demonstration for a day and putting their lives on the line in the face of an increasingly violent enemy."

Elizabeth also believes that the decades-long leftist denunciation of U.S. imperialism had the paradoxical effect of diminishing the impact of the left's exposé of the United States as an active player in the unfolding drama in Chile. It sounded so fantastic: the U.S. State Department, the CIA, ITT Corporation, orchestrating from Washington a massive conspiracy, with millions of dollars and hundreds of operatives, to undermine their democratically elected government. "Fantastic, but true," she laments. "Many simply dismissed it as paranoid rhetoric, preferring to put blinders on so as not to heed the signs."[1]

During the three months leading up to the September 11 coup, conditions became increasingly catastrophic. Elizabeth's political organization met daily to evaluate the latest events, to calculate how best to support the government, and to figure out how to protect themselves. "But we were so naive, we couldn't clearly identify what would happen. I remember meeting a friend one day, a sociologist, who advised me that we should learn from the experiences of comrades from other countries, the refugees among us from Brazil and Uruguay. 'If something happens,' he told me, 'we would have to burn our books, clean out our houses, disconnect from one another.' And I thought he was crazy. How in this country would I ever have to burn my books? Military dictatorship was something that characterized other countries, not Chile. This is a nation, I thought, where there is legality and where the armed forces are constitutionalists. We believed that; . . . Allende believed it. We thought we were different."

As it turned out, in the Southern Cone there were no exceptions.

The Ideology of State Terror

The military juntas justified the system of terror they imposed through an ideology that had been fine tuned for three decades after World War II. Its origins can be found in the Doctrine of National Security designed in Washington at the outset of the Cold War. Its aim was to preserve the hegemonic role of the United States in the Western Hemisphere and to protect the capitalist order throughout the Americas from external and internal threat. By the late 1940s, a division of labor between the United States and Latin American militaries had been elaborated: the United States would be responsible for the defense of the Western Hemisphere against outside aggression, and the Latin American armies would focus on the elimination of internal threats to stability.[2]

The Doctrine of National Security, which was expanded during the Kennedy administration in the wake of the Cuban Revolution, provided the rationale in subsequent decades for the U.S. government's development of counterinsurgency programs in its struggle against the spread of revolutionary movements in Latin America. Subversives were defined in broad terms to include anyone or any group whose aims were considered "inconvenient" to the existing system. The United States organized centers where North American ideologues taught the principles of counterinsurgency to Latin American armed forces. Special advisers, instructors, and CIA operatives fanned out over the continent to disseminate the message and the know-how. Beginning in the 1960s, the Conferences of American Armies met to coordinate security operations among the various Latin American militaries. From the Truman era through the Clinton presidency, thousands of Latin American military officers have attended special courses in the Doctrine of National Security and its tactics—including classes on the theory and practice of torture—at the School of the Americas, Fort Gulick in the Panama Canal Zone, and Fort Bragg in North Carolina.[3] Many of the officers who organized and implemented the coups in Argentina, Chile, and Uruguay had attended classes at these sites, developing collegial relationships and a mutual understanding of their historical task. They would cooperate when the time came to "go all the way" to implement the doctrine.

In the process, the liberals—the "soft-liners"—within the military would be forced to decide whether to acquiesce gracefully or get out.[4] The Uruguayan colonel appointed by the military to defend Marcelo after he was imprisoned was a case in point. Maren describes him as "avidly anti-Tupamaro." At first this officer scared her to death. She felt he was Marcelo's accuser rather than his defender. "But he was essentially a democratic man, and as the repression mounted, his personal ethic was deeply offended by the violation of human rights perpetrated by his military colleagues. After Marcelo was released, this colonel brought his daughters and wife for therapeutic consultations and also sent other associates for treatment. Shortly after, he took his family and left the country."

Ever since World War II, the United States has supplied heavy arms and lighter tactical weapons to Latin American militaries for counterinsurgency warfare against "internal enemies." As Defense Secretary Robert McNamara told Congress in 1963, "Our primary objective in Latin America is to aid, wherever necessary, the continual growth of the military and paramilitary forces, so that together with the police and other security forces, they may provide the necessary internal security."[5] It was argued that World War III—the battle against communism—had many fronts and included political, ideological, and psychological warfare as well as military struggle. Indeed, the U.S. military was so directly connected to the Latin American military apparatus that, three years into the Argentine junta's Dirty War against its citizens, it organized in Buenos Aires a course in fighting subversion, which included classes in physical and psychological torture, attended by many members of the Latin American armed forces. And in the seventh year of military rule in Argentina, U.S.

military personnel occupied offices in the army's headquarters, with separate telephones in the Operations Section, Overseer of Operations and Central Division.[6]

During the period of state terror, the economic policies of Argentina, Chile, and Uruguay were based on the free-market principle known as neoliberalism (in reality, a conservative philosophy, so called because it accepts the free-trade tenets of nineteenth-century liberal economic theory) advocated by the United States and Latin American business sectors and international lending and trading institutions. Advised by the "Chicago boys," neoliberal economic technocrats associated with the University of Chicago monetarist Milton Friedman, the military governments dramatically reversed the previous trend toward state-sponsored industrialization and opened up their markets to foreign competition. The Chicago boys' blueprint for an unfettered marketplace called for the elimination of protective tariffs, minimum wage laws, social entitlements, and government safety and health regulations, and for government intervention in or destruction of unions. When corruption and unproductive speculative investments resulted in economic crises, the militaries exacerbated their countries' cycle of indebtedness by borrowing large sums from an enthusiastic International Monetary Fund and World Bank, where U.S. interests predominated. The close relationship between the Argentine junta and foreign capital was symbolized by Ford Motor Company, which in a full-page newspaper ad congratulated the military as "Argentines of good will" who were turning the country around. Ford pledged its participation "in the efforts to fulfill the nation's destiny," concluding with a self-congratulatory "Ford gives you more."[7] Indeed, Ford gave generously to the junta: its local subsidiary supplied government security forces with the unmarked Falcon automobiles that were used in the illegal abductions of Argentine citizens.

From Juan Carlos's perspective, "The historical function of the Southern Cone dictatorships was to eliminate those sectors of the population capable of mounting resistance to the uncontrolled, free-market economics sought by transnational corporations and international financial and trading institutions." He emphasizes that the revolutionary armed movement had already been destroyed in Argentina when the military took power, and thus the Dirty War it unleashed was equivalent to the use of the atomic bomb in Hiroshima. "It wasn't necessary to vanquish the Japanese, who had already admitted defeat but rather to intimidate the Soviet Union: look what we have and what we're willing to do. . . . In the case of state terror in the Southern Cone, they utilized the ideology of counterinsurgency in a psychological war to attack all critical consciousness."

The mentality that engineered this ideological and military war against internal subversion was profoundly authoritarian. State terror was the product of a partnership in which U.S. political and military leaders shared a proclivity for authoritarianism with their Latin American counterparts. But because the violence occurred in Latin America, it could be depicted in the United States by government and media alike as the natural outcome of the inherently violent nature of the cultures to the south. The contributions of the U.S. government to the extreme political repression throughout the continent could be externalized onto other forces—immoral subversives, godless communists, bloodthirsty generals—and thus disavowed to its own citizens.

In addition to the Doctrine of National Security, each of the militaries in the Southern Cone brought to this partnership additional political and military theories garnered from their studies of nineteenth-century Prussian strategists and from their training with French veterans of the counterinsurgency wars fought in Algeria and Indochina.[8] In the Latin American terrorist state the authoritarian mind was fully developed, uninhibited, and self-indulgent in its grandiosity. Military leaders and followers alike shared a psychology characterized by a set of primitive defenses: the splitting of the world into good and evil—Western civilization versus subversion; the projection of everything bad onto a hated object—the subversive—with the consequent need to control it for fear of being controlled by it; and an infantile sense of omnipotence that promotes attacks on free inquiry and political difference, with a corresponding incapacity for empathy. Like European fascism, the Latin American terrorist state rejected the modern age with all its contradictions and was unable to abide political and philosophical pluralism. Repression of dissent was total. As the Argentine military succinctly put it, "Argentina has three main enemies: Karl Marx, because he tried to destroy the Christian concept of society; Sigmund Freud, because he tried to destroy the Christian concept of the family; and Albert Einstein, because he tried to destroy the Christian concept of time and space."[9]

The military juntas believed that World War III had begun. This war was not between democracy and communism, they argued, but rather between the entire world and left-wing terrorism. With their strong sense of corporate identity, army officers saw themselves as members of an elite organization and were contemptuous of civilians and especially of politicians. Democracy was, from their perspective, an inappropriate medium for winning the war against subversion. The militaries attacked all who might possibly be or become the enemy. The members of leftist organizations that had engaged in armed struggle to bring about change became demonized but were seen as the mere tip of the iceberg. According to the military, a vast subversive network of ideological conspirators had invaded every aspect of life, affecting the economy, the

judicial and educational systems, the labor movement, and cultural expression. As Argentine President General Jorge Videla put it to the press in 1978,
"A terrorist is not just someone with a gun or a bomb but also someone who
spreads ideas that are contrary to Western civilization." Videla's military colleague in neighboring Chile, President Augusto Pinochet, agreed, reporting
to journalists that minds armed with "envy, rancor and the irreconcilable
struggle of classes" were more dangerous than guns.[10]

The Argentine military elaborated a language that reflected the worldview
of their colleagues in Chile and Uruguay as well. Their Dirty War was needed
to cleanse Argentine society of the impurity of the subversives among the civilian population. Just as Hitler had seen the Jews as an "alien racial poison
in our bodies" and Marxism as "eating deeply into the national body like a
pestilence,"[11] the Argentine military described subversion as a disease infest-
ing the nation, which in turn was viewed as a living organism. Building on
disease metaphors that had been widely used in the postwar period throughout the Americas—in the 1950s the reformist government of Juan José Arévalo
in Guatemala had been referred to as the "Guatemalan cancer" and the Cuban Revolution had been called an "infection" in the Western Hemisphere—
the Argentine military alluded to an "epidemic" similar to the plagues that
had scourged the world in previous centuries.[12] "The social body of the country is contaminated by a disease that corrodes its insides and forms antibodies," claimed Admiral Cesar A. Guzzetti, minister of foreign relations. "These
antibodies must not be considered in the same way that one considers a germ.
In proportion to the government's control and destruction of guerrilla warfare, the action of the antibodies is going to disappear." Guzzetti went on to
justify military atrocities by arguing that right-wing terrorist acts were only "a
natural reaction of a sick body."[13] An Uruguayan psychologist who was imprisoned for thirteen months recalls that she and hundreds of other female
prisoners were kept in military prisons because they were considered a "contagious infection" from which common criminals had to be protected.

In Argentina the military's repressive strategy was called the Process of
National Reorganization, which offered a final solution to the problem of subversion. El Proceso, as it was known, identified for extermination not only
the carriers of the germ—defined as social discontent—but those directly exposed to it as well. The military saw themselves as modern crusaders, convinced that theirs was a "just war" carried out in defense of the "natural order"
designed by God. A popular handbook of military ethics encouraged the sol-
dier to think of himself as a "perfect Crusading Knight for God and Father-
land," in which "the punishment of the guilty is not an evil but rather an act
of goodness." Military discourse claimed that the authority for the Dirty War
came from God and that it was "a sign of love and mercy in imitation of

Christ, . . . compelling [subversives] to goodness."[14] This sanctimonious ideology justified the junta's illegal, forcible takeover of state power by redefining terrorism. The military turned the brutality of their rule into its opposite: a self-congratulatory conviction that theirs was a godly and generous act of redemption aimed at saving the souls of the sinner subversives.

An important part of the ideological arsenal of state terror was its public discourse on gender, disseminated through the mass media by all three military dictatorships. In their crusade to uphold the customary class, race, and gender boundaries that privileged the male upper classes, they asserted a patriarchal solution to the subversion of the established social order. In all three countries of the Southern Cone, since the turn of the century, middle- and working-class women had organized movements that had over time expanded female political, legal, and economic rights so that women could go beyond their customary roles as wives and mothers. However, like the Nazis before them, the military regimes reasserted an ideal feminine model of sublime domesticity and advocated traditional Christian and family values. Women were urged through ideological campaigns, sometimes buttressed by new laws, to withdraw from the public realm and return to the home. Femininity was defined as passivity, self-abnegation, and obedient adoration of the male sex, traits viewed as the necessary compliment to male glory and heroic dominance.

But the paternalistic aspects of military gender ideology were contradicted by the harsh impact of state terror on women. For example, in spite of the domestic ideal of true womanhood and official discouragement of women's participation in the public sphere, in all three countries the economic disaster resulting from free-market policies pushed women out of the home in search of paid work to augment their husbands' declining wages or to earn a wage when their husbands fell victim to unemployment. Women workers were subjected to increased exploitation on the job and, as male abandonment of families grew in response to political and economic repression, growing numbers of women found themselves heads of households, providing both financial and emotional resources to sustain themselves and their children. Moreover, the fundamentally misogynist attitudes of the military were expressed by officers and paramilitary forces, whose arbitrary arrests, rape, and torture of women fulfilled different functions: they were an official display of military domination over the civilian population, a self-indulgent ritual sport of off-duty officers, and a ritualized reenactment of power, which bonded the members of the military to one another. Female political activists, who represented the antithesis of bourgeois femininity, became a special target of the terrorist state. They embodied not only a revolutionary challenge to existing class relations but an assertion of self that challenged male hegemony in the psychological as well as the political domain. For this they paid dearly, and those who were among the *desaparecidos* became the victims in elaborate rituals of male domination exercised through psychological and physical torture. In addition, the state's ideology and practice legitimized an intensification of the customary relationship between machismo and violence in the culture in general. Many men who found themselves the hapless victims of an authoritarian state, unable to express their rage directly at the military forces responsible, displaced their aggression onto women, who were safer and socially more acceptable objects of male violence.[15]

Strategies of State Terror

State terror in Chile, Argentina, and Uruguay developed a strategy that made most of the population in each country victims of a doctrine of collective guilt.[16] The military governments engaged in a cleansing offensive against the enemies of Western Christian civilization, an important part of which was the construction of a public discourse aimed at paralyzing citizens with its contradictory and paradoxical content. The military's rhetoric turned the usual meanings of *order* and *violence* on their heads. Contrary to democracies, in which the function of government is ostensibly the creation and preservation of order through law and opposition to violence, terrorist states created violence (while attributing it to political opponents) and disrupted law and order (while claiming to enforce it). Society was redefined as a war zone, and the military and paramilitary attack on civil society was reflected in the militarization of ideology, which imposed a sense of catastrophic danger and constant unpredictability. Fear was reinforced by the promulgation of laws whose goal was to sever social and public ties by prohibiting individuals from gathering in groups or organizations.

Psychic dysfunction was reinforced by the media, whose skewed information created a sense of ominous threat. Paradoxically, newspapers, radio, and television operated under strict censorship, obliged to follow a rule of silence. They simultaneously plied the public with overwhelming amounts of information about military arrests, detentions, and executions, all calculated to convey a terrifying and dangerous reality. As Chilean psychologists explain, the terrorist state appropriated language itself to mystify the perception of the past and the present. *Clean* and *dirty* were words repeatedly utilized by the media to create an unconscious identification with a range of governmental policies and attitudes: UP murals on city walls were whitewashed away—cleaned—along with the past; public employees were fired—cleaned out—and those who lost their jobs were political enemies—dirty; progressive politics, Marxist books, and foreigners were all designated as dirty, enemy threats to the Chilean nation.

In Argentina, newspaper articles that began with accusatory headlines, such as "Parents: Do You Know Where Your Children Are?", described corpses of young people disfigured by bullets and torture found in city streets and along country roads. The papers identified them as hoodlums who had carried out illegal actions, forcing confrontations with the police or military. The deceased were accused of being common criminals or subversives who had broken the laws of the nation and whose violent attacks on society had been legitimately responded to by the authorities. Responsibility for their deaths was displaced onto their parents, who were accused of inadequately supervising their children and failing to rear them with the appropriate respect for authority and private property.

Policies of disappearing, torturing, and murdering significant numbers of citizens were aimed at imposing a passive consensus within the population. Everyone knew about the "secret" concentration camps, woke to see or hear about the disfigured cadavers of torture victims rotting in the streets or floating in the rivers, knew someone whose relative or friend had been disappeared. While the terrorist state spoke of the need to respect the family and social order, entire families were attacked, destroyed, and violated. Jacobo Timmerman, the noted Argentine publisher abducted and tortured by the Argentine junta, wrote that "nothing can compare to those family groups who were tortured often together, sometimes separately but in view of one another. The entire affective world . . . collapses. . . . Nothing is possible in such a universe, and that is precisely what the torturers know."[17]

As each of the Southern Cone countries fell under military domination, political refugees fled from one nation to the other seeking asylum. But the military and security forces pursued them, driven by the U.S. Doctrine of National Security, which favored respect for ideological frontiers over national boundaries. Uruguayans were captured, tortured, and murdered by Uruguayan officers in Argentina, and Argentines fell victim to security forces from their own country operating in Uruguay. A Chilean hit squad even pursued Orlando Letelier, former foreign minister under Allende, to Washington, D.C., where they assassinated him and his U.S. assistant, Ronni Moffitt, with a car bomb in broad daylight.[18]

Political repression went hand in hand with a deteriorating economic situation for most sectors in all three countries. The terrorist state imposed economic policies that favored elite groups at the expense of the popular classes, whose traditional avenues for seeking economic redistribution had been smashed. The World Bank and the International Monetary Fund, along with U.S. neoliberal economic advisors, imposed harsh measures to attract foreign capital and international loans. A docile and inexpensive labor force was a prerequisite for multinational investment, and those who challenged such policies were abducted or jailed. Uruguayan journalist Eduardo Galeano's pithy remark captures his compatriots' plight: "In Uruguay, people were in prison so that prices could be free."[19]

Labor unions were closed down, taken over by the government, or declared to be illegal, and workers, employees, intellectuals, and professionals no longer had legitimate means of defending their class and sectoral interests. Rising unemployment rates, forced wage cuts, and an escalating cost of living all reflected the assault on the working and middle classes' quality of life. People's energies were drained in the frantic effort to survive. With freedom of speech and all forms of organized collective struggle prohibited, any kind of resistance or opposition brought life-threatening reprisals. In Argentina, the military found willing allies in the Church hierarchy, some of whom were present during torture sessions, and among factory owners and managers, some of whom, as at the Ford factory, permitted illegal detention centers to operate on the premises.[20]

"This was the craziest time of our lives," says Juan Carlos. "Every minute Silvia and I would say, 'Let's go, let's go, let's go.' We fought constantly. . . . When I'd say, 'Yes, let's go,' Silvia would say no, and when I said no, she'd say yes. . . . We'd talk constantly about it, but we were paralyzed. At one point I said, 'Basta, I'm going crazy; there's no good solution, either way it's a catastrophe, so let's stay and take our chances.' Silvia agreed and we settled in." Almost all their contacts had been caught. The president of the Psychological Association, of which Silvia was a member, had been disappeared, and many of Carlos's colleagues in the FAP were also missing or detained. More people fled into exile, selling homes and other belongings for almost nothing in flea markets that were dubbed *férias americanas*. Juan Carlos bought a spectacular home and an office that was elegantly furnished with a balcony facing the neighborhood police station. He would water his plants and watch the military operatives come and go. He and Silvia had finally ended the torture of their indecision, and they told themselves that because they were cut off from everything political, they were safe. "We cleaned out our house of anything that could identify us with the left—books, posters, music. We focused on our patients and bought furniture, like good obsessives protecting ourselves from unwelcome thoughts and feelings. 'We were not doing anything wrong,' we told ourselves and denied that we were at risk."

In December, nine months after the coup, Juan Carlos and Silvia received a phone call from Cuba, where Silvia's brother, Leonardo, had been working as an epidemiologist since the early sixties. Silvia's sister-in-law, Beatriz, announced that Leonardo had suffered a heart attack and was in serious condition, and she implored them to come to Cuba right away. Unable to speak clearly for fear the telephone was tapped, neither Silvia nor Juan Carlos could determine the real nature of the message and concluded it might be a warning in code. Finally Beatriz implored, "For once in your life, please, don't say anything more and take heed of what I'm telling you. Leave immediately and go to Lima, where everything will be arranged and waiting for you." Chilled by her words, they concluded that Silvia's family in Cuba had learned something about their circumstances in Argentina that they did not know. They suddenly were faced with an irrefutable fact: they would have to leave the country. And it would have to be fast.

It took them three days. Juan Carlos announced to his patients that he had to leave Argentina for political reasons, explaining that as a professor in the university medical school, he was among the psychoanalytic faculty who had been threatened by the new military dean's directive "to leave the country and go to live in Tel Aviv, Paris, or Moscow." In response, several of his patients, influential political conservatives, generously offered to use their contacts to escort him and his family safely out of Argentina. It turned out to be unnecessary. As he had always imagined, they would benefit from having lived in a state of constant alert, prepared to leave on a moment's notice. With all the necessary documents in order, their major decision was where to go and what to take. Although they both wanted to go to Cuba, Juan Carlos was apprehensive that he would not be able to work as an analyst in Cuba's behaviorist-oriented mental health care system. "I felt too old to retrain myself and deliberated over a tempting offer from the Piaget Center of Genetic Epistemology in Geneva to work for a year as a child analyst. It was a wrenching decision, but ultimately our affinity with Cuba won out."

They packed in a frenzy, their choices about what to take reflecting their manic response to the sudden reordering of their lives. Laughingly, Juan Carlos describes how they anguished over how many suitcases, the weight allowed by the airlines, which few precious things to carry away, perhaps forever. "We took some clothes, and I took the goose-down pillow I'd had since childhood, which had belonged to my mother and her mother before her in Europe. . . . And Silvia, well, she fixated on a Swedish exercise machine she'd bought two days prior to our phone call from Cuba. It was a really complicated device that we'd thought would be the perfect accoutrement to round out our newly acquired bourgeois lifestyle. So that was what she chose to stuff into her suitcase. Its value was that she'd just bought it, and how could you leave behind a brand new thing like that? It weighed a ton, took up all the pounds the airlines allowed us to take on the plane! It was a testimony to our craziness. We'd never used it before nor did we after. But that's what we took into exile."

The next day when Juan Carlos, Silvia, and the two children went to the airport, many friends and family who had learned of their departure were there to see them off. "We went with the sensation that we would be gone for forty years because that is what happened to the Spanish refugees when fascism overturned the Spanish Republic. We wept, all of us, . . . and when we and the children boarded the plane, the four of us cried like babies all the way to Lima, Peru, our stopover to a new life." Several weeks later, when they landed in Cuba, they learned that Silvia's brother was in the hospital, recovering from a heart attack. The phone call had not been a code after all! No matter. They were safe. And the next eight years would prove to be the adventure of a lifetime.

Tato lasted in Buenos Aires several years into the Dirty War. "When the military finally came for me in March of 1978," he tells me, smiling, "believe it or not, my reaction was to feel outraged!" Tato had managed to survive emotionally by denying the danger and deluding himself with an omnipotent sense that he could stay, continue to speak out, and survive the wrath of the dictatorship. "More than denial," he says by way of self-criticism, "I employed an instrumental dissociation in order to go on. But my wife, Susana, was afraid, although she, too, escaped from her anxieties in her artistic activities." Tato felt that in staying he was sustaining a kind of political militancy by writing and producing plays whose themes would encourage people to think about the experience they were living through. "I told myself it would be all right, that I wasn't a guerrilla, only a playwright whose theater dealt with the human condition."

In 1977, his new play, *Telarañas* (Spiderwebs), opened, exploring for audiences the authoritarian characteristics in the family system that made its members receptive to fascism in the society at large. Immediately, Tato received a call from the authorities notifying him that he would have to close the production because, as they put it, he was an author without traditional Christian values. "To show you how much I denied my own vulnerability, I said to them in the most arrogant fashion, 'I can't do that. If you want the play shut down, you'll have to do it yourselves.'" Tato would pay a high price for this unfortunate miscalculation.

They came for him one day during a session of a psychotherapy group. His secretary interrupted the session to inform him that two men from the gas company were at the door downstairs. She signaled to him with a strange expression warning Tato that he was the object of a macabre reenactment of a scene in *Telarañas*, in which the paramilitary forces who come for the protagonists disguise themselves as *gassistas*. As he was telling his therapy group that he had to leave but that nothing would happen to them, he suddenly turned to see a hooded man standing behind him. Quickly, he leaped onto the balcony, where he caught a glimpse of two more hooded men in the kitchen below with two of his children.

"At that moment, panic overtook me. I did something truly mad. . . . I leaped from the balcony to the house next door and went immediately to the police. I reported that two robbers—I couldn't say an armed group—had invaded my home. Then in the midst of it all, I did something really intelligent, something I think might very well have saved my life." While the police set off to investigate the robbery, the police chief sat across the desk from Tato, "viewing me with respect as an unfortunate doctor whose home was being vandalized rather than as a Marxist enemy who was being persecuted by a paramilitary operation." With his heart racing, Tato courteously requested the use of the telephone. He called his brother but pretended that the person on the other end was Raul Alfonsín, a prestigious figure internationally known at the time for his work in the human rights movement. "He was someone the police chief had to take seriously, given his high profile, and I said, 'Look, Raul, I'm here at the such-and-such police station with Police Chief Lopez,' and then I responded as if he were indicating that he was coming right over. I was convinced, though, that they were going to kill me on the spot."

When the police and the paramilitary group returned to the station together, a really mysterious thing happened. "They were trying to figure out what to do with me, when one officer approached me and asked, 'Tell me, are you Catholic or Jewish?' When I replied that I was Catholic, the officer said, 'Very good, Doctor. Look, you walk slowly until you get to the big avenue at the corner. Then get out of here.'" Tato started to walk, terrified, but when he got to the corner, he saw that his brother was waiting for him, having interpreted the phone call correctly. "Then the worst period of my life began. He told me that they'd destroyed my house and taken all my personal documents so that I wouldn't be able to leave the country. But, thank heaven, they did not harm my wife or children. I lived for weeks in Buenos Aires, moving from one friend's home to another, waiting until my departure could be arranged. My political compañeros demonstrated lots of solidarity, and they helped me get to Montevideo. Once there, in exile, I felt that there was a historical thread linking my grandfather, my father, and me, one that wove together our fate as émigrés. It gave me an eerie sense to be in the same bar in Montevideo on the Avenida 18 de Julio that my father had frequented when he was in exile twenty-five years earlier. It seemed that becoming a refugee was part of my destiny."

From Uruguay, Tato went to Madrid, where he would endure exile for the next three years. However, he was never able, in spite of personal growth and professional success, to transcend the sense that "my life had been shattered by the profound psychic disruption of exile."

Forced Disappearances and Torture

Although Tato had escaped being abducted, thousands of citizens of Argentina, Chile, and Uruguay did not. Following in the tradition of the infamous

Nazi "night and fog" decrees, in which prisoners whose guilt could not be determined were transferred secretly in the darkness of night to undisclosed destinations, vanishing without a trace, the military governments ignored due process to simply abduct, torture, and murder citizens to whom they attributed the disturbing social, political, and economic crises of society. The *desaparecidos* became the metaphor for a dirty war. In Argentina, military discourse referred to "the incorporation of the enemy," and in line with the metaphor of disease and antibody, the enemy was in fact surrounded by the military, enclosed within it in the secret system of detention centers and concentration camps. The term used to refer to the strategy of disappearing people, *chupar*, means to suck, to absorb, to take in; *los chupados* were literally incorporated and taken in by the junta in order to be destroyed.

Why did the military choose this strategy? Why did they abduct individuals and families in often flagrant ways—openly witnessed by neighbors, coworkers and bystanders—only to claim later that they knew nothing of the whereabouts of those they had kidnapped? The *desaparecidos* served many purposes, not the least of which was the military's imposition of the culture of fear. By disappearing people, the dictatorships could deny their crimes because there was no concrete evidence: no bodies, no arrests, no formal charges, no trials, and no imprisonments. And, even more to the point, the military needed the *desaparecidos* because as long as people continued to disappear, each dictatorship could argue that the nation was still under siege by subversives, who continued to be caught. Indeed, the existence of an enemy was *the* raison d'être of repressive military rule. As scholar Frank Graziano has put it, "Were the Junta to neglect the constant invention of its Enemy, it too would soon be absent forever. The Hero thus found himself in the unhappy position of having a vital need for the very enemy he wishes to destroy."[21] The *desaparecidos* had an additional function: that of scapegoat. Military discourse depicted them as the embodiment of evil that had to be violently purged from the body politic, the community. Although they were members of the community, their persecution by the military was depicted as the purification of the community through the elimination of an evil rather than as violence directed against the entire community. Thus the ritual of disappearing people made the *desaparecido* the guilty one and attributed to the authoritarian regime and the community a measure of sanctity for having done away with the evil.

In Chile, although fewer persons were disappeared than in Argentina—approximately one thousand in comparison with an estimated nine to twenty thousand—the political and psychological functions were identical. The rumors of people vanishing made the security forces in Chile seem omnipresent and omnipotent. Elizabeth Lira indicates that "this policy of disappearing people evoked extreme states of anxiety in the community related to the sense that mysterious and uncontrollable forces were at work whose power everyone was impotent to contain." The individuals who disappeared left behind relatives—wives, children, husbands, mothers, fathers, grandparents—who were condemned to exhausting their energies in an endless search in the maze of federal, provincial, and municipal bureaucracies and police and military centers. Reminiscent of the universe in a Kafka novel, they were met with systematic denial of any knowledge of the whereabouts of their loved ones. Such fruitless endeavors often went on for years. The global effect of disappearing people was that it suggested "the inexplicable, the irrevocable, an absolute loss of knowledge."[22]

In Uruguay, with its tradition of the democratic rule of law, the terrorist state paid more attention to legal forms, even while it violated due process and norms of justice. The military established a classification system—called the A-B-C!—to place each Uruguayan citizen into one of three categories, officially recorded in the central archives. "A" citizens were considered ideologically reliable, so they enjoyed employment rights with a modicum of civil freedoms; "B" citizens were politically suspect and thus did not qualify for government employment and were subject to continual harassment by the security forces; and "C" citizens were pariahs with no civil rights or rights of employment. Every citizen lived in constant terror of being reclassified into the "C" category.

Although Uruguayan state terrorists indulged in kidnapping people from their homes and in public settings, more often they relied on the imposition of lengthy prison terms to terrify not only the prisoners but the rest of society as well. In a country with only three million inhabitants, from the mid-sixties to the mid-eighties, one out of every fifty citizens was imprisoned and one out of sixty-five was tortured. Although far fewer individuals were disappeared than in Argentina or Chile—an estimated two hundred—the large number of people who suffered lengthy imprisonment and unrelenting extreme mistreatment, including elaborate torture rituals, silenced dissent among all who feared the retribution of a brutal state.

Torture was, for the military in all three countries, more than a method of securing information by breaking individual prisoners. It was a political strategy, routinely practiced in a sophisticated and systematic way. It justified the military's war against the civilian population because it extracted confessions that "proved" the guilt of the *desaparecidos* and prisoners. Its object was not merely the body of the victim but the entire social body. The overriding politics of torture was not to make a few individuals talk but to silence everyone.

The coerced confessions obtained through torture often had little to do with the actual identity or political experience of a prisoner. Individual victims were so totally destroyed through brutal physical and psychological torture that they confessed to anything demanded by their captors. In Uruguay, as in Argentina and Chile, many individuals who were arrested had been engaged in only peaceful and legal activities, so that torture drove them to admit to crimes they never would have imagined committing. The destruction of the true past and identity of prisoners reenacted thousands of times represented for the dictatorships the proof of their world-view and of the righteousness of their actions. As Graziano puts it, "Ceremonial acts of cruelty, particularly when performed by regimes lacking legitimacy, make clear how a body in the political sphere can be exploited for the generation of power as it can be in the work place for the generation of wealth."[23]

The system of torture required a complex implementation, each point in the process demanding people with different kinds of psychological traits. For those who designed the system as a central pillar in the edifice of the National Security Doctrine, its key meaning lay in an authoritarian discourse that did not recognize the subjectivity of the victims. The extreme abuse was rationalized not as a wish to impose pain but as a necessary tool for securing the absolute subjugation of individuals perceived to threaten the institutions and ideology of the existing system. The second category of torturers were those who devised the torture strategies; they employed unconscious mechanisms of dissociation and denial in order to view their activity as if it were simply a particular form of work, no different from any other kind of employment. The third type of torturers, those who perpetrated the torture itself, experienced sadistic gratification from the attacks on the minds and bodies of their victims.[24]

Each torture ritual was called by a specific euphemistic name. In Chile, the *picana*, an electrified prod used on sensitive body parts such as genitals and temples, was called "the grill"; repeated dunking in excrement, urine, or polluted water, "the submarine"; a waterless technique of strangulation or suffocation, "the dry submarine"; and prolonged suspension with the body twisted around a pole, "the parrot's perch." In Argentina, Timmerman's torturers referred to his sessions as "having a chat with Susan [the torture machine]."[25] In all three countries the treatment was embellished in many ways: victims were beaten with fists and rubber and metal weapons; enclosed in pens with vicious dogs that came close to dismembering them; tied into sacks with cats. Prisoners were burned with cigarettes on the breasts or with scalding water on the anus and genitals. They were submitted to repeated gang rapes and mock and real executions in front of other prisoners and relatives. Pregnant women were often tortured, resulting in miscarriage and even death. Innovations in torture techniques included a calculated manipulation of human needs and emotions, including sensory deprivation or overload interspersed with frightening sounds and images of the victim's loved ones being tortured or murdered. The injection of chemical substances induced a variety of agonizing physiological and psychological states.

In many cases torture rituals became the theater in which the instrumental torturers were able to enact their aberrant sexuality and transform it into political power, revealing an intimate link between violence and eroticism. Torturers engaged in autoerotic atrocities, alternating between assaulting and caressing their victims' bodies. The *picana* symbolized their eroticized violence and power. Just as weapons in every culture have symbolized masculinity, the *picana* crystallized the phallocentricity of the torture ritual. Its electrified onslaught was focused on the male and female genitalia, the breasts and nipples, the anus and the mouth. Central to a variety of torture rituals, the *picana* was forcibly intruded into every orifice, its impact made more effective by wetting the body to better conduct the electrical discharge. Some torture sessions were punctuated by jokes, laughter, music, and sadistic excitement. Masturbation often accompanied the brutal assaults on a victim's body. Through it all, the *picana* was omnipresent, a perverse representation of an autoerotic form of sadism perpetrated on the objectified body of the victim.

The system chose the instrumental torturers well. Individuals were screened according to criteria such as obedience, discipline, intelligence, and family or individual anticommunist background. The torturers were often of lower middle-class or working-class origin, lumpen in mentality; their lifelong powerlessness was suddenly transformed into the powerful ability to destroy life. Indeed, they were taught to see themselves as absolute rulers over their prisoners' lives, not subject to ordinary constraints. The psychological profile of the torturer revealed an identification with those in power, strong fears or anxieties, an inability to tolerate uncertainty, and a proclivity for fanaticism. The torturer's capacity to engage in the sadistic ritual of torture is made possible by the mechanism of projective identification, through which the perpetrator unconsciously injects the hateful and destructive aspects of himself into the victim, where they can then be destroyed through torture. The accompanying feelings of persecutory anxiety only further stimulate the torturer's sadism toward his victim.[26]

Elizabeth believes that the training of torturers permits them to dissociate from their own emotions because a hierarchical structure takes moral and political responsibility for their brutality. However, she is convinced that each individual brings to the activity an unconscious motive—a personal passion and cruelty—that the system is able to mobilize. She gives the example of one torturer who was trained by the Chilean special security forces in torture methods and an ideology that depicted the UP and their goals as a cancer that had to be eliminated. "You know the worst thing of all?" he told her. "My father was a working-class leader, a communist . . . and he was an alcoholic

who constantly abused me. He beat me a lot from the time I was a little kid."
Elizabeth came to understand that this torturer had remained psychologically
enmeshed in a complex relationship with his father, who had mistreated and
devalued him. "In the position of the torturer, he fanatically abused men who
had the same politics as his father. What's more, he wanted to understand
where his victims got the internal resources to resist because it was a force he
wanted to know how to vanquish."

Individuals underwent special indoctrination to become torturers. They
were prepared psychologically for their work through basic training involving
infantilization and psychological castration by superior officers whose aggression they predictably came to identify with. Their brutality was seasoned
through courses on torture techniques in which they were required to torture
one another.[27] As Marcelo indicates, "We have to study modern torture, which
is not an act of barbarity. It is designed; it has a plan; it is not improvised.
Torture is a system in the sense that there isn't a single torturer, but a group,
a gang that enjoys a support system. It's as if they're intoxicated, getting drunk
among friends. Group cruelty is cathartic in that it increases the sense of power
of each participant."

The dehumanization of the potential victim was achieved through courses
that stressed the necessity of the torture work for national security. In his study
of German concentration camp guards, psychoanalyst Bruno Bettelheim
pointed out the importance of the perpetrator's dehumanization of his victim. He recalled—from his own experience—how concentration-camp guards
repeatedly said to their prisoners, "I'd shoot you with this gun but you're not
worth the three pfennig of the bullet." The importance of this ritual lay not
in its impact on the prisoners but in its affirmation for the guards of the worth-
lessness of their prisoners.[28] In Argentina potential torture victims were referred to as "delinquent subversives," the "enemy," "useful tools," "communist
dupes." Such terminology, by facilitating an ideological and psychological splitting between the good object (the military) and the bad object (the prisoner),
further diminished the torturers' respect for human life. The human capacity
for empathy and concern was stifled through the ongoing experience of torture and through the designation of the entire process in euphemistic terms.
The torture chamber was often called the "intensive therapy room," an individual to be killed had "gotten his ticket" or was a "transferee."

Obedience to authority was an important element in facilitating the perpetrators' ability to relieve their consciences. Individual accountability for their
criminal acts was eliminated through the formal assumption of responsibility
by superior officers, who signed release forms for kidnappings and torture. Argentine Admiral Emilio Eduardo Massera, for example, publicly urged his officers to apply extreme violence to the enemy and even took part in the first

secret operations of his special task force under the pseudonym Zero to demonstrate his approval of the work he had assigned to them.[29]

Once seasoned, torturers were allowed to perform unofficial or extracurricular tortures, which they devised to entertain themselves. In Argentina, low-ranking officers could indulge their perverse desires at any time with their helpless victims. Plunder, during or after an abduction, was also allowed. Not only people but their belongings were carried off as entire homes were ransacked and looted. In Argentina, the "spoils of war" often included babies, stolen and parceled out to childless couples among the military and their allies. This violation of family rights was justified by the messianic argument that the subversives' newborns would be brought up to respect the values of "Western and Christian civilization."

In 1973, Marie Langer had written in *Cuestionamos II* about the collaboration of a psychoanalyst with the Brazilian torturers. Such cooperation with state terror by health professionals, including physicians and psychiatrists, occurred in the Southern Cone as well. In Uruguay, for example, some were known to consistently violate the human rights of prisoners in a variety of ways. They gave physical examinations and turned their medical records over to the military, who would then know how much they could torture without killing the victim; they wrote medical reports so as to hide the evidence of torture; they deliberately denied assistance to ill or injured torture victims; and they prescribed psychopharmaceutical medications to intensify the psychological and physical torture of prisoners. They participated in the "good torturer/bad torturer" syndrome, playing the part of the empathically concerned bystander who encouraged torture victims to tell all in order to save themselves from more suffering. This tactic had the effect of confusing the torture victim, who found it increasingly difficult to retain a coherent sense of what was happening and why, as well as to distinguish between good and bad, enemy and friend.[30]

Once the captors were finished with their prisoners, they were usually "transferred"—strangled, dynamited, or shot in executions that were frequently staged to appear as if a shootout had taken place between them and security forces. Many prisoners were injected with sedatives and dropped alive into the ocean from airplanes or helicopters. Less often, individuals were released from prisons or clandestine concentration camps after charges were determined to be unsubstantiated and then dropped. This part of the drama was important because the released torture victim, the *desaparecido* whose absence became real in his or her reappearance, was the link between the military and the public.

In Argentina, Julia's eighteen-year-old son, Gabriel, was one of the thousands of *desaparecidos* who vanished into thin air from the streets of Buenos

Aires. On May 29, 1976, only two months after the generals had marched into the presidential palace to take control of the country, Julia was awakened by a telephone call in the middle of the night. "Julia," the wavering voice of an old friend punctured the silence, "I'm so sorry . . . Earlier this evening my daughter was walking with some friends downtown on Avenida Santa Fe when she saw the police grab Gabriel and haul him away." And, in a second, Julia's life turned upside down. Only then did she realize that all the horror she had been living with for so long had simply been a prelude to an unimaginable fear yet to come. As she sat there in the dark, paralyzed with dread, she could not guess that it would take eight long years to find out that her son had been tortured and murdered by the Argentine state.

Chapter 4

The Culture of Fear
and Social Trauma

Visible colonialism is a process that openly mutilates you: it forbids you to speak, to act, to be. Invisible colonialism, in contrast, convinces you that enslavement is your destiny and impotence your nature. It convinces you that "you cannot speak, you cannot act, you cannot be."
—EDUARDO GALEANO, *The Book of Embraces* (1992)

"WE WERE AFRAID. . . . I was afraid. . . . Many times marching with the Mothers in the Plaza de Mayo, I'd feel terrified when they would take our photographs, . . . and they would glower at us from behind their submachine guns. When I think about those years of terror, I remember that it was so hard to know at which moments people were specifically targeted and at which moments, not. . . . There were times when you'd be convinced they had picked you out of the group, and others when you'd think no, not me. . . . But you were never certain."

Diana Kordon is recounting for me her participation in the famous Thursday afternoon marches of the Mothers of the Plaza de Mayo in Buenos Aires. The group, so-called because of their weekly demonstrations in the plaza that faces the Presidential Palace, carried posters with enlarged photographs of their disappeared children, demanding publicly that the military junta reveal their whereabouts. "You took them alive," was one of their slogans, "we want them back alive." Diana and her husband, Darío Lagos, along with Lucila Edelman are members of the Team of Psychological Assistance to the Mothers of the Plaza de Mayo (Equipo de Asistencia Psicológica a las Madres de Plaza de Mayo)—known as the Equipo. We are sitting around a table in the Equipo's office in downtown Buenos Aires, where the three are explaining to me their emotional experiences and intellectual perceptions of the difficult years during the dictatorship. The sights and sounds of the office testify to the Equipo's continued activism since the return of constitutional rule in 1983. Its walls are plastered with posters announcing upcoming political and community events, and the hum of computers and fax machines can be heard from the adjoining rooms.

Diana is an attractive woman in her early fifties, her large green eyes expressive as she explains the Equipo's perspective on the nature of trauma in conditions of state-inspired social violence. Lucila, also in her early fifties, emanates a calm self-assurance as she listens and interjects specific details that seem important to Diana's narrative. I am struck by their modest demeanor as they describe their astoundingly courageous activities in the human rights movement during the height of the junta's repressive rule. Darío, too, clarifies points as the discussion proceeds. In spite of his imposing physical presence and forceful demeanor, he demonstrates a marked respectfulness toward the two women, referring appreciatively to Diana as "my loving wife and a real compañera in the struggle."

They remind me about the conventional meaning of trauma, which generally refers to the disruption or breakdown of the psychic apparatus when it is affected by stimuli, external or internal, that are too powerful to be dealt with or assimilated in customary ways. The individual who has witnessed or been exposed to threatened or actual death or injury responds with a sense of terror, horror, humiliation, betrayal, or some combination of these responses. A state of helplessness results, ranging from complete apathy and withdrawal to an emotional storm often bordering on panic. "This description of trauma," Diana explains, "does not specifically capture the nature of group psychological reactions to violence produced by state terror." Nor does the concept of posttraumatic stress disorder (PTSD), a psychiatric diagnosis of symptoms first noted in Vietnam veterans by U.S. psychiatrists. Lucila points out that many of the symptoms associated with PTSD are noted in populations living under military dictatorships, such as psychic numbing or a lowered threshold for anxious arousal. "But," she clarifies, "we do not think the concept of PTSD is an adequate one to describe the psychological impact of state terror. It makes a psychiatric problem out of a social phenomenon." Diana adds that "we don't even speak of trauma because that is usually understood to mean an intrapsychic experience. We use the concept 'traumatic situation' in order to represent the social sources of the psychological suffering produced by state terror. And we do not speak of victims [víctimas] but of individuals and groups that are affected [afectados] by political repression."[1]

The Equipo echoes the perspective of other political analysts. For example, Elizabeth Lira argues that "PTSD does not capture the ongoing nature of state terror, because there is nothing 'post' about it. We could speak of a 'culture of trauma,' although I haven't because we need to appreciate that certain things will traumatize some individuals and not others, depending on their personal histories. But there is a traumatic impact on the society. . . . I prefer to use 'the culture of fear' to emphasize that individual subjective experience is shared simultaneously by millions of people, with dramatic repercussions for social and political behavior." Julia Braun points out that although one can detect in the population at large or in individual patients a series of symptoms characteristic of PTSD, in state terror the syndrome is a "repetitive trauma," one trauma layered on another and then another. "The essence of social trauma," insists Julia, "is that it is not private but is a public and shared experience."[2]

The Psychology of Social Trauma

Indeed, the military dictatorships in the Southern Cone created a traumatic environment that affected the psychic structures of the self and the systems of attachment and meaning that link the individual to the community. Although the outcome of any traumatic situation tends to include attachment disorders, in these terrorist states, the general citizenry was affected. In conditions of extreme political repression, the population was forced to work out a way of understanding the rules, the cues, what made a good citizen and what made an enemy of the state. Citizens were compelled to feel that their homes, their jobs, their loved ones, their own lives were in jeopardy. They came to trust no one, to confide in no one, to seek self-preservation in isolation. Contact with others endangered everyone. Citizens' fearful hypervigilance resembled a kind of paranoid character disorder that was so widespread it looked like a national trait. Individual behavior in the terrorist state was characterized by silence, inexpressiveness, inhibition, and self-censorship, all of which resulted over time in depoliticization. In this situation, individuals became obedient and potentially punitive toward self and others. In Argentina, the masochistic submission to authority was contained in the widely heard response to the disappearance of someone: *"habra hecho algo"* (he or she must have been up to something).

People engaged in active self-censorship as well, going beyond the limits imposed by official prescriptions and proscriptions in an active endeavor to protect themselves. This personal vigilance led to the conscious creation of a false self, a partial and unrepresentative public portrayal of one's personality that was manufactured in order to survive the impingements of an environment that demanded extreme measures of adaptation. As a prominent Uruguayan sociologist writes, "Fear exterminated all social life in the public realm. Nobody spoke in the streets for fear of being heard. Nobody protested in the lines for fear of being reported to the police. One tried not to make new friends, for fear of being held responsible for their unknown pasts. One suspected immediately those who were more open or were less afraid, of being agents provocateurs of the intelligence service."[3]

The effects of this environment on children included an intensification of the fear of ghosts, states of confusion, fits of violence, all sorts of anxieties, learning disabilities, somatic disturbances, and accident-prone behavior. As several Argentine psychoanalysts evocatively put it, "Death and violence 'floating in the air' or witnessed by the child, institutional lies, disavowal on the part of a significant segment of society, having to move from one house to another, panic and confusion in the adults in charge of the child, the lies, the tendency to bring children up to survive rather than to live, the inoculation of vindictiveness, the relative social isolation so that 'he will not say' or 'they will not ask him,' so that 'he will not ask' or 'they will not tell him,' all contribute to the psychological disorganization of children growing up under state terror."[4]

Individuals who had participated in labor unions, peasant cooperatives, Christian base communities, women's groups, youth groups, or liberal and leftist political parties were forced to make an anguished choice. If they held firm to their political values and continued to commit themselves to struggle against the terrorist state, they paid the psychological price of living with constant anticipatory anxiety about their own and their compañeros' and family's vulnerability. But avoidance of the anxiety necessitated the abandonment of the projects that had given their lives positive meaning, had put into practice their values, and had contributed to their sense of community. This renunciation entailed a high degree of guilt and the rejection of the persons they once were, often experienced as the loss of personal identity. As Elizabeth Lira expresses it, "The loss is . . . of an idea of national identity centered around shared values and beliefs. The past seems lost within all the losses, symbolized by the dead, the disappeared, the tortured bodies, the broken hopes, the elimination of a future, the exiles, the disenchantment with politics. Each individual is conscious or unconscious of the losses and of the defenses that have been utilized to mourn less or to completely evade the necessary mourning."

In retrospect, Elizabeth, Marie Langer, Juan Carlos Volnovich, Maren Viñar all emphasize the unconscious defenses they employed as political activists to ward off anticipatory anxiety. They often refer to their recourse to denial, an unconscious defensive coping mechanism employed to prevent the conscious recognition of external threat. They also describe manic reactions, a defense characterized by inappropriately high spirits and hyperactivity that results in the conscious sense of accomplishment and omnipotent control over external circumstances; these feelings defend the self against the unconscious experience of loss and defeat. In a manic state, they were able to achieve a false sense of well-being, enabling them to deny both the unconscious fantasy and the external reality of terrifying danger.

Tato Pavlovsky, Marcelo Viñar, and the members of the Equipo stress especially their states of dissociation, an unconscious defense in which one group of mental processes is split off from the rest of a person's thinking or affect. This splitting permits the independent functioning of each group of discrete mental processes and thus prevents their customary integration from occurring. "I think," says Lucila, "that there's a good deal of reliance on the dissociative mechanisms under such circumstances. For example, we began to work in the office of the Mothers organization during a time when people who met, even socially, in groups of more than five were automatically suspect in the eyes of the military government and subject to arrest or other kinds of intimidation. And this was very strange. . . . We noted it often in the Equipo. . . . We felt completely secure when we were inside the office of the Mothers and became anxious only when we had to leave. It was absurd," she laughs, "because in fact we were actually in more danger all gathered together in a well-known human rights center. But this dissociation permitted us to be there."

These defenses were utilized by a pacified population as well, not in the service of political activism but as coping strategies in the adaptation to authoritarian rule. Elizabeth points to the psychological characteristics of citizens living in the Chilean militarized culture of fear. She asserts that "extreme vulnerability to arbitrary events beyond one's control produced a sense of personal weakness and a permanent state of alert, permitting no psychological rest. In conditions that appeared to be life-threatening, people felt helpless and defenseless. Equally compromising was the distortion of reality purposefully created by the dictatorship through its control over information disseminated to the public." The media's focus on military operations, its downplaying of other news stories, and its manipulation of terrifying rumors, which frequently exaggerated the degree of repression, functioned to convince the population of their collective powerlessness. Rumors of retribution against those who spoke out, while not necessarily experienced firsthand by many, exacerbated fantasies, which then functioned as internalized self-repression. Citizens became guarded and self-protective, and because they did not venture out into the social world as much, they could not employ the important psychological process of reality testing to contain their fearful fantasies. "The boundaries between the real, the possible, and the imaginary were all erased," Elizabeth explains, "and reality thus became confused and threatening, no longer able to guide subjective perception. The state's domination was achieved as citizens engaged in self-regulatory processes that inhibited critical thinking and oppositional behavior."

Forced disappearances and torture were essential to the military's strategy of imposing on the entire population—not only those who were actually disappeared or tortured—an acceptance of its absolute power. Many cultures have a centuries-old tradition of colorful, violent public sacrifice or spectacles of public punishment staged by those in power, who, by demanding the participation of the community as witness, impose on their citizens social involvement and responsibility.[5] But in Argentina, Chile, and Uruguay, torture was carried out secretly and clandestinely. Hidden from view and practiced on the *desaparecidos*, it nonetheless took hold of the public. As Graziano succinctly describes it, "Instead of cheering or gasping or screaming beside the gallows, the public voice reached only a hushed whisper risked in the shadows, a mumble of rumors diffusing the spectacle by word of mouth through a population that was itself diffused, confused, frightened."[6]

Torture created a multifaceted relationship between the military dictatorships and the population. The public became a participant-observer unable to do anything to stop it, as well as a potential (or actual) victim. The extreme anxiety resulting from this insoluble paradox often predisposed people to undergo a regression in ego functioning that led to a passive reliance on a repressive leader(ship), viewed as omnipotent and omniscient. In this sense, the authoritarian state became a container for the profound anxieties that had been mobilized during its unpredictable transition to absolute power.[7] The military dictatorships succeeded in infantilizing citizens psychologically, prompting many of them to deliver themselves up to a superior agency that would decide everything for them.

Identification with the aggressor was an important defense against the fear and anxiety stimulated by the continuous flow of disappearances and rumors of torture. For the witness/victim citizens who survived in the violence of everyday life, identification, at both the unconscious and conscious levels, with an arbitrary state power enacting its wrath on the *desaparecidos* permitted them to symbolically choose victims outside themselves to sacrifice—*algo habra hecho*. People could tell themselves that the *desaparecidos* were persecuted legitimately, that they must indeed be guilty of some terrible crime deserving of the punishment they received. Violent impulses—which intensified and multiplied during state terror at every level—could be thus projected onto the socially created scapegoat, who would then be destroyed. In Chile, even though many people never witnessed the forced disappearances, they were nonetheless haunted by the stark images of people being hauled off, screaming and protesting to no avail. All were faced with the moral dilemma of whether to denounce or witness silently the abuses of state terror. As one Chilean put it, "I worry more about the fascist within than the fascist without. . . . We became used to being in the cuckoo's nest, and we couldn't escape."[8]

The unconscious identification with officially sanctioned aggression was also revealed as the psychopathologically destructive behavior of the military and the torturers was gradually manifested within the general population as well. Among certain sectors military forms of thinking, feeling, and acting came to be accepted as normal modes of conduct. With social forms of response no longer available to permit the expression of aggression toward the real source of suffering and loss, aggressive attitudes and behavior were displaced onto less dangerous situations and onto safer objects in personal life. Explosive interactions increasingly characterized relations in work, family, and public encounters.

Many people simply refused to bear witness to the sinister events that unfolded before them. By disavowing reality, individuals shielded themselves from their consciences and the internal or external demand to defy the state's systematic violation of basic human rights. As parents, for example, altered their vocabulary and their vision of reality in response to their children's questions in order to protect them, they imposed denial, repression, and censorship within the family, which contributed to the creation of an apolitical and self-censoring generation. The psychology of disavowal thus functioned to sustain the politics of terror.

But what happened to people whose lives were directly affected by the state's repressive tactics of forced disappearances and torture? How did they cope with the catastrophic threat to their psychological equilibrium represented by such extreme situations?

Forced Disappearances and Social Trauma

Psychological reactions of relatives and friends whose loved ones simply vanished without a trace were complicated by the anguishing and usually futile attempts to trace their whereabouts. The state consistently disavowed any policy of disappearing people, and thus petitioners seeking help at police stations and military headquarters encountered either denial of their predicament or the half-hearted pretense of an investigation that yielded nothing. Energies were absorbed in endless appeals and the pursuit of the smallest clues that might produce any evidence at all of missing loved ones.

This nightmare, which engulfed the psychic and physical energies of thousands of families of the *desaparecidos*, began for Julia Braun and her husband, Mariano, when they received the 3 A.M. telephone call that announced the disappearance of their son, Gabriel. Stunned and then gradually overtaken by panic, Mariano pronounced, "It begins now, the cross we'll bear forever." He left immediately for the police station in their neighborhood, where the bureaucratic charade commenced. He was not permitted entrance, whereupon he rushed to another police station, only to be told by the officers who sent him home that there that was no record of his son's having been picked up by the police. Desperate, he and Julia phoned several good friends, who the following day helped to secure a lawyer and develop a network of contacts who might be able to help. But it was all useless.

"In subsequent weeks and months, we lived in constant terror that they would come for us or our younger son, Bernardo. We slept in the homes of friends and stripped our house of everything we thought might be indicting. We destroyed half our personal library, hundreds of books—not our psycho-analytic literature, but our political books. It was horrible: we burned them, tore them up, threw them out, put them in bags, and hid them. We felt they were on our heels, about to invade our home. But they never came! Because they didn't descend on us to search our home, as in so many other cases, it was as if the earth had swallowed Gabriel up . . . as if they didn't even realize it was our son they had." This pattern of unpredictability was implemented by the terrorist state to foster confusion, doubt, panic. "There was no logic to depend on, there was no basis upon which to act . . . and it drove us crazy."

In the beginning, Julia denied what she might have guessed to be true. In spite of the fact that she knew of Gabriel's friends and compañeros who had also disappeared since the coup and had not been heard from since, she convinced herself that the police would soon release her son. Even when several months had passed, she still believed they would return him alive. She realized that her own prison experience several decades earlier had surely been different from Gabriel's under the current repressive conditions. But she could not let herself imagine that the military were torturing her son. "I knew he would be having a hard time, but I could envision nothing concrete, I think because I couldn't have stood it. I also couldn't conceive of the nature of the torture itself. I thought they hit people, put them in isolation. I couldn't imagine anything else."

Julia's life settled into a grim pattern of days divided between work and the search for Gabriel. For months, like other families whose relatives had been disappeared, she and Mariano contacted lawyers and priests, wrote legal briefs and reports, visited barracks, jails, courts, the minister of the interior. "Daily life was divided between treating patients, searching for Gabriel, taking care of Bernardo, . . . fear, denial, persecution . . . eating out, going to movies, hearing bombs exploding, celebrating a birthday, visiting friends, wondering when they would come for us, hearing about the dead, the tortured . . . all mixed up together." They did not leave Argentina. They could not. They had to keep searching.

In 1978, after two excruciating years had passed with no news about Gabriel, Julia listened to a speech by the president of the military junta and came to a painful conclusion. She interpreted his words to indicate that all the *desaparecidos* were dead. "Gabriel's fate was suddenly sealed in my mind: at that moment, I told myself that he was dead. Mariano was horrified and insisted that it was I who was killing Gabriel. I felt terrible. But I realized that something had changed inside me, that, for me, the struggle to find Gabriel alive had ended. Yet I still had to do something."

Years later Julia would write about the psychological problems entailed in suffering the forced disappearance of a loved one. She would elaborate an analysis based on her own experience and those of the many people she observed and treated. She and other psychoanalysts would postulate that this mourning experience is characterized by unique difficulties. Those who suffer the disappearance of loved ones, they argue, can only partially work through the mourning process necessary for healthy mental functioning following traumatic loss. In contrast to the death of a relative or close friend, which usually stimulates community recognition of the significance of the deceased individual's life and death, when someone disappears as the result of governmental action, family and friends are left in a state of terrifying uncertainty, with no possibility of psychological closure.[9]

An important aspect of mourning is an acknowledgment of reality that ultimately entails a psychological separation from the individual who no longer exists. This mental process, which permits a gradual letting go of the deceased and the resumption of life in the present, is problematical and difficult to achieve when a family member has been disappeared. There is no confirmation of his or her whereabouts or proof of death. The family is caught in a terrible contradiction: a husband, wife, parent, or child cannot mourn without risking intense guilt, for without proof of death to go on with one's life is tantamount to a kind of murder of the disappeared loved one. However, to go on living and maintain the mental representation of the disappeared, to keep him or her alive, imposes a profound form of mental anguish. This terrible dilemma was one that Marie Langer noted among the refugee populations in Mexico from the Southern Cone and Central America. She called this unresolved mourning "frozen grief."

Not knowing about the actual fate of the disappeared person produces an intrapsychic elaboration that includes fantasies of the possible torments to the *desaparecido*'s mind and body, fantasies based on knowledge of the existence of secret concentration camps and other centers of torture. These fantasies cause acute anxiety and can result in the repression of fantasy life in general, which compromises mental functioning, especially in children. Life decisions are often frozen as the family waits for the return of the disappeared. The alternative reaction is the wish to free the victim from such suffering through the fantasy of his or her death, a wish that produces excruciating guilt feelings. In fact, the military dictatorship in Argentina demanded that the "missing" person be pronounced dead by the family itself in a variety of ways. For example, if the family needed to have access to money or property that was in the name of the disappeared person, they were forced to sign an official document declaring his or her death. For many Argentines caught in this dilemma, the psychological torture of a kind of arrested mourning often produced many apparently unrelated symptoms, such as psychosomatic ill-nesses, interpersonal conflicts, the inability to maintain healthy relationships, or a general alienation from one's immediate social group or society at large.

In Julia's case, at the moment she believed she had lost her son forever to the murderous forces of the state, she told herself that she had to act, had to do something. After Gabriel was disappeared, she returned to psychoana-lytic treatment, this time with a sympathetic analyst whose nephew had also been disappeared. "He was a kind person and a good analyst, and being in treatment helped me to keep my sanity. But I knew that I needed something more, that I had to engage with others who were suffering the same tragedy as I." For a time, Julia went to the Thursday afternoon marches of the Moth-ers of the Plaza de Mayo, and although she deeply admired their courage, her own fears at participating in this brazen challenge to the military government finally directed her to another kind of activism. "I am a psychoanalyst," she thought, "and all of this has to do with human suffering and pain. . . . I should use my skills to help."

Julia could see that her friend Graciela Fernández Meijide, whose son had also been disappeared, was benefiting emotionally from her work with the Per-manent Human Rights Assembly (Asamblea Permanente de Derechos Humanos). So when Graciela suggested that, for her own well-being, Julia be-come involved in a community health project organized by a colleague, Norberto Liwsky, she quickly agreed. Norberto was a pediatrician who had been disappeared in 1975 and brutally tortured.[10] After his release, he some-how found the psychological strength to return to his political activism. Now he was organizing medical services in a working-class community church, La Parochia Nuestra Señora de los Milagros, whose progressive priest had devel-oped a network of professionals to respond to the legal, health, educational, and employment needs of his poor parishioners. Julia immediately began to participate, and for the next three years she worked with the Parochia's popu-lation of working-class Argentines and immigrant workers from Bolivia and Paraguay. She went every Saturday for six hours and coordinated and super-vised individual therapy with children and group sessions with adults. "I felt utterly dismayed listening to these people's experiences, for if my story was terrible, their stories were fifty times worse. Many of their *desaparecidos* had been union activists, and not only had these women lost a son, a husband, an uncle, or a brother, they and their little ones didn't have anything to eat, no-where to live, nothing. Although it was difficult to sustain treatment in a for-mal and continuous fashion, the powerful impact of these Saturday afternoons at the Parochia lay in the fact that they provided the possibility of being to-gether, to live some hours in a place of solidarity, where we could speak about our traumas and listen to one another. Advice was given, help was offered . . .

some food . . . a little money. It was a shared space of suffering for all of us who'd been affected by the dictatorship."

Although the project had been designed to bring professional aid to the impoverished parishioners, Julia came to see it as a profound source of mutual support. "It was a therapeutic community," she says, "that helped to cure me." Thinking back on it, Julia believes that the experience was curative for many reasons. This kind of activism permitted her to achieve self-respect and a sense of integrity because it represented coherence with her ego ideal. She could also give to these people something she herself was desperately seeking and had not found before. Moreover, it was a significant source of continuity with her son because she was with people who shared Gabriel's values and political commitments. "We experienced a sense of gratification and mutual appreciation, they with me and I with them. And it was, as well, a profound source of reparation. I could help them with their losses in a way that I couldn't help the loved one whom I myself had lost."

Imprisonment, Torture, and Social Trauma

Most *desaparecidos* were subjected to violent torture rituals in the prisons and concentration camps that spread like tentacles throughout the Southern Cone. Designed to secure the complete submission of victim (prisoner) and bystander (society) alike, torture was used as a weapon of power by states that had failed to ideologically control their populations. Torture victims suffered thousands of deaths before their lives were completely obliterated. In Argentina, the omnipotence of the system was communicated through the torturers' attitude and behavior toward their victims. Their arrogant and sadistic domination was succinctly captured by one of Timmerman's interrogators. "Only God gives and takes life," he told Timmerman. "But God is busy elsewhere, and we're the ones who must undertake this task in Argentina."[11]

Torture makes use of the body as a vehicle with which to secure psychic submission to the absolute power of the state. As Marcelo Viñar has understood it, in the terror of the torture experience and its aftermath, a moment exists when the suffering undergoes a shift from the subject's extraordinary physical anguish to the more desolate experience of complete and total psychological helplessness. He has written that along with "the intensity of physical pain, including the sensory disorientation—the darkness, the hood covering one's head—and the rupture of all affective and loving ties with one's familiar and esteemed world comes the constant presence of a body in pain, agonizing, undone, completely at the mercy of the persecutor, who makes all other aspects of the world which are not central to the current experience disappear. We call this the moment of psychic demolition."[12]

This moment of demolition represents a traumatic threat to the victim's psychic structure. The imposition of a sense of total vulnerability entails multiple psychological repercussions. Because the victims have no possibility of defending themselves or others and are prohibited from expressing retaliatory aggression against the perpetrators, they often direct aggressive impulses inward. Self-blame and guilt are the result: victims reproach themselves for having been caught, for failing to escape, for being weak and showing fear. Guilt is experienced when victims break down under torture or survive it when others do not.

The psychological response to torture is greatly affected not only by the victims' personal psychological history but by their clarity and strength of morale, sense of purpose, and hatred of the authoritarian system responsible for the torture.[13] Marie Langer believed that the capacity to resist torture and its psychologically damaging impact may be the result of the victim's reliance on primitive unconscious mechanisms and the regression to infantile mental states in which order is made out of complex reality through psychic splitting of the world and people into simple categories of good and bad. "I think it's different than with the torturer," she argued, "whose more primitive mental functioning permits him to split the world into good and evil and then to violently attack the representation of evil in the political activist. The torture victim's task is to avoid confusional states by rigidifying his or her mental defenses in order to struggle not to be broken, not to give in, not to identify with the torturers." Langer thought this could be best accomplished when "the victim is able to maintain a clear distinction between 'good'—identified as the positive human values associated with the progressive ideology of equality and justice—and 'evil'—identified as the negative ruthless military dictatorship whose atrocities maintain an oppressive economic system."

Political prisoners who find ways to circumvent their isolation can reinforce this clarity of vision and their will to survive torture through the formation of deep attachments to those sharing their unfortunate fate. As the renowned Uruguayan playwright Mauricio Rosencof recounts of his own prison experience, even in the most awful of Uruguay's prisons, La Libertad, he and other political prisoners sustained their courage and hope by using their knuckles to tap poetic messages of solidarity to one another on the prison's cement walls.[14]

However, the torture system is designed to sabotage this capacity for resistance. Often the inconsistent and unpredictable application of violence and the constant threat of imminent death successfully undermine the victim's clarity of thought and relations of solidarity with other prisoners in favor of relations of domination and submission. In the wake of several threats of death followed by sudden reprieves, in some cases prisoners succumb to the paradoxical state of viewing the perpetrator as their savior. The assault on the body transforms itself into the successful assassination of the victim's psychological autonomy. Similar to Nazi Germany, the Latin American terrorist state was often able to bring about the complete psychological regression of the victim so that a pathologically symbiotic relationship developed between the torturer and the tortured. Some torture victims came to feel they deserved their abuse. Their self-esteem demolished, they ceased to believe themselves worthy of decent relationships and turned to the torturer for salvation.[15]

The ability to maintain psychic integrity in the face of torture has become more difficult with the increasing sophistication of torture weapons, supplied by some of the technologically advanced nations. But the extent to which terror, humiliation, loss of dignity, and physical anguish mark the victim depends on the structural characteristics of personality and the duration and intensity of the violence experienced. In this regard, Elizabeth Lira believes that in the victim's experience of helplessness the torture situation reproduces an already known but repressed universal infantile experience of helplessness and abandonment. Each individual's particular experiences in this state of early primitive helplessness affect and become enmeshed with the political and social experience as an adult under torture. This interaction of past and present partially determines the victim's reactions to the trauma.

Regardless of the psychic structure of individual torture victims, each suffers to some degree disturbing psychological sequelae. Symptoms are wide ranging in intensity and include sleep disorders, severe anxiety, psychosomatic illness, difficulty in thinking, loss of self-esteem, social withdrawal, decrease in productivity, abandonment of goals, and even premature death. In addition to the personal suffering these sequelae of torture represent, such reactions to trauma and even the specific symptoms associated with PTSD need here to be understood in light of the larger political goals of state-sponsored torture. Lira's point that "there is nothing 'post'" about this social trauma has to do with the legacy of state terror, which is that "the military dictatorships smashed important things not only in the torture victims but in the Chilean people in general. It destroyed the wish to construct a better future, the belief that it is possible, the conviction that people can do something worthwhile and make a difference. . . . This is the context in which prisoners were tortured."

Marcelo knows about imprisonment, torture, and its aftermath, not only from treating survivors but also from his own experience when he was sequestered a year before the military coup. In June 1972, the government's declaration of the Law on State Security and Public Order gave the armed forces carte blanche to launch a witch hunt for any progressive individual who could be accused of being part of the legal solidarity movement connected to the

Tupamaro guerrilla organization. They came for Marcelo two months later in the middle of a winter night. He and Maren were wrenched from a deep sleep by a group of armed men who had broken into their home. The terrified couple watched helplessly as the soldiers methodically ransacked their belongings, including their patients' files, searching for evidence. Of what? Neither Marcelo nor Maren knew. When they dragged Marcelo to the waiting van, they hauled off stacks of his clinical notebooks. Maren stared in shock as her husband disappeared. Later, when their six-year-old son, Daniel, realized what had happened, he whimpered, "Mama, do you think they're torturing Papa?" Maren asked what he thought torture was, and he replied, "Well, you get tied up and they hit you so much that you never, ever again can speak." As she recalls this reply, Maren chuckles bitterly, "It was like a summary of the goal of torture, to silence everyone. . . . It was terrible. . . . I told him that this was kind of what torture was like, but that we didn't know about Papa, that we hoped it wasn't happening to him."

For Marcelo, the entire experience of abduction and imprisonment was a prolonged torture. He insists on this interpretation. "Was I tortured? If you mean by that the infamous destructive attacks on the body, I have to say no. If I describe what my imprisonment was like, the answer would have to be yes—if a person is forced at gunpoint to go at 2 A.M. with ten armed men, in the cold of winter, after they've gone through your whole house, turning it upside down, without respecting your personal life. . . . They tell you they're taking you for a long time; they cover your eyes, handcuff you, tie your shoelaces together. They take you away; they don't tell you where. They don't tell you why. They isolate you and don't talk to you for a week. They make you do the *planton*, standing in one spot without knowing how long it's going to last. It goes on and on, interminably for five excruciating days. This for me is torture." He continues, "If I told you I was going to expose you to a very onerous experience for two months, you could accept it. But if I told you I was going to subject you to terrible things, who knows for how long, perhaps it will last forever, perhaps you'll die here, the situation of uncertainty and of the infinity of time, without limits, is very disorganizing mentally. The condition of sensory deprivation is itself a terrible torture. They deprive you of sight, of time and space referents, and they submit you to the unpredictable. For me this is torture."[16]

Marcelo describes how in such conditions one may even come to wish for punishment because at least it provides a concrete physical experience that punctuates the uncertainty. "As with head banging, the external pain helps to organize the disorganized internal world, but, in the case of torture, it's not self-inflicted." Echoing other prisoners, Marcelo emphasizes that torture is being deprived of knowing where one is, in such-and-such cell, in such-and-such prison, on such-and-such street. Although these facts may have no intrinsic meaning, they are profoundly important referents of one's location in the world. Knowing this, the torturers sadistically withhold such significant information from prisoners. "Often one of the only sources of orientation becomes the capacity to maintain control over one's sphincters. Enormous time is spent trying to control oneself to be able to pee or shit when they tell you you can and not to when they say no. Control over such functions can become everything, the central focus of orientation, the indicator of one's subjectivity. All the while, the effort reduces you to a completely infantile state."

As Marcelo indicates, torture is employed to impose on prisoners a "law of submission," every intimately small detail demonstrating to them their infantilized, dependent position. "One day I had the blindfold removed," he recalls, "with the instruction to look straight ahead at the wall. Here was my predicament: to obey and at least enjoy the relief of being able to see something, even if it was only a wall, or to resist and turn to see my persecutor. I obey because I am fearful of the punishment if I do not. I look straight ahead and time goes by, perhaps an hour. Suddenly I hear footsteps behind me, and before I realize it, I automatically turn to see who it is. They ferociously yank me away, punitively tie me up, and blindfold me again." Such apparently insignificant events function intentionally as psychological torture, ripping away from the prisoner any remnant of autonomy and dignity. "Who is going to risk dying because of not fulfilling one of these small details? And each time you obey, you acknowledge your impotence and their absolute power over you."

The torturers also deride prisoners about their isolation. "No one knows where you are," they taunt. "It doesn't matter what you do here or what we do to you, no one knows or cares. It's no use resisting. All your compañeros have talked. You've lost. You're lost. Everyone's given up on you. You're nothing because you've ceased to exist for others. You've been given up for dead."

How, Marcelo asks, and with what will the destroyed internal world of the torture victim be reconstituted? He asserts that two antagonistic realities fight for dominance in the victim's mind: the position identified with the torturer, who is incarnate in the present moment through his invasive control over life and death, and the other realities related to the past, now absent but promising coherence with the subject's identity prior to the torture, which she or he wishes to sustain but which is now gone, dead.[17]

In Chile and Argentina, the majority of prisoners disappeared forever. In Uruguay, the disappeared were imprisoned, and relatives had to suffer sometimes for months before locating their loved ones. For Maren, suddenly Marcelo was gone, absent, disappeared, and she had no idea what was happening to him. "We didn't even know where he was. I couldn't deny reality to my son. There had been a media bombardment about the capture of

Tupamaros, and about their grieving families, and everyone was talking about torture. So all the kids knew about it. Six months earlier, children had participated in the elections with their parents, going to festive Sunday picnics and then door to door campaigning for the Frente Amplio. Now it was all different. . . . We couldn't get together, couldn't go out. There were roving police picking people up, surrounding entire city blocks, hunting people down. The kids knew they had to stop talking openly. They showed a great deal of solidarity with their parents, but at a great cost of self-control and anxiety." Maren's extensive experience as a child analyst had taught her about the pathogenic effects of parental lies to children. She had treated many a mother whose husband, with no history of illegal activity, had been forced to go underground, who would tell her child that the father had gone away to work in the countryside. Sometimes when a husband had been taken prisoner, the mother would tell the children that their father had gone on a trip. "It is important, I think, to transmit reality to the child and to include her or him in the truth of what is happening. Children sense all of this anyway. Although it was difficult for the children to bear the truth, those who were lied to suffered in a worse way, their symptoms revealing that they understood much more than their parents told them. They often fell into depression, unable to symbolize what was happening or to elaborate it psychologically. If they are lied to, children are abandoned, alone without the truth."

As for Maren, the next two months were filled with nonstop action as she desperately fought to free her husband. "We didn't know where he was for two weeks. We were scared, and I just kept mobilized constantly, trying to do something, anything, everything I could. . . . I was in constant motion, going to this military prison, that military headquarters, filling out papers, standing in lines, trying to leave packages of clothing. 'No, he's not on our list,' they'd say. 'We have no record of him,' I'd be told. 'But . . . but . . . they took him away,' I'd insist. There was a Kafka-like unyielding quality to the legal and penal bureaucracies. It was made even worse when we learned shortly after Marcelo's detention that several days earlier a colleague, a surgeon, had been taken away and that, like many others, he'd been tortured terribly with the *submarino* in the freezing cold."

Maren's torture was not knowing where Marcelo was or what they were doing to him. In a large meeting of the Uruguayan Medical Association, physicians' wives exchanged stories about how their husbands had been arrested and what they were suffering. "We mounted an international campaign of solidarity. Marie Langer provided incredible help through FAP from Buenos Aires, contacting people throughout the Americas and Europe. Within two weeks international support began to arrive from colleagues. Some members of the APU were scared and withdrew from us, but others showed generous and courageous support. They started a letter-writing campaign for Marcelo and even went to the parliament to demand information. Many never stopped coming to my house to see me and offer their help. In similar circumstances, other people had found themselves isolated, alone, abandoned by their intimidated friends. I was lucky."

Marcelo was in prison for two months—not so long, comparatively, but yet eternal, an endless two months of daily experiences that bore the contours of torture. It would require years for him to work through the psychological sequelae. Afterward, he would write about it as his contribution to the Latin American literature on political repression. Even at the moment of his imprisonment, he recognized that it represented a complete undoing of all his understanding and beliefs about the world, "a loss in the reliability of thought," as he puts it. "I felt like a fool, that I believed in things that no longer existed. I was perplexed, and, in the face of the torturers, I came to see that the diversity of human nature was greater than I, with all my university education and psychoanalytic training, could understand. I felt that the world was more complex and different than I'd imagined. This was a violent destruction of the reliability of thought and perception."

Marcelo describes his emotional reactions to the torturers, which others have documented as well. He felt a wish to enact a vengeful retribution, "an eye for an eye, a tooth for a tooth." The torturers wanted to liquidate him, and he wished to do the same to them. Many prisoners tell of the wish to humiliate their torturers or of the fantasy of having the torturers in the same helpless position as they so that they might then demonstrate their superiority by renouncing the chance to torture them in kind. "My fantasy was to reverse the roles and for me to have total power over them. I would have them in the same helpless state, only to pardon them, so that their torture would be the realization of the differences between their humanity and mine."

Torture victims are sustained by another fantasy: the hope of leaving the prison or concentration camp and of reestablishing their former lives and social relations. But the fantasy and the reality are never the same. Marcelo's experience was similar to what is described by survivors of war and the Holocaust. "To be actually freed from prison," he says, "is not the same as the hopes one has kept alive during confinement. It is very difficult to transmit to others what has happened inside. People expect to encounter a hero or a traitor, but one isn't either of these. I don't deny that there are differences between the two, but I think reality is more complicated, in that it's very difficult to determine what makes one person able to stand the torture and what makes another break down. People also expect you to be the same person who entered prison, and that, too, is never the case." The tendency to see torture victims in terms that bifurcate them into good and bad, Marcelo argues, is problematic. He believes there is a thin line between the hero and the traitor, the one who has withstood the torture and the one who has broken beneath the torturers' weapons. In either case, the torture victim is never the same afterward.

When Marcelo was released, people came to ask questions, to hear his story. He tried to describe the experience, thinking that it was necessary for political and humanitarian reasons. "My testimony was very radical in its description of the destruction of human beings inside prison. My friends listened, but I later learned that some said I was exaggerating. Several claimed I had been taken to a five-star hotel because I wasn't tortured as much as the average torture victim. Others didn't believe me, saying that I manifested a traumatic neurosis and didn't have the capacity to judge objectively what had happened. And I talked a lot, sometimes a little compulsively, like anyone who has seen hell of any kind. It was like a hemorrhage. I communicated things in an overwhelming way, I think, reproducing the details of my brutal experience. Now, with twenty years' hindsight, I can see that I said things the others didn't want to or couldn't hear. They wanted to know, but only what they thought they could bear. They emotionally spit back to me the things I told them that they couldn't take in."

This psychological collision was terrible for Marcelo, who "felt [his] authority stripped from [him], like something inside had been broken." Maren confirms its profound impact on the couple's relationship. "I wanted Marcelo to be who he'd been before, but he had experienced two months that were like a hole in his life. He had no idea of what had happened outside during his imprisonment, as if history had abandoned him. A lot had gone on in the country during those two months—repression, people leaving, deaths, public demonstrations. I wanted to plug him into all that I had done in my life during his absence, the struggle, the battles, the mobilization of friends and colleagues. At the time, neither of us understood the disjuncture. I would get irritated at him because he seemed to have a fixed discourse, without variation. When people asked him whether he'd been tortured, he'd get mad. 'Having the *planton* is a torture,' he'd reply. It was as if he presented a story that hid the majority of things that had happened to him. 'Tell me about it,' I'd say. 'It's already passed,' he'd answer."

The impact on the family in general was dramatic. Years later, their son, Daniel, told his parents that he remembered his childhood as a happy one. It was filled with outings, camping trips, school, summer holidays, the house full of people—a life filled with vitality. "Then all of a sudden," he said, "it was broken."

Marcelo withdrew from much of his political activism, although he was determined to stay in Uruguay. "I didn't leave at once because I believed there were values one had to defend. It seemed worthwhile to hang on to one's small place in the trenches." Although Maren lessened her activities, she would not stop completely. For three years, she treated many children whose parents had been imprisoned like Marcelo. She is convinced that her own experience helped her understand them. Indeed, it seemed to her that the families sought her out as a therapist because they trusted her and believed she could identify with them. For her part, she benefited from this work by having to assume a therapeutic distance in order to help her patients deal with some of the same psychological problems she also experienced. Helping them think about their painful emotional reactions facilitated her capacity to bear her own. "It was therapeutic for me as well because it permitted me to leave my own trauma, my unthinkable situation, in order to think about theirs. It was a kind of reparation."

Maren buried herself in work, but one day her manic defenses broke down, and she suffered an episode of acute anxiety. She suddenly realized that she was in a highly compromising position: as a medically trained therapist, she aided families who were seeking permission to visit political prisoners by signing legal documents certifying that the children who could not see their imprisoned fathers were being adversely affected. "Because of my reputation, many families came to me to obtain these certificates, and . . . without my realizing it, in one month, boom, boom, boom, there'd be fifteen certificates signed by me. 'Oh, my god,' I thought, 'this is how they'll get me.'"

Marcelo also treated people who were in great need, militants who sought him out because they trusted him. "We were possessors of secrets," Marcelo comments ironically. "I knew many things. This is what scared me. But in Uruguay it wasn't that the military went after mental-health professionals in particular. As people were imprisoned, the interrogators would ask them to name their doctor, their dentist, their therapist, their lawyer. When the same name came up again and again, it was assumed by the military that this particular professional was a movement sympathizer, and they'd go after him or her. Their technical name for this was 'the destruction of the sanitation apparatus of subversion.'" As in Argentina, the Uruguayan military believed that the intellectuals and their ideas were responsible for the radical challenge to the system they were defending.

Following the birth of their second son, Juan, in March 1975, Maren grew more frightened. The repression was intensifying and people all around them were being arrested and abducted. "But I felt I couldn't be a coward and flee," remembers Maren. "And one day in desperation I said to Marcelo, 'Well, lots of kids grow up without mothers.' He grabbed me and shook me, 'Are you crazy?' he demanded. 'Listen to what you just said. How could you say such a thing?' I was thinking to myself, 'Look at all the mothers in prison, their kids alone and abandoned. I can't leave because of the pain of leaving them.' I was in a kind of panic."

The feelings of vulnerability grew. By July, Maren too had stopped all her political involvements. No one could do anything without risk. They could not meet with anybody in the street, in the cafés, or at home. The only thing they now dared to do was collect funds for people who were leaving the country. By December 1975, Marcelo was convinced it was time to go, but still they stayed. They began to take security measures and slept in different locales. "One night in February, they came to get us. They occupied our house. Fortunately we weren't there, and we were alerted by friends though a preestablished code. We don't know why they came, but we imagined it was the result of someone naming one or both of us under torture. Daniel, who was only nine, was with relatives outside Montevideo. We had to leave the country without him. It was all so terrible; poor thing, he knew what had happened, and it was several days before he could join us. This experience really marked him."

When the Viñars were forced out of Uruguay, they fled to neighboring Argentina, only to realize immediately that a military coup was imminent. Then came the decision about where to go next. Several months earlier, Marcelo had been invited by psychoanalytic colleagues to Paris for a year's sabbatical. Although neither spoke French, their only alternative was Mexico, where they would at least be with Mimi Langer and other South American refugees. "But we wanted to convert exile into an intellectual and professional challenge, like a compensation for so much loss. So we didn't choose Mexico, we went to France."

In early March 1976, a mere two weeks before the Argentine armed forces marched into power, the Viñars sailed for Europe. As they stood on the ship's deck watching the American continent slowly recede into the horizon, Maren realized that Marcelo was suffering more than she. For her, this exile was a continuation of her history; she felt as if she were following in the footsteps of her father, whose life had been disrupted several times because of his political convictions. It was like a commitment, a constant battle to which she was accustomed. And she had already experienced the loss of her country when she had given up Chile to be with Marcelo. But for Marcelo this forced departure was complicated by a personal tragedy. "It's terrible," Maren thought, shivering in the wet ocean air. "It's different for him. Marcelo is leaving his dying father in Uruguay. And I have my little baby—the future—with me, in my arms, on this ship, now. With Marcelo and my two children here, I feel less daunted to face our unknown future on the other side of the Atlantic."

Social Trauma and Human Destructiveness

As my Latin American colleagues and I talk, we keep turning back to the relationship between social class and psychology. "When you speak of the culture of fear or social trauma or the people of a country affected by authoritarian repression," I would ask, "to whom are you referring? Does the class that objectively benefits from military dictatorship suffer the effects of social trauma? How do we explain the terrible sadistic capacity of the torturer?"

Julia Braun responds to these questions by emphasizing that from her perspective "some people who approved the policies and ideology of state terror did not suffer. We may say that they could elude its implications. In fact," she tells me, "there are still individuals who actually say that the *desaparecidos* are on vacation in Europe! So when we speak of the 'culture of fear' or 'social trauma' or 'the Argentine people,' we are speaking of the majority who suffered, not the elite who were not harmed, who benefited from the stabilization of the traditional social order. But I also think it depends on the level of one's observation. It may be that if a wealthy person were on the analyst's couch, the analyst might detect the defenses that she or he had to mobilize in order to be shielded from feelings of empathy or guilt for the victims of the violence perpetrated in defense of his or her class interests."

Juan Carlos Volnovich holds the same view as Julia. "People who benefited from and agreed with the junta's project," he points out, "had to rely on the defenses of dissociation or denial in order to keep from recognizing the massive suffering imposed on the majority of people living in state terror." He believes that the need to organize one's mental life around these defenses has serious repercussions that impoverish the psyche. It is also Equipo member Diana Kordon's position that even the beneficiaries of the system were affected psychologically by the state's extreme violations of human rights. "To be a direct or indirect accomplice of massive assassination, of genocide, has to affect one's mental health in some way," she argues. "What we've seen in our experience is that even people who were directly involved in the repression have experienced sequelae, although few have sought psychological help. It is impossible that there is no impact. We know people who were torturers who have killed themselves and others who have reproduced very sadistic situations in their daily lives. For men—like the infamous Nazi doctors—who are capable of genocide all the while they are good family men, there is a primary schism involving profoundly dissociative processes. And those who were indirectly involved, if only by virtue of benefiting as a class, I think also manifested the impact in psychological terms. We could say that for them political repression is 'ego syntonic,' by which we mean that such actions and ideas are compatible with the standards of the ego or the self. In this case, the aggression and dehumanizing ideology associated with state terror are acceptable to the social sectors whose interests are represented. But it impoverishes them as human beings because their focus on economic security and class domination leaves other attributes lacking. We especially note the restriction of the capacity for empathy and love."

Marie Langer believed that the cruelty manifest in state terror was the reflection in group behavior of the human capacity for cruelty and destructiveness; the perpetrators unconsciously disowned their own sadism, projecting it onto their victims and rationalizing it ideologically. But she also warned about the dangers inherent in psychologizing social phenomena. She maintained that "the problem of aggression expressed through class struggle is best thought about as a political question, not a psychological one." But she, too, strove to understand the psychological meanings of political life. She recalled Freud's view that during times of war the principles that guide superego functioning, including "thou shalt not kill," are countermanded by the legitimization of mass murder in the service of a higher cause. "People who torture are not just pathological but are responsible for their actions," Langer claimed. "The instrumental torturers are usually people from the marginal classes whose sadism—which we all have, isn't that true?—has been mobilized by class resentment. They are ordered to discharge—displace, we would technically call it—all their resentment for their powerlessness, which was perpetrated by the system that marginalized them, onto the middle-class political activists and the class-conscious union militants. They operate on the basis of extreme dissociation reinforced by the prevailing anticommunist ideology."

Always in Langer's mind was the comparison between the Nazis and the Argentine torturers. From her point of view, the Germans were the more rational. They exploited the labor of the Jews in the camps, and those who could not work were put to death in the gas chambers. It was inhumane, to be sure, but they did not regularly torture inmates in the camps. The Argentines, she believed, acted more sadistically. "In Argentine state terror, people were tortured sometimes for years, and to what end? To diffuse terror in the population. The Argentine generals even killed people of their own class—families who were part of the opposition—including their own sons and daughters who had defected. The fathers, with their fear of losing everything to socialism, practiced filicide. I think the elites acted out of a kind of social guilt related to their historical role as the class whose privilege was based on the exploitation of the majority. They suffered persecutory fears of retribution by those they had brutally oppressed and went after them and their radical political allies with a vengeance."

Mimi pointed out that the elite and the Generals congratulated themselves for the Dirty War and that their allies in other social classes justified the repression as a necessary tool for the cleansing of Argentine society. "But," she added, "we shouldn't forget the other responses. People also simply denied reality, which often permitted them, through identification with the repressors, to vicariously express their infantile sadism. And I know many people who, in order to remain in the country during the dictatorship or to return because they could not bear living in exile, had to disavow what they knew to be true."

Tato Pavlovsky agrees that Argentine society under state terror manifested a pattern similar to that of Nazi Germany or any nation ruled by dictatorship: some of the population acquiesces to an authoritarian power. He cites Wilhelm Reich's classic study, *The Mass Psychology of Fascism*, to make the point that dictatorship does not exist without the complicity of the population. As he had elaborated in his play *Telarañas*, Tato argues that it is important to understand the subjective receptivity to fascism. From his perspective, the existence of an authoritarian consciousness among many sectors—including the middle and popular classes—stemming from bourgeois patriarchal society and its values predisposes people to identify with the forces of a repressive authority. "For example, when I returned from exile, I encountered my family, who had remained here during the military government. Nothing bad had ever happened to them. They had lived well, and they had no idea that there was even a problem with the dictatorship! There were so many people like my family, who had never lifted a finger, who had done nothing. On the other hand, I saw many people, including psychoanalysts, who were very traumatized, very affected, who had been courageous and valiant to stay here . . . people who were overjoyed to see me again, who wanted to struggle together, to do something meaningful. It was as if there were two countries."

Especially interesting to Tato is the discourse of those who benefited from state terror, "those who said, 'I didn't live badly during the dictatorship; it went well for me economically—I had my little weekend country home—my children went to a good private school . . . there was order, there was no crime.'" This way of thinking, says Tato, is congruent with the bourgeois position in capitalist society, and it represents an ego-syntonic way of responding. "But such attitudes are shared by other social classes as well, who identify with the values of the dominant class. It's similar to what's been written about the Greek torturers. You couldn't find a more bloody dictatorship, but the torturers in Greece were more or less normal young men who were trained to have ideological convictions about their work." Tato thinks about Rosencof's chilling description of his incarceration in Uruguay, in which he describes how a torturer could listen to a game of soccer on the radio with him and then subject him to the most unbelievably sadistic torture rituals. From Rosencof's perspective, the torturer did not suffer from any extreme pathology but had been ideologically trained to view him as an enemy of the Uruguayan nation. "I agree with Rosencof," says Tato, "and I think the torturer, in fact, doesn't have to be a sadist. That's what I tried to show in *Señor Galindez*, where I compared two torturers, both of whom were good examples of pathologically sadomasochistic personalities, with a third one, a nice young man who was in no way particularly aggressive but who had been deformed intellectually by his special forces training. To me, repression is a very complex phenomenon. Rosencof suggests that our biggest challenge is to understand what is in the heads of people for whom kidnapping, torture, beatings, the *picana* are syntonic with their affective and intellectual relationship to the world."[18]

During the years of the Chilean dictatorship, Elizabeth Lira strove to comprehend the complexities of the mental processes and social dynamics of aggression and violence in state terror. She asserts that in the first years following the coup the global environment of fear affected everyone because there was such randomness to the violence of the military as it methodically imposed its complete and arbitrary power over the citizenry. Only later, when the repression became more systematically aimed at political dissidents, was it clear that the military state protected some sectors and that these groups, although they might not necessarily like torture, found a way to rationalize it as a necessary evil to rid society of a "subversive cancer." And many who benefited from the coup could even claim that the danger had passed, in this way disavowing the continuing violent attacks on the sectors specifically targeted for repression. Elizabeth is reminded of the behavior of many Germans during the Nazi regime who simply denied that their government was carrying out genocidal policies against entire ethnic populations.

Elizabeth came to believe that there was nothing personal between the torturer and the tortured, only a symbolic relationship between the state and the "subversive." But in addition to the political motive of a system, she holds that the impersonal activity is fueled by what the torturers bring to the task in terms of their personal passions and cruelty. She, too, is reminded of the psychological studies of the Nazi doctors that postulate a phenomenon called *doubling*. More extreme than dissociation, doubling refers to the existence of more than one ego, as if there are two subjects: one who is decent to people and a good family man, and the other who is perverse and capable of the most heinous crimes against humanity. "When I began to hear about the torture, from the perpetrators and from the victims, I felt I could hardly manage my reactions. I was filled with anxiety. . . . I had terrible nightmares. But as I began to think about its meaning, what it entailed, how to denounce it, what we could do in the world so it would end, I could more easily listen to their stories."

Psychoanalytic Practice under State Terror

In all three countries, psychoanalytic treatment was affected by the advent of state terror. Marcelo explains that for the full exercise of psychoanalysis—"the talking cure"—which demands the articulation of fantasy life, a certain level of basic human rights in society is a necessary precondition. Free association, he stresses, is the fundamental rule of the psychoanalytic process, requiring that the patient attempt to relinquish conscious control over thoughts, wishes, and feelings so as to communicate to the analyst whatever comes to mind. The patient must often overcome conscious feelings of embarrassment, fear, shame, and guilt in the process. The analyst infers from the sequences, patterns, and content of the patient's associations the unconscious influences and conflicts underlying them. In the persecutory culture of fear, free association—and thus the practice of psychoanalysis—was seriously compromised because the distinction between psychic reality (fantasy) and external reality (state terror) collapsed. "In order for sadism, aggression, and so forth to be freely manifested in a patient's fantasy life, there has to be a guarantee that it's not happening in reality," says Marcelo.

In the culture of fear, not only was free association compromised, but patients also tended to increasingly repress thoughts and feelings that, if consciously acknowledged, might prove too painful or dangerous. Moreover, the conscious resistance to revealing information that might potentially be used to menace one's self and family, which characterized people's functioning in general, did not cease to operate at the analyst's door.

The work of the analyst was limited in other ways. As conditions deteriorated, the analytic function became more difficult to provide. When patients spoke of traumatic personal situations arising from the social conditions of state terror, analysts' ability to listen was compromised by associations to their own concerns, conflicts, and fears produced by the same conditions. When Julia's son was disappeared, for example, she attempted to separate her private life from her work as an analyst, to leave aside her terror, anxieties, and fears for Gabriel when she was with her patients. She strove to practice psychoanalysis as she had been taught. "Close the office door and try to understand my patients' terror related to the political repression as if my own terror were my private experience that should and could remain outside. I tried to arm myself psychologically in order to do the work and to keep everything the same—the schedule, the office, my own mental condition and physical appearance. I don't know how I did it or what I did! It was a terrible strain. . . . I think I had to constantly disavow my fears that the police or military might interrupt a session to take either or both of us away. Several years later, my work with the Parochia represented a tremendous emotional relief to me because I didn't have to hide behind the goal of psychoanalytic neutrality."

After his release from prison, Marcelo found it difficult to maintain the rules of neutrality and to keep his personal life from invading his patients' concerns. As the repression in Uruguay mounted, even though none of his patients left treatment with him for fear of being associated with an ex-prisoner, the possibility that he might still be "in the hornet's nest" was disturbing to both patient and analyst alike. "One of the reasons that I ultimately decided to leave the country was that I could not practice under those conditions. I realized I couldn't discriminate between what was happening to the patient and what to me. Sometimes I reproached myself: if only I were stronger or better analyzed. At other times, I thought that the situation required a superhuman effort and that I was only human. For example, I was profoundly disturbed by the sounds in the environment: if a bus stopped, I got distracted wondering if it were just a city bus or something more sinister. One time during a session, two taxis stopped in front of my house, and I was convinced it was the armed forces coming to get me again. It turned out to be a priest who came to fetch me to treat a drunk who was threatening to harm himself with a knife."

Learning about aspects of a patient's life that might be of interest to the authorities put the analyst at risk of arrest, torture, and possible death. Some analysts did experience these forms of repression directly related to their work. In Argentina, on many occasions, analysts' offices were invaded during sessions, and patients were summarily arrested and carted off, sometimes never to be seen again.

But there were additional professional concerns: how to respect the injunction against imposing the analyst's perspective or point of view on the patient, as well as the mandate to focus on the patient's subjective reality rather than external events. Even the politically conscious analysts struggled to respect these aspects of prevailing psychoanalytic theory. It was often impossible. Marcelo recalls that he encouraged some of his activist patients whose lives were in danger to break off their analyses and flee the country. "In one case, a politically active friend of mine did not listen to his analyst's admonitions to leave the country immediately, and he paid dearly with seven years of prison and torture. Only years later, after studying psychoanalysis in France, did I finally understand that the world of unconscious fantasy is a mestizo—mixed breed—between the instincts and social reality and that the borders are much more porous than we used to think."

Juan Carlos also faced the conflict between professional responsibility to psychoanalytic technique and his ethical concerns about his patients. This problem emerged especially when he treated political activists who were in increasing danger as the repression in Argentina escalated. Concerned by what he viewed as a troublesome lack of attention to personal security on the part of both the Montonero leadership and their grass-roots activists, he felt obliged to help his activist patients become conscious of the need to take precautionary measures to protect themselves from military persecution. "I realized my patients were in a state of denial about their extreme vulnerability. I'd intervene in ways that were not a direct expression of my opinion but rather my interpretation of the patients' unconscious concerns that emerged from their discourse. Based on their associations, I could ask the important questions, which is, after all, the role of the analyst. 'Isn't it interesting that with what you're describing it never occurred to you that you might be in danger?' 'I wonder whether you're aware that when you talk about the revolutionary leadership, you're speaking as you do when you're describing your childhood and how you felt your mother didn't take care of you.'"

Yet another problem facing progressive analysts was the omnipresent threat that one of their patients might be an informant. Maren describes what happened to a psychotherapy group of adolescents when one of the patients' father was abducted. "Dealing with it was very difficult, and there was a great deal of censorship in the discussion. Free association wasn't possible because everyone knew that it took only one traitor within the group for a disaster to befall us all. The moral responsibility under such conditions was tremendous, and it was finally necessary to stop doing group therapy completely." On other occasions, patients become informants or collaborators. Maren relates one such incident about a high school boy who was taken prisoner and tortured. He became a hero, a symbol of resistance, and there were many demonstrations on his behalf. "When he was released, he sought therapy with me," recalls Maren. "But there was something about him that made me feel he was hiding, not telling the truth. I was frightened, and when he said he'd chosen me as a therapist because I was trusted by the left, I tried to minimize this connection in his mind. He didn't come back, and very soon after he was imprisoned again. Almost immediately he became a policeman and was often seen on the streets in our neighborhood, pointing out specific people to the military. When they later came for us, we hypothesized that it might have been he who denounced us."

In Chile, therapeutic issues confronting Elizabeth emerged within the context of her own journey back to psychology and of the role of the therapist in the human rights movement. She recounts how during the several years following the coup, she was involved in solidarity work, helping people get out of jail, leave the country, or obtain economic help to feed their families. "It was really scary because you didn't know with whom you were working; everything was anonymous for our own protection." She herself was always potentially in danger because of her history of militant activities with peasants, one of the sectors targeted for repression by the military. By 1976, she was once again drawn to psychology "because of my need to understand the subjective aspect of everything that had happened." A friend loaned her some books about Marxism and psychoanalysis, including one edited by Marie Langer that made a profound impression on her.[19] After that, she began to work in FASIC (the Catholic Foundation of Social Aid) in its psychiatric and medical section, where treatment was offered to former prisoners, families of the *desaparecidos*, and torture victims.[20] "That was when we began to write. In 1983, we put together two volumes of articles attempting to analyze what we observed, and Mimi wrote the introduction. We used pseudonyms for our safety and distributed copies of the volumes clandestinely within the country and internationally at congresses on human rights."

FASIC offered some degree of safety for Elizabeth and her colleagues who worked with torture victims. For several years, she and other mental-health professionals listened to testimonies by hundreds of people who had been illegally imprisoned and tortured. It was an anguishing process. "It was so sad, men and women so young: twenty, twenty-two year olds . . . so destroyed. I had a hard time psychologically containing both for them and for me something that was almost uncontainable. And we had no reliable therapeutic model to depend on to intervene clinically." The FASIC therapists began to tape their sessions, as well as testimonials of torture victims, so they could systematically study the psychic meaning of torture and its treatment. They read about the Nazi Holocaust and began an ongoing dialogue with therapists from other countries who practiced under similar conditions in order to elaborate a psychosocial analysis of state terror. "We noted similarities and differences between this experience and the Holocaust but felt lost because most of what was written dealt with the long-term effects on victims rather than with treatment interventions."

For Elizabeth and her colleagues, treatment issues were connected to the struggle to end the dictatorship. The testimonials were important for the victims because through them the reality of their experience could be validated by the therapists, who confirmed their sense of themselves and the world. Together they engaged in a political act by sending these testimonials to international human rights organizations and the United Nations to expose and denounce the dictatorship.

In an effort to develop treatment interventions for victims of state terror and to research and publish analyses of the culture of fear and its sequelae, Elizabeth and her colleagues from FASIC formed ILAS (Latin American Institute of Mental Health and Human Rights) in 1988. By this time, each had acquired psychoanalytic training. As Elizabeth says, "I came to realize that behaviorist treatment models were of no use in addressing the *afectados* of state terror and that only a psychoanalytic conceptualization of the psychic apparatus and psychoanalytic clinical techniques could make our therapeutic work effective. But I also became convinced that the patient's relationship with the analyst under these conditions needed to be thought of as more complex than simply a matter of transference. In fact, the patient-therapist relationship was often a transformative one, in which the patient learned to be able to depend on the analyst not only for psychological support but for practical help in resolving problems related to basic necessities like finding work, locating housing, and searching for the *desaparecidos*."

When working with victims of state terror, the notion of neutrality appeared totally irrelevant to Elizabeth. "We shared a political view with our patients, which helped us understand the depth and meaning of their trauma. We can't forget that in Chile we actually had won something in the election and presidency of Allende that then was brutally ripped away from us. And that made the issue of loss different from [that in] the other countries in the Southern Cone. It was difficult for an analyst who didn't feel that the Allende government had constituted an extraordinary social project to comprehend how its loss could represent a profound catastrophe. Such sentiments in a torture victim would simply be devalued by a therapist who didn't understand this. The therapist who could identify with this experience—without necessarily telling the patient—could use it to work very productively. We have found the patients' knowledge that we are on their side to be fundamental to the working alliance. Without it, how could they speak, thinking that you might be on the side of the enemy? Because ILAS is publicly connected with the human rights movement and politically opposed to the dictatorship and state-organized violence, the patient who comes to us for help is never confused about our alliances. This shared context permits the patient to risk entering into the treatment and disclosing traumatic experiences related to torture and forced disappearances. In this sense, the therapeutic relationship is itself reparative."

The Equipo and the Mothers of the Plaza de Mayo

"From the beginning, we were clearly identified with the Mothers' struggles to locate their disappeared children and grandchildren," Lucila says, "which is what made it possible for us to develop this unique therapeutic team effort on their behalf." Darío explains that their initial connection with the women who would later form the Mothers organization occurred shortly after the coup in March 1976, when Diana contacted some of them in the course of gathering names of *desaparecidos* for an Amnesty International delegation visiting Argentina. "It was in December," he recalls, "and after Diana and several colleagues delivered a list of names of university professors and students who had been disappeared, they were followed and on the point of being detained. Luckily, the Amnesty delegates were alerted. Their immediate return to the scene prevented the arrest of Diana and the others because the military, already concerned about their international reputation as human rights abusers, feared a scandal."

During the next several years, Diana often encountered women as they anxiously traipsed from church to ministry to barracks seeking information about their disappeared children and grandchildren. Although Diana used a pseudonym in her human rights work, when some of the women learned that she was a psychologist, they asked her to meet with one of the mothers who was depressed. Diana began to meet her informally in relatively safe public places like churches and cafés. Soon there was a chain reaction because other mothers who heard about Diana's expertise created a permanent demand for her services. "Later," recalls Diana laughing, "when the Thursday afternoon marches in the Plaza de Mayo started, sometimes I'd be walking around in the march listening to a mother tell me about a disturbing dream and helping her understand its unconscious meanings!"

Out of this experience, Diana recognized the need to work with the Mothers as a mental-health professional, not just a political activist. "That was the origin of the idea of forming a group, a team," says Lucila, "and Diana suggested the idea to Darío and me. Of course, we were very enthusiastic. We began immediately to deal with basic questions, such as what should be told to the children whose parent or parents had been disappeared or how should we deal with the problems that emerged in the marital relationship of parents of a *desaparecido* or what could be done to help people tolerate the uncertainty and anguish of not knowing about the fate of their disappeared children and grandchildren. We quickly realized that these efforts would best be realized through the creation of small groups composed of the families themselves so they could participate in the elaboration of these issues."

The three organizers of the Equipo were not new to political activism, for each had been involved in the radical movement of mental-health professionals that developed in the 1960s and 1970s in Buenos Aires. Their personal histories mirror the patterns of many psychoanalysts of their generation. Diana, whose grandparents had immigrated to Argentina from Russia and Rumania, grew up in a politically progressive family who lived in a working-class neighborhood that had benefited greatly from the Peronist government's pro-worker policies. After graduating from high school, Diana entered the intensely politicized student environment of medical school, and she quickly came to identify with the left and Marxism. Then in the early 1970s, like many fellow medical students, she received an important professional and sociological education as a resident at Lanus Hospital. Lucila too is a second-generation

Argentine whose grandparents arrived at the turn of the century from Russia, Rumania, and Austria. Lucila's mother was one of Argentina's best known leftist activists in the feminist movement from the 1920s on, and she had imparted her progressive values and principles to her daughter. "She left me an important legacy," Lucila notes, "for which I am grateful, although I must admit it has often been hard to be the daughter of the famous Fanny Edelman!" Darío is a fourth-generation Argentine of Spanish and Austrian heritage who also became politicized as a university student. During the early 1960s, medical school introduced him to professional training as well as leftist activism. His theoretical and clinical understanding of the relationship between social ills and individual sickness was honed in practice when he worked as a physician in a working-class community. Both his and Lucila's experiences as physicians among the poor stimulated their interest in psychology when they observed how frequently their patients' physical symptoms and requests for medical intervention seemed to be influenced by emotional difficulties and problematic social situations.

All three founding members of the Equipo developed a special interest in mental health. Their psychological training took place within the context of the great social turbulence in Argentina in the late sixties. They were among the young generation of mental-health professionals who were active in the Organization of Mental Health Workers, which was created by Marie Langer and other political analysts after their departure from the APA. Diana remembers her work as a student on the committee to develop the CDI curriculum. "It was fascinating to work with Mimi Langer in the CDIs, where we tried to develop a socially conscious psychoanalysis, one that would be responsive to the great social crises facing the country. We studied Freud, Klein, [R. D.] Laing, [Jacques] Lacan, Marx, and Althusser. It was incredibly exciting intellectually. And we were also developing activist projects, one of which was to put pressure on the state to implement programs of primary prevention. Hundreds of mental-health professionals went into the communities, much like the social workers in the United States, to respond to the psychological and social needs of the poor."

Later, following the coup in 1976, when conditions became extremely repressive, the three focused on human rights work and treatment of victims of state terror, often at great risk to their own personal safety. Finally, in 1979, their efforts coalesced in the formation of the Equipo. They began to work in a formal manner with the Mothers of the Plaza de Mayo, providing them with psychological assistance in their struggles to confront the terrorist state.[21] The women who were engaged specifically in the search for their disappeared grandchildren had formed a separate organization, the Grandmothers—*Abuelas*— of the Plaza de Mayo.

Like their counterparts in other Latin American countries where Mothers organizations have fought for their disappeared children,[22] the women who became activists in the Mothers and Grandmothers of the Plaza de Mayo came from diverse backgrounds. Some had prior experience as political activists, while others were middle-class professionals and working-class women with no political experience. The majority were homemakers from all social sectors with no previous activity in the public realm. When they began to gather in the Plaza de Mayo in April 1977, the issue that united them was their commitment to their children and grandchildren and their unswerving refusal to passively accept their forced disappearance (and torture or murder) by a terrorist state. On behalf of their loved ones, with their own lives in constant danger, they tenaciously confronted the armed forces.

These women viewed their activism in very specific ways. They did not see themselves fighting in the tradition of the women's rights movements that had emerged at the turn of the century to demand social, economic, and legal equality with men, nor as part of the radical and socialist feminist movements that had made their appearance during the early 1970s. In fact, the Mothers repeatedly stated that they did not identify themselves as feminists but rather as a group of women whose activities were not politically motivated. Indeed, they purposefully designed their discourse to reflect their traditional domestic roles: theirs was a struggle on behalf of motherhood and in defense of children. This self-presentation, symbolized by the white head scarves that became the motif of their struggle, coincided with the military's official rhetoric about Christian society and family values. Ironically, the military's adherence to the patriarchal ideal initially compromised their ability to respond to the Mothers with outright repression. Moreover, from the start, the armed forces' own prejudices against women led them to view the Mothers as an inept group of housewives, whom they disparagingly referred to as the locas (crazy women) of the Plaza de Mayo. The military's paternalistic underestimation of women prevented them from recognizing the Mothers as a potential threat to their authority, and this tactical error gave the women the time they needed to organize themselves. Even when the armed forces did attack the organization by kidnapping some of its members in late 1977, the Mothers' determination could not be broken. And although theirs was not a political struggle as they saw it, in the process of confronting the state, the Mothers educated themselves politically about the alliance of forces complicit with the military. They came to understand how the Catholic Church, the judiciary, and the capitalist sector cooperated with the crimes of the junta and then hid them from Argentine citizens.

The Mothers took up the search on behalf of their desaparecidos because, as they often publicly declared, as men their husbands were more vulnerable to the reprisals of the state. Their husbands, as well, had to maintain their jobs and thus could not risk being fired for missing work as a result of the labor-intensive search for their children and grandchildren. Many of the women speak warmly of their husbands' comradely support and willingness to take up the extra burden of housework so that their wives could go to the jails, police stations, hospitals, judges' chambers, and government bureaucracies to hunt for clues, file papers, and lodge formal denunciations. Diana explains that the women's activism created great solidarity among them, an important source of comfort in this grim activity, which generally yielded nothing. "The solidarity often included their husbands, who did not participate themselves for a variety of reasons. Often the men stayed away because of the very real fear that they would be easier targets of the military and police than the women, but there was also the factor of psychological demoralization that many men felt in the face of their impotence to protect their children. And some mothers and grandmothers found it necessary to take to the streets and the plazas with little or no support from their husbands, who felt unconsciously threatened by their wives' activist stance." For those women who were forced to deal with their husbands' passivity, fears, or even resentment of their own burgeoning assertiveness, conflicts in the couple relationship added additional stress to the politically provoked emotional burden of the loss of their children or grandchildren and their anxiety and fear for their own lives.[23]

However, membership in the Mothers organization has been extraordinarily positive for its participants. The Equipo members have written that the significance of this political activism must be understood within the context of the intended goal of state terror, which is the imposition of silence and total social isolation. Equipo members describe the pathological effects of complying with what they call "the silence rule," including extreme dissociative phenomena, the denial of reality, learning problems, and the impoverishment of fantasy life. The value of the Mothers, they argue, is their refusal to accept the terms of the terrorist state, their articulation of the existence of a responsible party that has disappeared their children, and their demand for an accounting from those responsible. Their slogans symbolize this posture: "They must appear alive"; "They took them away alive, we want them back alive"; "Punishment to culprits."

Although recognized as an important public stance, this political position of the Mothers brought debate within the organization and the Equipo. "We talked a lot about it," recalls Diana. "Many nonactivist therapists argued that families needed to mourn the loss of loved ones, to give up the *desaparecidos* as dead, in order to maintain their psychological connection with the real world. But we felt that for many people it was impossible to presume that their loved ones were dead, especially since we knew nothing about their fate.

In that sense, we thought that what passed as 'neutral' psychological theory on mourning was an unconscious capitulation to the dominant discourse of state terror. This was a very complex question, and we supported the right of each family to go through their own subjective process about how to live with the situation of having had a child forcibly disappeared."

The Equipo has argued that, in their coming together to act, the Mothers give up the narcissistic dyad "I and my child" or "I and my grandchild" in their common concern for all the disappeared children and grandchildren. The Mothers do not seek revenge; their action is beyond the realm of retaliation. They demand the return of law and its ability to contain arbitrariness within the social order. They have occupied a geographical space—the Plaza de Mayo—where for centuries Argentines have assembled when fighting for their political rights. They have marched, their white kerchiefs indicating peace as well as the diaper—eternal symbol of mother/child unity—their large photographs of the disappeared a defiant message that their children are indeed *presente*.[24]

Diana and her colleagues postulate that the Mothers organization sheds light on the relationship between political resistance and mental health. They note that women such as these have been better able to work through the traumatic loss of their loved ones, in part because for them their activist group has become a new privileged relationship, and they have been able to give a new meaning to group links beyond the family. Many of them have emerged from the limited sphere of the home to assume new forms of active solidarity and to identify themselves as socially engaged human beings for the first time in their lives. "The struggle for peace and justice means another type of relationship with the [child]. . . . The ego ideal system has been altered: to be a mother now means 'to fight for all our children' or 'to fight for life.' "[25]

The Equipo has noted that these activist women tend as a group to be better able to elaborate the trauma they suffered and to deal with the general impact of state terror than their husbands and those mothers who have not engaged in an organized confrontation with the political forces responsible for their traumatic loss.[26] As Diana points out, "Political activism does not necessarily eliminate the need for psychological attention. However, when we first began to work with the Mothers, we expected that, given their traumatic losses, they would all need psychotherapy. That was not the case. We discovered that, in and of itself, their involvement in the Mothers organization is potentially healing, precisely because the individual who has known traumatic loss is no longer cut off from the group. Her loss is no longer individualized, detached from its historical context, but is now part of the collective process that produced it and can now potentiate its reparation. The Mothers' transcendence of isolation and their commitment to act as historical agents are essential to the resolution of the pathological effects of social trauma."

Not only the Mothers about whom they write but Equipo members as well illustrate the positive use some individuals are able to make of social trauma. Their courage permitted them to preserve a sense of personal integrity and coherence with their ego ideals, which in turn empowered them. Hopefulness was nurtured as a result of their capacity to sustain a connection with others who shared their commitment to human rights. Marcelo and Maren Viñar have been especially interested in this human capacity for a creative response to traumatic situations. They have criticized the idea that the victims of the culture of fear are inevitably impaired, irrevocably changed for the worse, doomed to suffer lives deprived of creativity, productivity, and joy. The Viñars suggest that those who were the *afectados*, affected by the disappearances and torture in the Southern Cone, did not necessarily emerge "damaged" from the experience, as is implied by the diagnostic notion of "traumatic neurosis." Such a designation, they argue, may be more helpful to the therapist, whose work is framed by the comfort of a diagnosis, than to the victims, who can be hurt by the assumption that they have necessarily been psychically impoverished. The Viñars argue, "The person who has lost loved ones to the repressive state or has been tortured or forced into exile can emerge from such traumatic situations much worse off or much better off. The individual is altered, to be sure, but we ask the question How? It may be that [one] matures as a human being. Extreme situations may deplete or enrich the subject, whose creative and symbolic capacities are either dramatically compromised or enhanced. Trauma is by its very nature something that resignifies one's life, not in the symptoms or the sequelae of the injury, but by the meaning one attributes to it through the psychic elaboration of the experience."

The Viñars' own responses to the traumatic events in their lives testify to this assertion. In addition to the social trauma they suffered within the citadel of state terror, they, like many other political analysts, were forced into exile. Far from home, they were obliged to deal with the additional trauma of making a new life for themselves, isolated from all the familiar cultural, historical, and familial indicators that are the profoundly important referents of one's location in the world. Like Juan Carlos Volnovich and Mimi Langer, they faced yet another challenge in the process of resignifying their lives. Through their capacity to embrace and transcend the potential pathological effects of this fundamental life disruption, liberation psychology would survive, not only in the courageous work continued by the analysts who stayed in Argentina, Chile, and Uruguay, but in the projects of a socially committed psychoanalysis created amid the vicissitudes of exile.

Chapter 5

Liberation Psychology in Exile

Exile, once it begins, never ends . . . ever. One experiences it as an internal migration that lasts forever.

—MAREN AND MARCELO VIÑAR

IT IS A balmy summer morning in June 1984. Marie Langer, Ignacio "Nacho" Maldonado, and I are ordering espressos at the bar in Mexico City's international airport as we wait to board our plane for Managua, Nicaragua. Mimi has invited me to accompany her and Nacho, the two coordinators of the Internationalist Team of Mental Health Workers, Mexico-Nicaragua, as they return to the tiny Central American country whose revolution in 1979 has made it a target of President Reagan's new cold war policies. For the past three years, the Internationalist Team has sent two or three of its members for ten days of each month to teach and supervise in the Sandinistas' new mental-health system, an endeavor that has brought new meaning to life in exile for Mimi and Nacho. We are excited to be going to Nicaragua, but a little anxious as well in anticipation of flying through nature's turbulent Central American winds and over the U.S.-sponsored war in El Salvador.

Soon, because it has become my custom to take advantage of free moments in Mimi's busy schedule to pursue our ongoing exploration of her life and work, and perhaps stimulated by the airport environment, I direct our attention to the theme of exile. Nacho, Mimi's close friend and a fellow veteran of the movement of political analysts in Argentina, has also lived in exile in Mexico City since 1974. A gentle and soft-spoken man in his fifties, Nacho contributes his own recollections as I pursue threads of previous conversations about Mimi's arrival in this country a decade earlier.

"It's hard to describe," Mimi begins, her deep blue eyes becoming serious as she recalls her own complex feelings. "It's a daunting experience, arriving in a country and knowing from the moment you set foot on *tierra firme* that you are not here out of choice. Even more important, you have no idea how long your stay will be or whether you'll ever return home. You don't know what to feel, and in the beginning you oscillate from relief and excitement to fear and trepidation. At first you try to deny the gravity of the situation. Many of us plunged into a kind of defensive euphoria, playing at being tourists. 'Did you see how lovely Mexico City is?' 'Did you visit the pyramids—what beauty!' But our startled reactions to the sudden sound of an ambulance siren or the backfire of a car punctured the fiction that we were here on a planned vacation. We had come from a nightmare, and at night, when we slept, for months that nightmare persecuted us."

Nacho points out that after a while "the nightmare invaded our waking hours, and then we were even more psychologically disturbed." He and Mimi recall the impact of newspaper reports that detailed ongoing atrocities in Argentina. "There were the typical scenes," says Mimi. "An activist would comment anxiously to a compañero, 'Did you read that Haroldo went crazy under torture?' A distraught mother would tell a friend, 'You know the child my little girl plays with? Her mother just learned that they killed her husband.' And I'll never forget the evening when, during a meeting of a Freud study group, one of the female participants answered the phone, listened quietly to the voice on the other end, gasped, and began to scream, 'No, no . . . my god; they've killed my brother.'"

As exiles continued to learn about the horrors at home, the denial associated with the first phase of happy tourism shifted to a kind of depersonalization. Mimi recalls that "many friends and patients described 'out-of-body' experiences, observing themselves from outside as they went through the motions of daily life. And then there were the sudden attacks of self-reproach. One would walk the streets, thinking, 'What am I doing here? What is this city?' Or sit on the edge of the bed staring at the cheap ceramics purchased a day earlier with wild enthusiasm, thinking, 'But am I crazy? How did it occur to me to come here? I have to go back right away.' And then there were the slim hopes stimulated by rumors: 'Did you hear about the demonstration in Cordoba?' And 'What do you think? If the strike in Rosario continues a little more, will it be possible to return?'"

Worst was the guilt that everyone suffered, independent of their own histories, their political situations, or the circumstances of their leaving. It did not seem to matter whether they had left after being released from prison or had been deported by the government or had departed with permission from their political organizations or had simply decided to flee. All the refugees suffered the pangs of guilt for having fled and survived when others could or would not. "The anguish of this 'survivor guilt' was bound up with our grief for the lost political project that was such a fundamental part of our lives," Nacho adds. "With its disappearance, we also lost our self-esteem. You could hear the self-recrimination in the frequently uttered remark, 'We are all deserters.'" Mimi nods in agreement. "I remember my worst moment in exile. It was the night I went to a solidarity meeting of the Chilean exiles to hear President Salvador Allende's sister, Laura, speak. She told about how she had been taken prisoner because she hadn't left Chile after the coup. Because she was from such a prominent family, she wasn't tortured, but one night they threw her, naked and blindfolded, on a pile of tortured bodies for the night. When she was released, she continued her activism in the opposition struggle. I went home that evening and collapsed on my bed in tears. I felt a terrible desperation because, unlike Laura, I had abandoned my commitments. I had not continued to struggle, and in Argentina people were suffering and dying."[1]

Mimi and Nacho are describing significant aspects of the psychological impact of exile.[2] The forcible uprooting of individuals and groups from their country of origin is experienced as a profound rupture that threatens the stable functioning of the psyche. Exile from everything familiar is a life crisis that stimulates emotional reactions comparable to the helplessness and futility felt by a baby or young child at the absence or loss of the parent, who is needed to help manage frustration, anxiety, loneliness, and fears of separation.[3] Indeed, much like the defenseless child, exiles experience the loss of a containing environment when they are suddenly separated from their homeland, with its familiar and predictable language, cultural signifiers, and social relations. A state of psychic disorganization may result, especially if unresolved conflicts associated with earlier experiences of extreme vulnerability and loss are reawakened. Manic overcompensation in the form of an exaggerated enthusiasm about the new environment, such as Mimi describes, is frequently the first—and a fragile—line of defense against a host of disturbing states of mind. Or the opposite may occur: the exile cannot adapt to the new situation and rejects the culture, language, and people through an exaggerated devaluation, while nostalgically idealizing the country left behind.

A variety of symptoms appear frequently among an exile population, including disorientation, confusion, acute self-doubt, nightmares, insomnia, the inability to focus, depression, anxieties, paranoia, and dissociation. Some individuals become accident-prone, as if reenacting the experience of being attacked by a harmful environment. Often psychological conflict is displaced onto the body, and psychosomatic problems emerge. Higher rates of fatal diseases, including cancer, are found among exiles in comparison with the general population. Somatic disturbances are frequently related to digestive symptoms, as if new foods—symbolic of the new experience in general—cannot be "digested."[4] Marcelo Viñar recalls how, after living in Paris for a time, he received a letter from a friend whose philosophical advice hinged on eating as a metaphor for "taking in" the experience of exile. "I am happy to hear that you are in the process of putting down roots," the friend wrote. "One cannot continue to nibble a little at each thing, as if in passing. It's necessary to sit down at the table and partake of what life offers us." His friend went on to advise Marcelo to embrace his current situation. "One must weave a kind of density and thickness around what is provisional in life," he counseled. "You and I have lived in a country that will never be the same. Something else will exist in the future. Other youth will make their history, others who will not be us. We must learn to live this grim existence that fate has dealt us. If not, when a new day dawns, we'll be asleep or daydreaming."[5]

His friend wisely suggested that Marcelo recognize and accept the change in his life circumstances. He advised Marcelo to grieve the loss of his country and his own place in it, his own past identity, so as to get on with his life in the present. This mourning process is one of the central challenges facing the exile, who must struggle to relinquish both the fantasy and the reality of what has been lost in order to make a psychological investment in the new situation and in new social relations.

Like any life crisis, exile is a transitional period in which deprivation and loss may chronically undermine mental health or else create the possibility for growth, depending on how the individual has negotiated early experiences of helplessness, separation, and loss. Some exiles find it difficult or impossible to overcome internal and external obstacles to adjustment, manifesting psychological and physical symptoms that reflect and maintain the vicissitudes of the crisis. Some experience an outbreak of latent pathologies, which often provoke serious psychological disturbances. Others are able to overcome the initial depressive and anxious responses to exile, which temporarily compromise the psychic structure, and work through the mourning process related to lost loved ones and lost aspects of the self. Their resilience represents a positive use of the crisis of exile for the further development of creative and integrative capacities.

Such was the case with Marie Langer, Juan Carlos Volnovich, and Marcelo and Maren Viñar, all of whom were able to turn exile into an opportunity for growth and enrichment. As if sown by the wind, these activists landed in far-flung places whose distinct cultural and political circumstances presented new terrain on which to elaborate their various versions of a socially committed psychoanalysis.

Mexico: 1974–1987

Almost from the start, Marie Langer was able to resolve the significant issue of economic survival in exile. "Mexico," as she puts it, "proved to be a hospitable host." Well known among her Mexican colleagues, many of whom had trained years earlier as psychoanalysts in the APA with her, Mimi was

welcomed by the academic and professional communities alike. "Shortly after my arrival," she tells me, "I became a professor in clinical psychology in
the postgraduate program at the National Autonomous University of Mexico,
where I supervised therapists who worked in institutions throughout the city
offering low-fee or free treatment. It was very gratifying, for, in a way, this
supervision was a continuation of our work in the public hospitals in Buenos
Aires, where we brought quality mental-health treatment to the working class."
Mimi also became an honorary member of the Mexican Association of Group
Psychotherapy and developed a private practice that included refugees from
the Southern Cone and Central America. This work with refugees taught her
more about the psychological responses to state terror and exile. "I had patients from the sophisticated European cultural centers of Buenos Aires and
Montevideo and others from the indigenous highlands of Guatemala and El
Salvador, which gave me the chance to observe the role culture plays in shap-
ing the psychic responses to political repression."

In spite of the relative ease of her professional adaptation, Mimi continued to experience the disconcerting anxieties and depressive affect typical of
other exiles whom she knew and even treated. At times she obsessed about
her departure from Argentina. Had she left too soon? Could she have withstood torture had she been abducted by the Triple A? Would she have been
killed had she stayed? It was hard to escape the doubts and the deep sadness
of feeling adrift, cut off from her friends and the movement in Argentina. "I
came to understand years later," she says, "that the exile community was composed of two groups: first, those of us who had great difficulty in adjusting to
the loss of our political project. We became compulsively involved in the work
of denouncing the dictatorship. It wasn't only that the right wing had won
that was difficult for us but the fact of our defeat that we found so hard to
accept. The worst example of the inability to acknowledge that the enemy
had won and that the revolutionary forces had been routed—in fact, a serious denial of it—was . . . the self-destructive counteroffensive mounted by the
Montoneros in 1978, during which hundreds of Argentines returned from exile
to fight against the military, only to be slaughtered."

Mimi explains that the second group in exile did not remain politically
involved but instead assumed an extremely conservative lifestyle, working hard,
sending their children to the best private schools, and buying homes and cars
that demonstrated their material success. "They, too, found it difficult to accept defeat at the hands of the military, but their reaction was to reject their
radical politics and return to the conservative ways of their childhoods. In
psychological terms, we would say that they dissociated the aspect of themselves related to their progressive politics acquired in young adulthood and
returned to the life style and values they'd grown up with. We all need our

self-esteem, and these people could feel good about themselves through an adaptation to values acquired early on in their conservative upbringing and internalized as superego morality and expectations. For me, this was impossible. My self-esteem was related to my ego ideal, which I felt I had betrayed by abandoning the struggle and my compañeros in Argentina."

Thus Mimi's ability to adapt to exile depended on the possibility of maintaining continuity with the politics she had been forced to leave behind. She needed to find a way to practice the tenets of liberation psychology in response to the conditions in Mexico. Resilient, she soon found a place for herself in the Argentine solidarity movement, where she and other mental-health professionals carved out an important activist space on behalf of the survivors of state terror. By 1974, among the thousands of Argentine compatriots already in Mexico, a network of individuals was organizing resources to respond to the needs of refugees who continued to arrive. They arranged for housing, clothes, work, and even psychological assistance, which was secured from Argentine analysts and their Mexican colleagues in the Círculo Psicoanalítico Mexicano. In January 1976, a group of these activists met in Mimi's home to create an organization that would formalize their work. Soon they inaugurated the Committee in Solidarity with the Argentine People (COSPA) and rented an old, Spanish-style, two-story house in the heart of Mexico City to provide a center, called Casa Roma, for their activities.

COSPA had a variety of functions, ranging from practical and psychological help for Argentines just beginning their lives in exile to crisis intervention for those already established who experienced a sudden disruption in their adaptation to their new homeland. Committees of exiles gathered information about the Argentine military government in order to formally document and publicize its gross human rights violations in a variety of international professional meetings and political conferences. From its inception, COSPA sponsored weekly *peñas*, festive evenings featuring music, dancing, typical Argentine food, and often reports and discussions of current developments in Argentina. These Saturday night events, in which the children were prominent participants, were attended by exiles from Latin American dictatorships and their Mexican compañeros, all eager to be together to share their songs and their pain. As one Mexican journalist described it, "The *empanadas* [typical Argentine meat pies] are delicious, the conversation better . . . [but] behind the joyfulness, the humor, the enormous solidarity, now and then one can feel the tragedy, so intense at times it is almost palpable. It happens, for example, when the person introducing the musical groups suddenly mentions, as if in passing, the death of a compañero in Argentina, the exile of another, the torture of yet another."[6]

Shortly after COSPA was founded, Mimi and her colleagues organized its mental-health commission, which later became the Argentine Mental Health Workers in Mexico, in order to develop a program of therapeutic assistance to adults and children from the Southern Cone. Through COSPA's Secretary of Social Assistance, their efforts were coordinated with the volunteer labor donated by family physicians, a variety of medical specialists, and sympathetic staff in Mexico City's hospitals and medical laboratories. "Because COSPA was located in a spacious house, it could serve as a temporary residence for recent arrivals or expectant mothers about to give birth. On occasion, it became an improvised residential clinic for refugees who arrived in acute states of psychological crisis or for people already living in Mexico City who required therapeutic interventions on learning of disappearances, tortures, or deaths of loved ones still in Argentina." The mental-health workers also supervised and offered treatment when needed at COSPA's preschool, where more than one hundred children from different Latin American countries were cared for while their parents worked. "The solidarity movement was extremely important to all of us," Mimi stresses. "It helped us as much as it did those who received our assistance. Our ability to recuperate, to whatever degree possible, the victims—the enemies—of the military dictatorships gave us back important aspects of our lost political project."

Exile meant other possibilities as well. In Mexico Mimi reestablished old friendships with European colleagues and made new friends with feminists from Europe, the United States, and Latin America. Young activists were drawn to her, impressed by her vitality and rare blend of wisdom and openness to new ideas. Gratifying as these relationships were, Mimi, widowed for about a decade, lamented the lack of people her own age able to remain involved in a similar life project, as well as the absence of an intimate sexual relationship with a man, which she related to the social taboos against sexuality in older women. But she derived much pleasure from her family, who remained a close-knit clan. She saw her two daughters and their families often since they, too, lived in Mexico City. Her sons frequently brought their families from Buenos Aires to visit. As always, they shared Mimi with the other passions of her life. "I remember once," she says with a mischievous grin, "how my older son, Tommy, jokingly complained about how I'm not one of the full-time grandmothers, like his mother-in-law. 'You're just a part-timer,' he told me. Well, I felt a little hurt, but I had to admit he was right. I told him that maybe I'm more like a grandfather because I continue to work and be involved in the world."

Mimi's "world," by the late 1970s, included growing numbers of refugees from repressive military dictatorships in Guatemala, El Salvador, and Nicaragua, who were flowing into Mexico seeking asylum. Gradually the Argentine Mental Health Workers in Mexico extended solidarity activities and therapeutic assistance to these Central American exiles. In the autumn of 1978, Mimi and her colleagues had their first direct contact with the Sandinista revolutionaries, who waged war against the repressive Somoza dynasty, which had ruled the tiny Central American nation of Nicaragua for half a century. A group of sixty Sandinistas had been granted asylum in Mexico for several months before they returned to the struggle in their country, and many were suffering the cumulative psychological consequences of growing up in a dictatorship and fighting in the revolution to oust it from power. The young men and women had survived horrific abuse at the hands of Somoza's National Guard and were experiencing many symptoms, including alcohol abuse, depression, insomnia, and acute anxiety. The Argentine Mental Health Workers in Mexico had been contacted by an exiled Nicaraguan physician in the hope that they could help.

"We were uncertain about how they would relate to us," recalls Mimi, "so we decided to first meet with the entire group of them in the day-care center of COSPA. When we arrived, there they were, most of them so young, patiently waiting, chatting among themselves. One boy was strumming a guitar, and others were singing along. We realized that we would have to find a way to help them feel at ease and trust us, so one Argentine compañera began to tell of her own experience of jail and torture. Others of us spoke as well, each explaining our firsthand knowledge of political repression and why we were here in exile. Gradually the Nicaraguans, who had no familiarity with psychotherapy, warmed to the idea of being able to speak with a professional who might help them understand their emotional turmoil."[7] In the days and weeks that followed, a variety of therapeutic interventions, including private and group sessions, helped alleviate some of the Nicaraguans' symptoms, many of which were related to the fact that they had had no possibility of mourning the loss of relatives and compañeros who had been disappeared or killed by the National Guard. Mimi and her colleagues deepened their understanding of what she would call "frozen grief" in the context of political struggle. Although she could not know it at the time, this experience was to be but the first in an enduring connection to the Sandinista Revolution.

In later years, Mimi believed she had been fortunate that her political activism had forced her to leave Argentina before the military coup occurred "because it saved me from the experience of having to endure the dictatorship in silence, humiliation, impotence." She concluded, in fact, that those who stayed—who experienced the tribulations of internal exile—had much more courage than those who left and who had been able to benefit in many ways from external exile. In this regard, when democracy returned to Argentina in 1983, Mimi chose to remain in Mexico because she was deeply involved in the exciting project of helping the Sandinista Revolution build

Nicaragua's first national system of mental-health care. She was thrilled to be developing the tenets of liberation psychology in this new context, where it shifted from being an oppositional movement to one that worked in concert with a government whose values and goals paralleled its own.

Adaptation to exile in Mexico was facilitated for Mimi and other political refugees from the Southern Cone by the country's proximity to Latin American revolutionary movements and its familiar language and history. But, for refugees from Argentina, Chile, and Uruguay whose flight took them to faraway continents and unfamiliar cultures, exile was experienced as a global rupture with the past and a demand to create not only a new life but a new self. They would have to begin again, learning to talk, behave, play, and work within a new cultural and social matrix.

France: 1976–1990

Early March seemed an appropriate time for Maren and Marcelo Viñar to arrive in Paris, for the city's late winter rains and gray, overcast skies mirrored their gloomy state of mind. Although they had chosen France as their country of exile because French colleagues had been willing to help them find a professional niche outside Uruguay, they had not foreseen the devastating impact of trying to survive in a society whose culture, language, and people they knew nothing about. It took months, indeed years, for them to adapt to exile. During their decade and a half in France, the Viñars elaborated a politically informed psychoanalytic conceptualization of exile based on their astute observations of their own experience and their clinical work with adult and child refugees from all over the world. The central concerns of liberation psychology, such as the importance of social as well as individual reparation, formed the basis of the Viñars' significant contributions to the growing literature and international dialogue about the psychological impact of political repression and exile.

"Imprisonment and exile were the two most difficult experiences in my life," Marcelo says solemnly, looking at me over his reading glasses. "There were two especially painful aspects of exile. The first was what I call a narcissistic collapse, like a kind of undoing of the self. And the second was the loss of security, which is related to my origins. I was a child of the middle class, with very protective parents who supported my growth and development. As an adult, I built a successful professional life. I was *somebody*—Dr. so-and-so— who was recognized as a specific individual with a specific status in the social group. The disruption of this 'place in the world,' which I had taken for granted before it was suddenly ripped away from me in my late thirties, was devastating. We have written about how exile in this sense is a violent and decentering rupture, especially for those who have fulfilled a social role highly valued by themselves and their community. One loses the many-sided mirror in which he has created and nurtured his own image, his public persona, his celebrity, if you will. In exile, what he once was no longer exists. No one knows him, no one recognizes him. He finds himself in a new scene from an unfamiliar play with unknown actors. This is a true identity crisis."

An additional painful aspect of exile for the Viñars was economic insecurity. Although they and their children never went hungry, their economic situation during the initial years in France was precarious. "Even though as exiles we were privileged to have a group of colleagues who showed us great solidarity," Marcelo says, "the deep insecurity we felt about our very survival came as a tremendous shock. I know that I am speaking as an intellectual and a professional and that perhaps a worker who has known insecurity from birth on would respond differently. But in my case, exile plummeted me into a situation of helplessness that was extraordinary." Eventually Marcelo obtained a position in a psychiatric clinic that provided a minimal salary. His work with schizophrenics was demanding and difficult, but rewarding. "I always tell a funny story that has much of reality in it," he remarks. "After about a year in the clinic, everyone said I was the best psychiatrist there because my patients got better. Actually, I think they improved because they had a doctor to take care of rather than a doctor who took care of them! They were the nurses and therapists desperately needed by their depressed psychiatrist! This reversal of roles created a very strong link among us. My own psychological precariousness wound up facilitating a good therapeutic relationship among us. The other side of the coin had to do with the rumors that circulated about me. I later realized that to them I symbolized the Latin American hero."

The anguish of the first years was exacerbated by having to learn to speak and read French, not a word of which either Marcelo or Maren had known. Marcelo extrapolates from his own struggles to learn French that one's relationship to language is of key significance in the exile experience. His view echoes what has been noted elsewhere about the psychological impact on immigrants who are obliged as adults to learn an entirely new language. The adult must tolerate reexperiencing the initial helplessness of the child struggling to acquire language, which is the bridge to becoming an active participant in the social world. One's place in the world is ordered, after all, through the linguistic system of verbal and visual signifiers. Some adult immigrants learn the new language fairly easily, perhaps as a defensive maneuver to cope with their feelings of impotence and exclusion from social interaction. Others resist learning the new language, which may reflect their guilt for abandoning their parents' tongue.

"Each language has a code of customs, laws, relations," emphasizes

Marcelo, "and to speak in a language implies knowledge of more than words, [of] other things as well about the culture that produces it. One might be able to understand the dictionary and at the same time not know much at all. Alienation comes from not being able to interpret the meaning of words but, even more important, the meaning of gestures, references, and social relations. It is an unforgettable experience. Very soon after we arrived in Paris, Maren and I wrote about being strangers in a strange land. The sensation of being lost is horrible. Once you've been a stranger, a foreigner, you always carry this somewhere inside. It never goes away. One is irreversibly a stranger. One never returns to the nest, to one's home, one's homeland, nor to the illusion of completeness. That is lost forever. What remains is a rupture between the individual and his links, and there is always, forever, something lacking." When, after living in France for almost a year, Marcelo began to treat his first patient—an Argentine—they were able to conduct the analysis in Spanish. This experience represented for him the return to a state of thinking. "It gave me immense pleasure and joy to once again use my full mental capacities."

Language can become a wedge between parent and child in the exile family. The fact that children acquire the new language more easily than their parents often leads to mutual bad feelings. Marcelo remembers how in his own childhood the Uruguayans laughed at his immigrant parents and their friends for their "gringo" way of speaking Spanish. In France he relived the experience, only this time as the inept adult who was ostracized. He recalls how his younger son would feel ashamed of him when he spoke French and would pull at his pants leg and beg him not to speak. Sometimes his children spoke French rapidly together so he and Maren could not understand them, or they spoke French between themselves and Spanish to their parents, as if to establish an authority relation that countermanded the customary one between the generations.

The jealousy and envy of the older generation often turn into an accusatory and condemning attitude toward the children, whose relative ease in absorbing the codes of the host culture makes them seem like traitors to their parents' ideals. Marcelo points out that "there is often lots of conflict between parents and their adolescent kids. The parents have a nostalgic discourse about the *patria*, the ideals, the revolution. The children say, 'We were too young, it wasn't our life.'" Marcelo believes exile taught him something valuable about his children. "With respect to the theme of political repression, for example, I remember growing up in my small Uruguayan town and being taught about the Holocaust and the oppression of Jews. But we kids would walk the streets and there was no anti-Semitism, no one pursuing the Jews. I think this discourse about the Jewish people, persecuted and forced to be immigrants, functioned in the children to secure either submission to our parents' discourse or rebellion and family misunderstandings. Now it was my turn to be a foreigner, a minority, and to demand that my children recognize and hold alive the memory of why we were exiles. I realized later that I wanted them to sustain in their minds an identification with my generation's values and struggles, with the revolutionaries who had been repressed. And they, poor things, saw nothing of this in Paris and sought only successful adaptation to their new world. Their parents' nostalgia could only create a powerful familial breach."

However, the opposite pattern also existed. Marcelo and Maren have written about parents who attempted to protect their children from the reality of the past. They avoided speaking of the conditions that prompted their exile—of the prison or the torture—in the false belief that they would save their children from suffering. As Maren explains, "Keeping them from this information only results in taking away their possibility of locating themselves in their own history, only denies them access to knowledge that can permit the psychological elaboration of an experience they have lived through and, like their parents, been deeply marked by. Isolated and abandoned by this lack of communication, these children often remain permanently alienated from their past and their culture."[8]

The family in general, the Viñars have argued, suffers many pressures in exile and is forced to play a contradictory role. On the one hand, it provides the context in which its members work through the mourning process, in which the threatened and vulnerable identity of each can be experienced as having survived the crisis. On the other, it is the stage on which is dramatically enacted all the aggression unable to be expressed elsewhere. "The family," they have written, "bears the mark of the social catastrophe. In place of the mutual support that would facilitate cohesion, miscommunication and isolation are often paradoxically unleashed among its members, dissolving the illusion that they might recover from the magnitude of having been forcibly uprooted from their country, helpless to defend themselves. Each detail, each small frustration, intensifies the enormity of the loss. It is manifested in the explosions of aggression between husband and wife, parents and children, and within old friendships and even the exile community itself."[9]

The Viñars experienced tensions in their own relationship because of their different attitudes toward exile. For a number of years, Marcelo fell into a depressive nostalgia for the life he had been forced to abandon. "Five years after we arrived," he comments ruefully, "suddenly one spring day, with the tree-lined streets ablaze with color, I realized that Paris is a beautiful city! I felt so resentful that Maren was enjoying it. For some time already she had been going to museums and feeding her aesthetic sensibilities, while I still walked around in a gray fog." Maren smiles as she recalls the dissimilarities in their rhythm of adaptation to Parisian exile. She reminds me that in her childhood she had learned from her father and the Spanish exiles who had stayed with her family that one has to go on, to sustain one's ideals, one's hopefulness, one's life.

"For me," Maren says, "becoming an exile didn't devalue me. I don't know whether this is related to gender roles, but I'm certain I was helped by my conviction that I had to continue functioning as the wife, the mother, keeping everything and everyone together. I couldn't have a narcissistic crisis with a baby just learning to walk! The children forced me to keep going, they were like a prohibition against having a breakdown! The first year and a half were really terrible. Things didn't improve. I couldn't get work, and the unpredictability seemed as if it would last forever. Conditions in Uruguay worsened, so there was little hope of an alternative. Finally the moment arrived when I told myself, 'I have to stay here; I have to adapt; this is my life.' And so I began, easier and sooner than Marcelo, to enjoy aspects of being in Europe in the heart of such extraordinary culture." Maren began to let herself feel enthusiastic about the challenge of starting over at almost forty. She became engrossed in the process of undergoing the additional training necessary to practice in France. Over the years, both she and Marcelo treated exiles from many different countries, which deepened their understanding of the dynamics of exile. "France, exile, was a profoundly maturing experience for me, as it was for Marcelo. It was ultimately important for him to have lost that kind of self-contentment, the illusion of complacency that was inherent in his life in Uruguay, where it was easy to feel that 'we are so terrific, such fabulous people, everything is so wonderful!'"

Like everywhere Latin Americans congregated in exile, Paris had a solidarity movement in which the Uruguayans participated. In Paris the movement was complex and, from Marcelo's point of view, riddled with contradictions. The movement generated important activities, including the exposé and denunciation of the military dictatorships across the Atlantic. As in Mexico, it provided a much-needed source of material and psychological support for Latin Americans so far from home. At times it could function as a kind of microsociety, however, where refugees shielded themselves from the demands of adaptation to their new society and culture. Some never learned more than a few words of French and refused to develop friendships with French citizens. They complained about the nation that had given them safe harbor, as if it, rather than conditions at home, were the cause of their geographic and social dislocation. At times their negativism seemed justified by the ambivalent or hostile attitudes of the French, who were offended by the invasion of their politically exiled guests. Over all, though, the solidarity movement was a great source of comfort, even for those like Marcelo and Maren who eventually succeeded in situating themselves within French culture and social relations.

Maren remembers that through the solidarity movement she joined a women's group whose members were from many Latin American countries. The group provided much-needed emotional and practical support. "When I got sick, or my kids got sick, what could I do? My compañeras came; they helped me. And I helped them. We depended on one another. The strong bond of unity we built made me think a lot about how gender influences one's experience of exile. Women who remained housewives and stayed home to care for their children had something concrete to devote their energies to, something they were building for the future. It was we women who had to deal with the schools and the parents of other children, we who had a long-range project through raising the children. The men often had no equivalent psychological investment."

But in the cosmopolitan European capitals, exile also provided new opportunities for women and, in so doing, challenged traditional gender roles among the Latin American refugees. Many women who had not been involved politically in their own countries joined their activist sisters in the solidarity movements. And women now had access to work possibilities like the men, sometimes at higher wages than their partners. Maren treated many couples who experienced conflicts when the husband's sense of masculinity was undermined by his wife's superior work situation or wages. Many middle-class couples found themselves for the first time without the cheap female domestic labor so plentiful in underdeveloped Latin America, and they were forced to divide the work in the home, traditionally done by women, between husband and wife. In this regard, Marcelo recalls the pleasurable aspects of this period in Paris, when increased domestic responsibilities were tiring but emotionally fulfilling. "Evening meals, for example," he recounts nostalgically, "required the collective participation of all of us—Maren and me and the two kids. That meant that every evening we'd spend about two hours all together working, eating, and talking." Downward mobility thus provided the Viñars with a daily ritual fostering a familial intimacy not achieved in their more privileged life before or after exile.

In the end, both Maren and Marcelo recognized that each was able to use the experience of exile to grow personally, professionally, and politically. They matured intellectually through their connection to French psychoanalysis, whose unique perspectives on psychic life and psychopathology, permeated by radical political critiques of bourgeois social structures, added provocative dimensions to their writings and public presentations on the political and psychological meanings of state terror and exile. But when the military governments in the Southern Cone gave way to popular pressures for a return to democratic rule, like other exiles, the Viñars were faced with the difficult decision of whether to return to their country. In spite of the expanded horizons exile had come to represent for them, ultimately they opted to return to Uruguay.

The Viñars have written widely about the significance of returning from exile, of going home again. "It's complicated," muses Maren. "In the final analysis, we developed many connections in France and strong ties to the French people. I also had many women friends there. To return means that you break this link; you destroy the world you've constructed. I still don't know to this day," she chuckles, "how we could do it. Sometimes I feel more intensely the rupture entailed in coming back than the original rupture of forced exile. The exile was obligatory; this return was chosen. Marcelo wanted to be here, but it was a difficult decision for me to make. And it took me five years to feel good about being back in Uruguay." Marcelo listens pensively and then adds, "In reality, it's not a return. It's another departure." Maren agrees. "Yes," she says, "it's a going back to begin again. One goes back to Uruguay. But Uruguay is another country. Those who stayed are no longer those you left, and you are no longer who you were when you went away. In the final analysis, one does not go back, one actually goes away again."

Cuba: 1976–1984

Juan Carlos could not know when he set foot on Cuban soil in December 1976 that he, too, would later face the choice of returning to Buenos Aires and leaving behind the life that he would create during his eight years of exile in Caribbean socialism. At the moment of his arrival in Havana, he knew only that he felt disoriented. The warm greetings from Silvia's sister-in-law, Beatriz, and several medical colleagues of her brother, Leonardo, who had come to the airport to welcome them, barely punctured his state of disequilibrium. What was he going to do? How would he practice his profession? How would they survive? As they left the airport, one of the Cubans asked what work Juan Carlos wanted to do while living in Cuba. He responded that he was a psychoanalyst and that he was worried about having to learn a new skill at his age. "I know I can't practice psychoanalysis in Cuba," Juan Carlos explained, indicating that since the early days of the Revolution, when most psychoanalysts had left the country, Soviet behaviorism had been the prevailing orientation within Cuban psychology. But his Cuban acquaintance exclaimed enthusiastically and, as it turned out, quite prophetically, "Look, man, you can do anything you want here in Cuba."

And so it was. The following day Juan Carlos and Silvia were informed that they could work within the Cuban health system where and how they chose. Surmising that their good fortune was due to the fact that Leonardo and Beatriz had lived and worked in Cuba since 1960 and that they themselves had spent previous summers working in health and educational projects on the island, they were now faced with the real possibility of staying in the country. "This was truly a weighty decision," Juan Carlos remembers, with the usual twinkle in his eye. "Given the hostility to Cuba orchestrated by the United States and ruling elites in Latin America, we wondered what would happen to our chances of returning to Argentina someday if we lived our exile in Havana rather than in Geneva, where I'd also been offered work. The conflict was resolved in a funny way. We talked together about how if we, who considered ourselves Marxists but had failed to bring about revolutionary changes in our own country, could not adapt to socialism in a Latin American country that had made the revolution, then to hell with Geneva: we should just go to Las Vegas and never again mention Marxism! Well, we decided to stay in Cuba, to test our principles and coherence. We took it on as a challenge. I felt I was putting all of my pride, my integrity, on the line."

The Volnoviches took up the test of living in socialism at a propitious moment. By the mid-seventies, the quality of life for the average Cuban had improved dramatically from what it had been under the U.S.-supported dictator Fulgencio Batista. In an era of chronic unemployment throughout the rest of Latin America, the Cuban Revolution's economic development strategy provided full employment with a host of workers' benefits. Its internationally acclaimed social programs, including universal free education from kindergarten through university, free medical care, and free child care, had raised Cubans' standard of living. Even while bureaucratic centralization produced inefficiencies and waste, the government's emphasis on investment in capital goods and technology had achieved long-term development goals that eluded Latin America's market-driven nations. Periodic shortages of basic necessities were dealt with through a rationing system, which was a conscious strategy to provide an equitable distribution of available goods to all citizens and to avoid the price inflation that ravaged the poor in the rest of the countries of Latin America. Even so, when shortages did occur—to a good extent the intended result of the U.S. embargo of Cuba—it often meant waiting in long lines for food and other basic commodities. Daily life was also affected by the deterioration of Havana's infrastructure, with its periodic interruptions of electric, water, and gas services. At the same time, Cubans enjoyed increased access to culture through the government's encouragement and financial support of production and distribution of the arts. Cuban cinema, literature, music, and visual arts boldly developed innovative form and subject matter that entertained international as well as Cuban audiences. The Volnoviches shared in the benefits and the difficulties of life in socialism during their years in Cuba, which brought them and their children a sense of accomplishment and plea- sure that surpassed in many ways what they had known in cosmopolitan Buenos Aires.

For several years before they moved into their own apartment, the Volnoviches lived with Beatriz, Leonardo, and their three children. "It was a miracle: two families, one of which was going through the pain of exile, liv- ing together in one house . . . and we never fought! We created a kind of com- mune. All the kids slept in the same room and developed a close relationship with one another. It helped Silvia and me a lot, as well, for we learned from our in-laws the specific cultural codes of Cuban social relations." So although they had Argentine and Chilean friends in the exile communities in Havana, Juan Carlos and Silvia were integrated into Cuban society. They lived and worked as Cubans, with the important exception of being allowed to use dol- lars to purchase a car, which improved the logistics of daily life by eliminat- ing the need to depend on the city's overcrowded public transportation system.

"I know it's hard to believe now," Juan Carlos says, "especially given the growing difficulties in Cuba since the late 1980s with the fall of the Soviet Union and the intensification of the U.S. embargo, but life was easy on the island. Even then, people outside Cuba had the impression that we were suf- fering, and our friends in exile elsewhere would write, pitying us for the hard life they presumed we led. Ironically, lots of things were actually better than ever for us. For example, we'd been accustomed to living in Argentine con- sumer culture, with our kids always demanding, 'Buy me this, buy that, buy that.' In Cuba, from the beginning, they must have intuited there was a dif- ference. There were few commodities, and they simply stopped thinking about them. Instead, their attention was directed to other things. They both got very involved at school and made many new friends. Yamila enthusiastically stud- ied art, and Roman became a champion swimmer. As they got older, they, like their Cuban compañeritos, learned about and felt passionately identified with struggles for social justice throughout the world. This was truly wonder- ful for Silvia and me, to see our kids growing up in an environment that en- couraged them to care about the same things that we did. It provided us with an intergenerational continuity that was extremely gratifying."

Juan Carlos smiles as he thinks about his friends' misplaced concerns. Convinced that he and Silvia were suffering and deprived, they would send them books along with a variety of personal items from abroad. In fact, he says, life seemed easy. For one thing, they marveled at the fact that they could go to sleep at night and wake up in the morning, an experience they had long forgotten in Argentina because of their constant hypervigilance during the final several years before exile. Juan Carlos had also felt for over a decade that he never had time to read, and now in Cuba it felt like a privilege to have access to the most recently published books from all over the world and time enough to read them.

"The biggest privilege of all, something I didn't realize at the time, was that our situation was different from that of our friends scattered throughout the world—Mexico City, Paris, Madrid, Venice, Rio—many of whom felt obliged to adjust to environments that demanded an abandonment of their political practice. In contrast, living in Cuba permitted us to maintain coherence with the same ideals as before. So exile for us was not an interruption, an abandonment of our life project, our principles. It's true there were cultural differences between Argentina and Cuba. . . . We felt it in everything—the language, peoples' attitudes, social custom. But it represented a continuity with the Latin American revolution. I know of many exiles who lived elsewhere and who, although they continued to work with the human rights movements, felt they had to 'cleanse' themselves of their previously committed revolutionary politics. This meant that when they eventually returned to Argentina, they could focus on creating successful careers and a bourgeois lifestyle. Our choice meant we couldn't 'cleanse' ourselves of past sins, but instead we 'dirtied' ourselves even more. We couldn't deny our revolutionary past, we simply added more 'stains' to it."

Living in Cuba meant adjusting to the struggles being waged against traditional sexist culture and on behalf of gender equality. In 1976, the Cuban constitution had included a new Family Code legalizing a radical reordering of traditional male privilege in all domains of life, including equal pay for comparable work, access of women to traditionally male careers, reproductive rights, and paternal responsibility for all children, including those previously considered illegitimate. "Although equality between men and women was clearly not yet a reality, I did observe how in one generation the Revolution represented a great change for women," Juan Carlos recalls. "There were significant differences between mothers and daughters in that regard. For example, an illiterate peasant woman might have a daughter who was the best student in her class or a youth leader who was honored by appearing alongside Fidel on television. There were many palpable differences like that."

However, the Family Code's most revolutionary article stipulated that domestic labor and child rearing were the equal responsibility of women and men whether or not women worked outside the home for wages. This aspect of the Family Code challenged the customary sexual division of labor in its most intimate domain and sparked dramatic conflicts among many Cuban couples as they struggled, negotiated, and resisted the metamorphosis it represented. Within this political context, Juan Carlos and Silvia designed a family life radically different from the one they had led in Buenos Aires. "Silvia and I get into arguments about that aspect of exile," Juan Carlos says. "She claims I was very happy, but I say she doesn't understand the effort it represented to me. I felt much more pressure to do my part to make a good home life. From the time I was two years old, we'd had two domestic workers at home, and later either Silvia or a housekeeper would take care of the housework. I didn't know what it meant to have to shop, cook, wash dishes, make beds, wash and iron clothes. This may sound strange, but it was traumatic for me!"

Juan Carlos continues, "In Cuba, we both worked as psychoanalysts in hospitals. Silvia held a responsible post at Havana's maternity hospital, where she specialized in the psychological aspects of pregnancy and childbirth. She became a highly recognized professional, probably more than I, which was the reverse of our experience in Buenos Aires. Nonetheless, we were both on tight schedules, obliged to arrive at work punctually. Like factory workers, professionals had to clock in, and if you acquired a certain number of tardies, it would be announced in hospital meetings, and you'd feel humiliated. So, in the mornings I'd wake up, take a quick shower, and rush to get to work on time. And I'd get home earlier than Silvia, who left work later and picked up the children on the way home. I'd walk in at 4 o'clock in the afternoon, and the house was exactly the same as I'd left it in the morning, exactly! I realized it had never been that way before. I'd leave the house to study or work, and when I returned, everything would be organized: the house clean, the meal ready, the clothes washed and ironed. For me, it was the most natural thing in the world. In Cuba I realized with a thud what feminists mean by 'the invisible labor of women.' I also came to understand what they mean when they say, 'The personal is political.'"

So it was that Juan Carlos developed new skills, including housework, shopping, and cooking. When Silvia and the children came home in the afternoon, the house was clean, dinner was on the table, and they all sat down for three hours of eating, chatting, reading, and studying together. "In spite of the fact that our apartment was small and the furnishings quite simple, we'd decorated it with care, and it had a real artisan feel to it," Juan Carlos says. "Silvia, Yamila, and Roman all say that this period of integrated family life represents the happiest years they can remember. And I felt proud that I was up to the task of doing my share to create this experience for us."

Juan Carlos was also "up to the task" of carving out a psychoanalytic practice within the Cuban health system. When he was first told that he could work where and how he wanted, he knew immediately that he would choose to work at Havana's General Pediatric Hospital under a psychiatrist who had been trained psychoanalytically in Chicago before returning to his native land in the 1960s. "I hadn't forgotten my visit with Dr. José Perez Villar during a prior trip to Cuba. I can still see it in my mind's eye: the two of us sitting and talking together in his office, while I was transfixed by the three enlarged photographs hanging behind him on the wall. The first photo featured the founder of the Cuban Communist Party, the second Che Guevara, and the third Sigmund Freud! The way the photographs were arranged, Che and Freud were staring at each other! I thought, 'If Freud only knew that here in revolutionary Cuba he'd be hanging on a wall exchanging a long meaningful look with Che!'"

In the department of child psychiatry, Juan Carlos began to treat adults as well as children. His Cuban colleagues, who understood nothing of psychoanalysis, and his patients as well, who had never even heard the term, were bemused by a doctor who wanted to see his patients four times a week. Juan Carlos's esteem rose in the eyes of his Cuban colleagues, however, when successful interventions with several patients who happened to be well-known physicians resulted in "cures" of psychosomatic and hysterical symptoms. Indeed, he acquired a reputation for being somewhat of a magician! Soon he was treating adults and children who came to the hospital from the neighboring communities, as well as prominent individuals in the arts. "Because I gained prestige as an analyst among writers, artists, and musicians, Silvia used to joke that my salary should be paid by the Ministry of Culture rather than the Ministry of Health!"

Like the Viñars in France and Mimi Langer in Mexico, Juan Carlos had the opportunity to treat Latin American exiles and to develop projects that represented continuity with the tenets of liberation psychology. He treated Argentine, Chilean, and Uruguayan children whose parents had been disappeared or killed by the military and who had been sent to Cuba for safekeeping. This work became an important focus in 1978, following the deaths of hundreds of Argentine activists who had returned home from exile to take part in the Montoneros' ill-fated counteroffensive against the military junta. The gravely misguided strategy, which ended in disaster, left numerous children in Argentina and in exile orphaned. Four hundred of these "war orphans," ranging in age from infancy through adolescence, were brought to Cuba that year. A residential center, occupying two enormous old mansions in Havana, became the new home of those children who had no relatives residing in Cuba. During the following five years, as many as forty or fifty children at a time lived at the center with their Cuban and Argentine caregivers.

Although this center was the focus of Juan Carlos's attention during its five-year existence, in 1979 he was diverted for some months by an opportunity to be part of an international medical brigade organized in Mexico to provide medical care to the Sandinista forces fighting the Somoza dictatorship in Nicaragua. Much as an earlier generation of physicians—including Mimi Langer—had traveled from many nations to provide medical care on the battlefields of the Spanish Republic's struggle against Franco's fascists, now

Juan Carlos could join medical colleagues to provide similar support for the Sandinistas. "I remember thinking when the Cuban government prohibited its citizens from going to Nicaragua in any capacity that the dictum didn't apply to me because I was an Argentine! And, as a physician, at last I could contribute something to a Latin American struggle against dictatorship that had a chance of succeeding." Soul-searching discussions with Silvia ensued. What about her and the children? What would happen if he were wounded? Or killed? Was this foolhardy adventurism or the realistic extension of the principles that had guided their adult lives? Finally they agreed that the liabilities were outweighed by the fact that Juan Carlos could be of real, concrete help in saving the lives of combatants fighting for a just cause. So it was decided that he would travel to Mexico, where he would be trained as an anesthesiologist before going on to Nicaragua.

Juan Carlos spent the four months leading up to the Sandinista triumph in a liberated zone in the north of Nicaragua; he lived and worked in an emergency hospital converted from a monastery and run by nuns sympathetic to the revolution. With little sleep and nothing but rice and beans to fuel his exhausted mind and body, he participated around the clock in seemingly endless emergency operations on wounded Sandinistas. "In spite of the fact that war was a grueling experience," Juan Carlos tells me, "I was thrilled to be a protagonist of history." After the Sandinista triumph and the countrywide celebration, which "was one of the most amazing events I've ever witnessed in my life," Juan Carlos worked for months as a pediatrician, directing the treatment of malnutrition and infectious diseases among Nicaraguan children in the north of the country and establishing parenting classes for their parents. Although the work gave him much pleasure, the separation from his family was painful. Explorations with Silvia about whether to move to Nicaragua resulted in the sober estimation that it would be unfair to uproot their children, now happily integrated into Cuban life. So Juan Carlos returned, somewhat reluctantly, to Havana, leaving the heady excitement of building a new society to the Nicaraguans and the thousands of other volunteers who had come from around the world to help. Before he departed, he made some initial contacts with the new Nicaraguan Ministry of Health that would facilitate the future work of Mimi and the Internationalist Team.

Once back in Cuba, Juan Carlos resumed his role at the center of exiled Argentine children. He supervised the work of the staff responsible for taking care of the children, including the weekly meetings of all personnel, from caregivers to janitors; these meetings dealt with the psychological and organizational aspects of the functioning of the center. The goal was to provide the children with a caring home environment—in British psychoanalyst [D. W.] Winnicott's terms, "a holding environment"—and to integrate them into Cuban society. One of the requirements was that the staff be divided equally between females and males so that the children would bond with both sexes. "It was rather like a kibbutz," recalls Juan Carlos. "We organized the program so that the very small children would be cared for by the same one or two adults, and the older ones by the adolescents in the community, much like an extended family. We were creating the model as we went along, and this pattern emerged spontaneously. The kids attended Cuban schools, and when they'd return in the afternoons, they would participate in other activities, including discussions about Argentina so they wouldn't lose their connection to their roots."

Juan Carlos was the project's chief therapist. He observed the children at play to determine which of them needed psychotherapeutic attention and then treated them at the hospital. Some of the children suffered from serious symptoms, and at times Juan Carlos had to begin treatment with children whose background—mother's and father's history, birth, infancy, traumatic event, and so on—he knew nothing about. He treated children who urinated and defecated all over themselves, who suffered panic attacks, who had psychosomatic conditions he had never before seen. Some were completely mute, and others stared into space, unresponsive to their environment. At times he was uncertain of appropriate diagnoses, and he often wondered whether he was observing symptoms of trauma or schizophrenia.

"It was very difficult to treat them, but the amazing thing was they improved very rapidly. Each one reminded me of a little dying plant that in response to sun and water begins to thrive. I was curious as to why they made such good progress, and I wrote to colleagues, including Maren Viñar, who were also treating children in exile with less positive results. I thought a good deal about how the social context interacts with individual psychology to determine the prognosis of mental health. I developed the hypothesis that an important factor was the different experience the children had in Cuba as opposed to France or other bourgeois environments. For example, the kids in other countries like France often lived with grandparents who were depressed, mourning the deaths of their children and thus unavailable emotionally to their grandchildren. In addition, the kids would learn the host country's language easily and would probably feel reluctant to bring their friends home, embarrassed by their grandparents, who spoke with accents, and fearful lest their political history and the reason for their exile be exposed. More likely than not, they would be ashamed of their parents' political activism because in Europe Latin American exiles were often demeaned and rejected, stereotyped as guerrillas, who were mistakenly equated with terrorists. Also, many children were being raised by reactionary grandparents who told them that their parents had been disappeared or killed because of their misguided politics, blaming them for their fate instead of the armed forces and warning their grandchildren that the same would happen to them if they became activists."

Juan Carlos believes that the Cuban political environment had a positive effect on the children living there. "In Cuba," he continues, "the exile children experienced an admiration among the Cubans for the ideals, if not the strategies, of their activist parents. Even more, their parents were considered fallen heroes in the struggle against right-wing authoritarian repression. They were respected. After all, they were like Che, who, let's not forget, was an Argentine. I concluded that this ideological coherence was an important factor in the improvement of the kids in Cuba because the environment encouraged rather than negated the children's positive identification with their lost parents and the struggle for which they had given their lives."

The children's residential program continued until 1983, when, with the return to democratic rule in Argentina, its organizers made the decision to locate the children's biological families for the purpose of reuniting them. Relatives began to come to Cuba to fetch the children, and at times the staff found it painful to relinquish them, especially when it was to grandparents or aunts and uncles who were insensitive or hostile to everything the children and their history represented. "I'll never forget a particularly difficult case," says Juan Carlos. "One child's grandparents who came from Buenos Aires to get him were wealthy industrialists who were extremely right wing. They met with me before seeing the child, and in the course of our chat told me a little of their story. They said that in the early seventies their daughter had become involved with a Montonero, who, they were convinced, had filled her innocent head with terrible ideas about social change. These people were very influential and had friends in the military. They told me how after the coup they had decided to reveal the whereabouts of their daughter's compañero to their military connections, hoping to rid her of his 'evil' influence. As a result, the military had pursued the daughter along with her compañero and assassinated them both, leaving their infant an orphan. It was to these grandparents that we had to give the child we had nurtured for years! In cases like this, we felt terrible because we had come to love these children. . . . They were like our own kids. We worried about the impact of relatives whose psychological ambivalence and ideological hostility toward these young people would likely trouble and confuse them, reversing the progress they'd made in dealing with the traumatic events of their early lives."

The work Juan Carlos did over the years in this unique children's project was an extension of his earlier socially conscious psychoanalytic praxis. It also gave him extensive firsthand experience with the psychological effects of political repression and exile, which he would utilize when he reestablished his practice in Buenos Aires.

When the Argentine military relinquished the government to civilian rule in 1983, the Volnoviches faced the possibility of going home. For almost a year and a half, they struggled with their conflicting feelings about returning to Argentina. "Now, with the military back in the barracks and a democratically elected president in power, how could we not return to our culture, our home?" Juan Carlos says. "We had been very happy in Cuba, although I, more than Silvia, missed Buenos Aires and my professional life there. We anguished about it, in terrible conflict. But finally we decided to return. The key factor had to do with the kids, who were now adolescents and actively resisting the idea of leaving their life and their friends in Cuba. We concluded that we had to leave while we still had the power to decide for them because we couldn't bear the idea of a future in which we would live apart from them in different countries."

Finally, in December 1984, the Volnoviches returned to Buenos Aires. There, like the Viñars in Montevideo, they discovered that the return was more painful than the departure had been and that their fantasies of the future had been based on frozen memories of the past. In fact, what they had nostalgically clung to during their years of exile no longer existed. Everything was different: Buenos Aires, the struggle, their friends who had survived, the hole left by those who had been killed or were still in exile, and even they themselves. Only by coming to grips with this reality and mourning the multiple losses it implied—including the life they had left in Cuba—were they able to create a new one of meaning and relevance for them and their children.

Nicaragua: June 1984

Over a week had gone by since our arrival in Nicaragua, and I was witnessing the invigorating effects on Mimi of her participation in the creation of a national mental health program within the context of revolution. Typical of her previous trips here, our days and nights had been filled with demanding work, punctuated by lengthy midday meals and late evening dinners with colleagues and friends from all over the world. Their energetic discussions ranged from the difficulties of realizing the long-range goals of their various projects to the Sandinistas' ability to survive under the U.S. economic and military assault. Although they were anxious about the future of Nicaragua, none could know at this moment that the Sandinista experiment would collapse within just six years, undermined by U.S. policy.

"You can see why I love it here," Mimi was saying to me as we gently swayed in our wooden rockers in the shaded central patio of the Internationalist House, where we were staying during our time in León. We were taking a late afternoon break, trying to escape the stifling summer heat. Outside the sun relentlessly baked the yellow-hued stone buildings and streets of colonial León, where the Internationalist Team had been working for the past week. As we chatted amid the verdant and lush plants that overran the colorfully tiled patio, we could see the kitchen and dining area, where the two cooks were preparing the evening meal for the dozens of volunteers—agronomists, physicians, social workers, artists, engineers, filmmakers—who had come from all over the world to assist the Sandinista Revolution. These *internacionalistas* lived in the maze of rooms lining the enormous square patio; each one contained a bed, a small bookcase, a portable radio, and boldly colored political posters. The modest accommodations of the Internationalist House were more than compensated for by the liveliness of the inhabitants, all of whom seemed delighted to be participating in the construction of a new society. Mimi looked quite content as she described what being in Nicaragua meant to her.

"You know," she reminded me, "it's been a year now since a democratic government replaced the military dictatorship in Argentina, and I could go back if I wanted to. Sometimes I miss my life there—family, friends, the special excitement of Buenos Aires. But I could never leave this work. It's the most important thing I could be doing, the most wonderful challenge of my life." She paused to sip her drink. I waited, rocking slightly in order to feel the air moving around me and thinking about how happy Mimi seemed. Then, as if revealing a precious secret, she confided, "I realized on my second trip to Nicaragua what the experience is for me. I realized that here I am not old nor young . . . I am atemporal . . . and I live it as if the Spanish Republic, the old Republic, had won, and I am collaborating in the reconstruction. It is . . . a continuity . . . and finally, and suddenly, I am there."

It was easy to see why Mimi felt this way. Nicaragua was fairly exploding with the energy of people engaged in projects they believed would develop the country and bring pleasure and productivity to their lives. It was a particularly interesting time in the brief history of the Revolution, for the country had adopted a new electoral law modeled on key components of the French, Italian, Austrian, and Swedish electoral systems, and its many political parties were engaged in a spirited campaign in anticipation of the elections in early November.[10] The optimism of the people was palpable. Everyone seemed on the move, their busy days filled with long hours of work, followed by political meetings of unions, the women's and youth movements, the revolutionary neighborhood committees, and the "popular" Church organizations.[11] "Compañero" was the familiar greeting used by everyone identified with the Revolution, indicating closeness and mutual respect for all who shared the values and goals of the difficult and exhilarating political process.

In truth, there was much to be done. When the Sandinistas ousted the repressive Somoza dictatorship on July 19, 1979, they inherited a country whose class and ethnic relations bore the weight of five centuries of colonial-ism and neocolonialism. In the fifty years leading up to the Revolution, Nica-ragua had been characterized by extreme economic inequities, brutal political repression, and subservience to U.S. geopolitical interests. The majority of its nearly three million inhabitants lived in abject poverty, with a per capita an-nual income of $897 and an illiteracy rate that reached 70 percent in some areas. Those conditions had inevitably produced a mass-based revolutionary movement whose goal was to overturn the structural inequalities in Nicara-guan society. When the Revolution triumphed, about 1.5 percent of the popu-lation had been killed, with an additional 110,000 disabled and almost 50,000 children orphaned. Crops had been ruined, and schools, hospitals, medical centers, and houses had been damaged or entirely destroyed. In response to these conditions, the Sandinistas designed a strategy to reconstruct the coun-try within the context of their Marxist conceptualization of the structural causes of underdevelopment. The model they chose was based on the prin-ciples of political pluralism, a mixed economy, and a nonaligned foreign policy.[12]

Although the Sandinistas represented the largest constituency in the country, minority parties to the left and right battled over their different points of view in the National Assembly, each pressuring the government to go faster or slower in the implementation of reforms. The private sector resented the new taxes that had been imposed by the Sandinistas in order to pay for the many social programs aimed at improving the health, education, work, and living conditions of the Nicaraguan people. The achievements were notable. By 1984, illiteracy had been reduced from 70 to 13 percent. Women were tak-ing part actively in political affairs, and in 1983 the high priority given to health won Nicaragua the World Health Organization's praise for the great-est achievement in health care by a third-world country.

Mimi was continually incensed by U.S. policy toward Nicaragua. "That cold warrior Reagan you have in the White House," she would say indignantly, "just can't bear it when a tiny country whose fate has been determined by the 'monster to the north' since the mid-nineteenth century finally says 'enough'—*basta! We* determine what goes on in our country!" Indeed, in spite of the po-litical democracy and economic reformism instituted by the Sandinistas, the United States had declared Nicaragua to be a communist threat in the West-ern Hemisphere. In order to avoid out-and-out invasion by U.S. forces, which the Pentagon believed would be unpopular with U.S. citizens, Reagan imple-mented an alternative strategy known as Low Intensity Conflict (LIC).[13] LIC was a combined psychological, economic, and military assault used against gov-ernments considered to be a threat to U.S. interests. Reagan sabotaged the Nicaraguan economy with an embargo that made traditionally imported goods scarce in the hope that the erosion of the Nicaraguan people's standard of living would alienate them from their government. The United States also organized and armed the Contras, Nicaraguan mercenaries led by the ex–National Guard who were attacking and destroying newly built rural schools, clinics, and agricultural cooperatives. The Contras killed and wounded not only soldiers but also hundreds of civilians, Nicaraguans and foreigners alike, in the process; the tortured and butchered bodies were purposely paraded in order to psychologically terrorize those who survived.[14] Behind the massive front door of the Internationalist House, for example, the entryway was covered with photographs of Pierre Grosjean, a French physician who had come to Nicaragua to study and treat mountain leprosy. Handwritten poems taped to the wall angrily decried the Contra forces' murder of Pierre in a nearby country village as he was participating in a vaccination campaign for the local inhabitants.

Hardly anyone escaped the emotional turmoil produced by the country's volatile conditions. Alongside the obvious exhilaration of many Nicaraguans actively involved in the Revolution's many social projects, there was also tension and conflict. In fact, when the Revolution triumphed, it inherited the psychological as well as the political and economic contradictions of a country ruled for over half a century by dictatorship. Thousands of adults and children suffered the traumatic sequelae of having lived under the terror and repression of Somoza's fearsome National Guard. And many were severely depressed in response to multiple losses of loved ones sustained during the revolutionary struggle. Traumatic neuroses and psychoses were commonplace, with symptoms that included listlessness, emotional withdrawal, anxiety, intellectual impairment, paranoia, and damaged self-esteem.

After the triumph, some of the more transient nervous disorders diminished, especially among activists whose participation in revolutionary reconstruction projects offered a form of psychological reparation because they were achieving the goals of those who had died. But the Revolution also exacerbated psychological problems because of the profound alteration it was stimulating in the traditionally hierarchical relations between the classes, sexes, and generations. For example, as Mimi had pointed out to me numerous times, "the Sandinista commitment to the struggle for women's equality is noteworthy, and feminists in North America and Europe are right to admire it. But we must remember that while change creates benefits, it . . . stimulates fears and anxieties as well. By challenging traditional male dominance in Nicaraguan culture, the Sandinista platform adds stress to the most intimate emotional relationships of the men and women whose collaboration with one another is needed in the difficult task of developing their country."

However, another characteristic of the Sandinista Revolution was its recognition of the importance of people's psychological health, and it set about to develop a national system of mental-health care for all Nicaraguans. At the time of the triumph there were only one psychiatric hospital, one medical school, twelve psychiatrists, thirty to forty psychologists, and one electroencephalograph machine in the entire country. The Sandinistas immediately initiated the construction of a number of health facilities and programs to train a new generation of mental-health professionals, social workers, nurses, and educational psychologists. The Ministry of Health (MINSA) endorsed a strategy of preventive care, which became available through a network of hospitals, community clinics, the newly established Centers for Psychosocial Attention, and the Sandinista mass organizations, such as the women's movement, the peasant unions, and the neighborhood committees. Putting psychology at the core of the revolutionary state's health policy was a strategy that Mimi and her colleagues heartily endorsed. According to MINSA, mental health is the product of a dialectical relationship among the biological, psychological, and social aspects of life, and psychology should therefore be a part of all the health services and should be taught as an aspect of all specialized training. This perspective was the theoretical basis for the Internationalist Team's collaboration in Nicaragua.

"We began our work," Mimi had explained to me, "when the dean of the León Medical School attended a conference in Mexico, where he heard us speak about our work in Argentina during the late sixties and early seventies. He was very excited by our approach to mental health and requested that we come to León to train and supervise physicians, psychiatrists, and students at the Medical School. We agreed, [but] since none of us could move to Nicaragua because of work and family responsibilities in Mexico, we devised this team effort, which permits us to come in twos and threes for ten days each month. All twelve of us meet every Monday evening in Mexico to provide continuity in our work. We started in 1981, under contract to the Nicaraguan National Autonomous University, the Mexican Metropolitan University, and the National Autonomous University of Mexico. We have developed projects at the psychiatric hospital and children's hospital in Managua and the university hospital in León. But since then we have also worked directly with MINSA and are involved in all kinds of mental-health projects." The Nicaraguan work was being financed partially by the Pan American Health Organization, and in addition Mimi raised funds through annual trips to Europe, where she reported on the Internationalist Team to enthusiastic audiences of progressive psychoanalysts willing to donate money to a project they believed had great social value.

From Mimi's perspective, the experience of the Internationalist Team in Nicaragua represented the first time in history that the Marxist and psychoanalytic dialogue transcended intellectual discourse to become a concrete praxis that was supported, rather than attacked, by the state. However, the complex and contradictory process of reconstructing a society under conditions of extreme poverty was challenging Mimi and her colleagues to reassess their political and psychoanalytic posture, which had been devised years earlier under different circumstances. They had less time to ponder questions related to the convergence of Marxist and psychoanalytic theory. Instead, they were absorbed in the thorny practical problem of how to adapt psychoanalysis to the conditions and urgent needs of a tiny, poor Central American country undergoing radical social transformation, with few resources and many competing priorities. As Mimi put it, "When we left [the Argentine Psychoanalytic Association], we defined ourselves as Marxists, Freudo-Marxists. I believe none of us now is fixed on that: we are much more pragmatic. For example, we ask about Nicaragua, 'How can one be useful to Nicaragua with certain psychoanalytic concepts?' We don't ask, 'Is Nicaragua Marxist, and how can we connect theoretically as Marxist psychoanalysts?' We are not interested in that kind of question, which has lost much of its appeal."[15]

As I saw during the many days of our stay in Nicaragua, Mimi and her colleagues in the Internationalist Team were interested in elaborating central concepts in psychoanalytic theory and technique that would provide the basis for training and treatment within the specific culture of Nicaragua, the limited economic conditions of underdevelopment, and the financial constraints of the revolutionary government. I had observed her in a variety of settings during the previous week in Managua as she taught classes to psychiatric residents, social workers, psychologists, and nurses. She was especially gifted as a teacher, one who could make the fascinating—but often fantastic-sounding—fundamentals of psychoanalytic thought accessible to students who were introduced to them for the first time. She told me during our stay in Nicaragua that the team was drawing up a list of the basic psychoanalytic concepts they believed to be essential to an understanding of how the mind works. These concepts provided the foundation of the psychoanalytic training of the Nicaraguans, who had to develop therapeutic modes feasible in their country, such as brief individual, group, and family treatment. "We call them our ten commandments," she joked, and added that she planned to write an article called "Psychoanalysis without the Couch" to elucidate the ideas.[16]

"Ten basic concepts?" I laughingly responded. "Well, just think about what you'd have to include," she told me, now serious. "We teach about the unconscious and how it may be demonstrated through interpretations of slips, dreams, fantasies, and delusions, and how even our ideology is partly unconscious. Then we elaborate how the human mind is characterized by conflict and how even while people fight for change, they are simultaneously frightened of it. We show how all symptoms have a primary and secondary benefit. It is also important to see that the mind is essentially contradictory and that, as Winnicott shows us, even the mother who loves her baby also hates it. We teach that the history and sexuality of our childhood are important because they are repeated in the present, mostly without our conscious awareness. The same is true for transference, in which we project internal representations of important early figures in our lives onto those in the present, distorting current relationships in the process. We think it is essential to teach about countertransference because every therapist should understand what he or she brings unconsciously to the therapeutic relationship. As we've always argued, no one is neutral. And finally, we believe it is very important, especially in a revolutionary situation like [that in] Nicaragua, to show how every individual has many aspects to his or her personality. Each of us is wonderful, but also a bit mad. Each loving, but also perverse. We are all heroes, but also cowards. And we need to accept rather than deny this so we can learn how to deal with conflict and fear. We also have to understand guilt and how to diminish it because guilt usually paralyzes people and doesn't serve as a good basis for commitment to anyone or anything."

I realized I was observing Mimi and Nacho practice what they preached. I was reminded of how they supervised two cotherapists doing group therapy in a community clinic in Managua the previous week. Both therapists believed that their patients all manifested the sequelae of the collective trauma of Nicaraguan life under the Somoza dictatorship. Mimi and Nacho painstakingly showed the Nicaraguan therapists how to pursue the unique meaning that each individual attributed to his or her traumatic symptoms and how it was related to early life experiences and constitutional endowment. They also emphasized the importance of intervening through interpretation rather than by using the directive approach favored by the Nicaraguans.

I recalled, as well, the supervision sessions in the psychiatric hospital in Managua during which Dora, an astute young social worker, presented a case to Mimi and Nacho. Their interpretations captured the essence of their psychoanalytic conceptualization of psychopathology and treatment interventions, as well as their appreciation of the centrality of the social context of individual mental illness and reparation. Mimi brought to her supervision of Dora her special interest in the role of women in Central American societies, which she had learned about through her treatment of Salvadoran and Guatemalan refugees in Mexico and through her friendships with some of the Sandinista Revolution's famous women leaders, such as Dora María Tellez.[17] She learned even more through her clinical interventions with female patients in Nicaragua who sought treatment for depression, anxiety, and psychosomatic illnesses. Here she observed the psychological manifestations of the problematic family

structure in Nicaragua, which was characterized historically by male abandonment. The widespread pattern of female-headed and female-centered households had produced contradictory patterns. As feminists from the United States
and Europe noted, this phenomenon had strengthened women by promoting
independence and self-sufficiency, enabling them to care for themselves and
their children as well as preparing them to participate in large numbers—and
in leadership positions—in the Revolution. But Nicaraguan women also felt
disempowered by the widespread practice among men of forming more than
one family—*la familia grande* and *la familia chica*—either simultaneously or se-
quentially. Consequently, many women harbored intense feelings of resentment toward men, the result of which was their tendency to form their closest
affective ties with their children, whose strivings for independence were often experienced by their mothers as a threat and were thus resisted. Mimi believed that the Revolution's support of women's rights would help women to
struggle together against these entrenched patterns, and she was glad to have
the opportunity to provide psychological treatment to female patients living
in a society whose government supported the fight against patriarchal structures and values.

Mimi listened to Dora's case presentation with this political context in
mind. Dora reported that her patient was a seventeen-year-old girl who had
become agoraphobic after suffering two psychotic episodes. Dora was treating
the patient, her mother, and her two married sisters in family therapy because
they all lived together along with the sisters' husbands and children. All three
daughters claimed to adore their dominating mother and viewed their family
as loving and conflict free. The father, who had another, common-law, wife,
and children with whom he currently lived, was participating in the therapy
sessions as well. The patient's older brother had been killed in battle by the
National Guard just prior to the triumph of the Revolution, but his death had
not been recognized by the community, which had chosen to rename its street
to honor another fallen combatant.

Mimi discussed the unconscious mechanisms at work in Dora's patient
and her family. She suggested that the patient's psychotic episodes might be
understood as the container for the otherwise denied aggression of the mother
and daughters. The married daughters' dependence on their mother had prevented them from establishing their own households, and they were unable
to express any aggressive feelings toward the mother, whose failure to maintain a relationship with her husband drove her to rely on her children for ful-
fillment of her emotional needs. The patient's symptoms, which kept her
regressively dependent on her mother, also unconsciously legitimized the
mother's overprotective hovering. In addition, the patient's agoraphobia, which
was sometimes reflected in the fear that her mother might be harmed if she

left her alone in the house, was a manifestation of her desire to protect her mother from her own unconscious aggression by never leaving her side. In addition, the patient's illness had succeeded in bringing the father home in order to participate in the treatment. Mimi indicated that the therapeutic work needed to address the mother's feelings toward her rejecting husband, the unconscious conflict between mother and daughters, and the guilt related in part to the unexpressed desire of the daughters to attain psychological independence. Mimi went on to demonstrate how the patient's symptoms should also be explored as a manifestation of frozen grief related to the death of her brother. "Your identified patient," she told Dora, "cannot go outside, but the rest of the family can't 'come outside' themselves to mourn their loss." Treatment for the family therefore would also have to encourage grieving for the dead brother.

Mimi was convinced that in a society where the state, political ideology, and mass organizations encourage people's involvement in social struggle to improve the quality and substance of their lives, psychologically disturbed individuals can benefit from political activism. Thus, an assessment of the social context was also a part of the suggested treatment plan. "We are lucky here in Nicaragua," Mimi reminded Dora, "for in addition to psychotherapy, this family can rely on political resources as well. We can encourage the patient, her mother, and her sisters to become involved with AMNLAE." Mimi was referring to the Association of Nicaraguan Women, the Sandinista mass organization that took a special interest in education, child care, family life, and employment of women, and that was spearheading the struggle for women's legal and political equality. AMNLAE had developed consciousness-raising groups for women, had successfully fought to require men who abandoned their children to pay child support, and had won passage of a new law that required both men and women to participate equally in household and child-rearing tasks. By becoming involved in the organization's many activities, both mother and daughters would have an opportunity to develop a new sense of autonomy and self-esteem through mutual, supportive relations with other women engaged in the social world outside the family.

Mimi also recommended to Dora that she think about the community resources for this family to help them deal with the problem of frozen grief. "This family has not yet experienced the community's recognition of the deceased brother, and their capacity to mourn him can be greatly helped through public acknowledgment of his death and his importance to the Revolution. The Neighborhood Committees for the Defense of the Revolution and the popular Church," she advised her supervisee, "can both be mobilized to provide community rituals that can facilitate private mourning."

Mimi and her colleagues, in fact, were working directly with the mass organizations in their primary prevention campaigns. One example was the Sandinista brigade program, through which individuals from different sectors of Nicaraguan society were organized and trained in specific health and mental-health projects. The brigade workers—*brigadistas*—were referred to as the multipliers—*multiplicadores*—because they worked among the people of their sector, providing services such as vaccinations against infectious diseases, education in sanitation, instruction in mother and infant health care, and therapeutic intervention for psychological problems. The Internationalist Team taught the *brigadistas* basic principles of how to help individuals experiencing emotional difficulties. The *brigadistas* became involved with specific psychological issues and brought people together in groups to share common problems. They were involved, for example, in establishing such groups for mothers whose children were fighting in the war against the Contras and who needed a chance to share their anxieties and fears. The *brigadistas* also organized people who were working two and three jobs to replace those who had gone to the front to fight. Many were under extreme stress and were burned out—*fundidos*—with symptoms that included headaches, hypertension, alcoholism, insomnia, anxiety attacks, and family distress. The *brigadistas* were trained to help them in simple ways by providing them the chance to participate in group discussions and relaxation classes. *Brigadistas* were also trained to recognize individuals who might be suffering from trauma and to offer them the opportunity to speak about their feelings in an emotionally safe environment.

While we had been in Managua, Mimi and Nacho met with psychologists who worked with *brigadistas* in the squatter settlements around Managua. The target population in this project were recently transplanted peasants from the Nicaraguan countryside and refugees from El Salvador, mainly women and children, whose flight from the civil war raging in their country had separated them from husbands and fathers who had either been disappeared or killed by the military or who were fighting with the revolutionary opposition, their fate unknown.

The psychologists' specific task was to train *brigadistas* to recognize the psychodynamics of persons suffering from frozen grief. They studied this phenomenon with the Internationalist Team and helped the *brigadistas* design comic books that taught their cohorts how to detect the symptoms characteristic of people whose functioning was impaired by their inability to mourn. The comic books demonstrated basic techniques the *brigadistas* could employ to encourage such individuals to express their feelings and to gradually feel less isolated and more connected to their current situation and social relations. The psychologists proudly showed Mimi and Nacho a sample of their instructional comic books and related a poignant story about how a *brigadista*'s interventions with several depressed Salvadoran mothers had resulted in their becoming more psychologically available to their small children and actively involved in their new community in Nicaragua. As I was listening to their discussion, I began to leaf through the comic book; my attention was caught by a frame in which the animated character representing the *brigadista* suggests to the depressed peasant he is trying to help, "I understand, compañero; it's O.K., you may cry without feeling embarrassed. I want to hear your story; I understand, for I, too, have lost people I love. I will listen as long as you need me to." In the next frame, the peasant begins to weep, and the *brigadista* gently touches his shoulder, patiently waiting. Such compassion, I thought, such humanity.

"Here in León," Mimi was saying, and her words brought me back to the present, "the most fascinating experiment is the university medical school's work-study program. I think it is a brilliant approach to training future physicians in a holistic approach to illness. I wish medical training programs everywhere would incorporate it." She smiled as she recollected the morning's lengthy meeting with the university medical school's staff and how they had planned the Internationalist Team's psychological component for the third and fourth year of medical school. The work-study model was a revolutionary challenge to traditional medical training models in that it focused on a specific theme each year—physician attitudes toward patients in the first year, school-aged children's needs in the second year, contagious diseases in the third year, and mother and child health in the fourth year—and involved students in a variety of research and collaborative activities in the community so as to familiarize them with the social context of physical disease. "The students learn about the psychological dimension of each year's focus through our classes," Mimi told me, "and then their internships take them out into community organizations and schools for practical experience directly related to the psychosocial theory we teach them."

Our discussion reminded me of the previous afternoon's seminar with pediatricians, in which Mimi and Nacho had spoken about the psychological dimension of the doctor-patient relationship. They had described the transference that occurs in the child's relationship to the physician and how as it shifts in the various developmental stages from infancy through adolescence, the physician needs to use different techniques to interact successfully with both child and parents. They had also encouraged the pediatricians to explore their own psychological motivations for their professional choice, as well as their feelings about their work, both of which were important resources in managing their emotional reactions to patients. They suggested techniques for organizing small group discussions that would provide them with mutual support as they handled the pressures of their profession.

As I observed Mimi working in the different programs the Internationalist

Team was developing in Nicaragua, I could not help but be struck by her boundless energy and buoyant spirits. The tiny Central American country's revolution did seem to be the perfect environment in which this Viennese-Argentine analyst could integrate her politics and professional expertise. Mimi was passionately committed to Nicaragua, and I was slowly realizing that her dedication emerged from a mature assessment of what is possible rather than a naively romantic sentimentality. As a Marxist, she deeply believed in the need to create social structures that nourish all human beings in an environment of equality and justice, and for that reason she was angered by U.S. efforts to overturn the Sandinista government. As a psychoanalyst, she understood that even human beings committed to the most revolutionary goals might fail to achieve them for psychological reasons, and so she was not disillusioned when the Sandinista leadership or its followers manifested personal or political limitations or contradictions. "If I am asked what psychoanalysis is for, beyond transforming symptoms, I always say 'in order not to lie to oneself any more,'" she said. "If I go to Nicaragua I think I am not lying to myself, although I know of the existing contradictions. I try to weigh things up and say, despite the contradictions, that I am in favor of the Sandinista Revolution, because the positive far outweighs the negative."[18]

Sitting together in the momentary tranquillity of that late afternoon in León, neither one of us was thinking about the future. We did not yet know that in several years Mimi would be diagnosed with inoperable cancer. But some time earlier in Mexico when we had spoken about aging and death, Mimi had told me, "I don't want to die without meaning; I want to live until the end. So when the dangers of the Nicaraguan work become undeniable, . . . [I think about how] there is an important difference between a worthwhile death and one that has no value. . . . I believe this very much, and I believe that my life has been worthwhile, within my own limits."

Mimi often referred to her favorite poem, written by Turkish revolutionary Nazim Hikmet, whose passionate verses, many of them written in prison, made him one of the great international poets of this century. She quoted the poem in her contribution to *Cuestionamos II*, "Woman: Her Limitations and Potential," and it brilliantly captures her own attitude of engagement in the world:

> —"Oh, to be able to go to sleep now
> And to awake within a hundred years, beloved . . . "
> No, my love, not that; I am not a deserter.
> My century does not frighten me.
> My miserable, scandalous century,
> My spirited, great, heroic century.

> I never complained of being born too soon.
> I am of the twentieth century. I feel proud of this.
> I am happy to be where I am:
> In the midst of our people
> And fighting for a better world . . .
> —"To be a hundred years from now, my love . . . "
> —No: much sooner than that and in spite of it all.
> My agonizing and renascent century,
> My century, whose last days will be beautiful,
> This terrible night that crushes the shrieks of dawn,
> My century will be ablaze with the sun, my love,
> The same as your eyes.[19]

Mimi Langer's life was, indeed, of this century, and she lived intensely and with meaning until the end. Unlike the Viñars and the Volnoviches, she decided not to return from exile. She opted to remain in Mexico because of her gratifying work with the Sandinista Revolution. In the three years following our trip to Nicaragua, Mimi continued in her role as the co-coordinator of the Internationalist Team. She returned to Nicaragua many times and traveled to Europe to raise money and counteract the disinformation campaign against the Revolution. As she continued the work that gave value to her life, by 1986 she was also battling the cancer that was consuming her. Experimental cancer treatments gave intermittent hope to family, friends, colleagues, and compañeros who found it painfully difficult to contemplate the world without her. When she and I were together, our discussions revealed the shifts between her desire to live and her rational acceptance of death.

Finally, in the fall of 1987, Mimi returned to Buenos Aires to live out her life in the home that she had been forced to flee thirteen years earlier. Just before she left Mexico, she received an invitation to participate in a conference, "The Driving Out of Reason and Its Return," organized by the Austrian government to honor prominent figures in the arts and sciences who had been forced to leave the country after the Anschluss in 1938. Mimi was saddened that she could not attend, but she was now too ill to travel. Her letter expressing her regret to the organizers was read publicly to the participants in the conference, who responded with an ovation acknowledging her contributions to psychoanalysis and human rights.

Once again in Buenos Aires, Mimi was in the familiar environment of her home, now also occupied by her older son and his family. Although in an increasingly weakened state, she stubbornly resisted her doctors' orders to rest. In the final several months of her life, she welcomed her many friends and colleagues who came to visit and even agreed to be interviewed at length on film by several members of the Internationalist Team about her work in

Nicaragua. Although exhausting, this was a precious opportunity, on the brink of her death, to achieve continuity with the values by which she had lived her life. On December 22, 1987, Mimi Langer died at home, surrounded by her family. To the end, she was an active participant in history.

Memorials took place in Argentina, Mexico, and Nicaragua, honoring Mimi's contributions to psychoanalysis and Latin American social struggles. She would have been especially moved to know that her compañeros renamed themselves the Marie Langer Internationalist Team of Mental Health Workers.[20]

WHEN EXILE ENDED for our other protagonists, liberation psychology in the Southern Cone was to face new challenges. For those who returned from abroad as well as for those who lived through the dictatorships in internal exile, the new democratic regimes would come to represent the most recent chapter in the Latin American story of oppression and struggle. Popularly elected presidents in Argentina, Chile, and Uruguay would negotiate the re-integration of former military violators of human rights into civil society and become the overseers of ever-deepening economic crises and social violence arising from the growing gap between the haves and the have-nots. Our protagonists would become actively engaged in human rights struggles, whose aim would be to address the psychological legacy of the culture of fear and to posit a politics aimed at individual and social reparation.

Chapter 6

Democracy and Social Violence

*I live with a circumstantial pessimism
and a fundamental historical optimism.*

—DIANA KORDON

THE THIRD-FLOOR office of the Grandmothers of the Plaza de Mayo is a converted apartment that fronts the busy Avenida Corrientes in the commercial
center of Buenos Aires. The drone of the congested traffic below provides a
steady acoustic background to the sounds of women answering telephones, typ-
ing letters, and organizing an upcoming event of solidarity with the Haitian
people. The walls of the rooms are covered with large photographs, colorful
artwork, and posters from human rights groups from all over the world. They
are visual testimonies to the valiant struggle the Grandmothers have waged
since the late 1970s to locate their grandchildren, who were forcibly disappeared by the military during Argentina's Dirty War. I am here with Estela
Carlotto, a retired primary-school teacher, and Rosa Roisinblit, a retired ob-
stetrician. They are the president and vice-president, respectively, of the organization, and they have been telling me their personal histories and how,
seventeen long years ago, they came to be activists in the opposition to state
terror.

It is impossible not to be impressed by these women, whose age and tragic
histories are hidden by their contagious vitality and sense of purpose. They
both emanate the intelligence and determination that have molded their emotional pain into an effective activism on behalf of human rights. Estela's com-
posure and attractive elegance are complemented by Rosa's intensity and ironic
expressiveness. But their stories are similar: each experienced the trauma of
having had her pregnant daughter forcibly disappeared and assassinated after
giving birth and her newborn grandchild appropriated by the Argentine armed
forces. Both grandmothers have spent years using all legal and scientific means
at their disposal to try to locate their disappeared grandchildren. Neither has

yet been successful, but because of the efforts of their organization, more than fifty of the estimated four hundred babies who suffered similar fates have been located and returned to their legitimate families.

As we pause for several minutes to have a *café*, we reminisce about the human rights conference the Grandmothers had organized several years earlier.[1] Estela comments appreciatively about the presentations of the psychologists, who had described their work with the restituted (reunited) children and their biological families. She feels they helped the public to become aware of the complex psychological issues involved in this unique situation, especially the impact on the children of learning the truth about their history and about the families with whom they grew up. As she speaks, I recall the several psychoanalysts who had elaborated the idea of trauma and its different meanings in the particular situation in which children have been disappeared and located years later by their families of origin. They had distinguished between the nature and meaning of two different traumas: the first was the "destructive original trauma" suffered by the children when they were stolen (right after birth or as small infants or toddlers) and raised on the basis of a family secret (lies they were told about their origins by their appropriators, who were often the assassins of their biological parents); the second was the "reconstructive trauma," an inevitable aspect of the revelation of the truth about their origins and their abductor "parents," but nevertheless the kind of traumatic experience that facilitates the psychic and social reconstruction of one's existence and provides the foundation for an identity and life based on the truth.[2] I tell Estela and Rosa that I vividly remember the moving final plenary session, when many of the restituted grandchildren came up on the stage with flowers to embrace each of the Grandmothers present. One boy read a poem to the audience describing how much they love these women, whose collective struggle had given them back their true identity; all of them have become these children's grandmothers. Estela and Rosa smile. "Yes," they say, "these are the gratifying results of our hard work."

As we resume our interview, I ask each woman to describe how she became involved with the Grandmothers organization. Estela begins, "I had been searching in vain for some concrete clue about my daughter Laura's whereabouts after she disappeared. I had even gone to the hierarchy of the Church and the generals to plead for her life, but with no results. We knew what was happening to the *desaparecidos*, how they were being tortured and how the military then put their unconscious bodies in bags to haul them off, murder them, and dispose of the remains. We had no idea what was happening to Laura, whether they were torturing her or whether they had already killed her. The uncertainty and sense of impotence, with nothing concrete to do, and the terror of what might happen to the rest of us—my husband and three other children—were unbearable. Then I learned about the Grandmothers, and in July 1978 I began to go to their meetings. This was a crucial turning point for me, the chance to feel part of a group. The women were very warm and open, and they had many creative ideas."

Although the circumstances of her daughter's disappearance were different, Rosa's frustration was similar to Estela's. "In my case, I actually received a phone call shortly after Patricia's disappearance in October of 1978 from someone who told me that they had my son-in-law and my pregnant daughter. He told me that I should prepare for the arrival of my grandchild, whom he claimed they would deliver to me after its birth within the month. He said they would be in touch and hung up before I could ask any questions. Do you know what psychological torture is? She was my only child. I waited by the phone, but there were no more calls. Six months passed, and nothing. When the baby would have been one year old, still nothing. That's how it's been to this day. I went everywhere, inquired every place I could. Finally, in 1979, the Permanent Human Rights Assembly put me in touch with the Grandmothers of the Plaza de Mayo. When I began to work with them, I felt an enormous solidarity, even though each of us had a different life experience. We were from different social classes and had various levels of education. But, despite differences of religion, politics, and skin color, our great pain united us."

I asked how they had mobilized their courage to participate in the Thursday afternoon marches in the Plaza de Mayo with the Mothers and Grandmothers, especially in the beginning, when the repression was indiscriminate and the military's reaction to the women's open challenge to its policies was unpredictable. "I've always been afraid," responds Rosa immediately, "but my love for my daughter and my grandchild was greater." Estela nods in agreement, looks contemplative, and then says, "You know, it's complicated. I was always frightened, even in the years before the coup, when there was all that political activism on the part of the young people. Laura and my younger daughter, Claudia, began to be politically active in high school, and they continued at the university. I respected them and their friends for their earnest preoccupation with social issues. I saw that they were a generation with great maturity and social commitment. They would come to my home to make the huge banners for their demonstrations. But intermingled with their serious political activism was an enormous capacity to have fun, to fall in love, to dance, to play music. I witnessed this, and I admired them for it. But that doesn't mean that my husband and I weren't scared for them. I was anxious even before the military took over the government, but afterward, and especially after Laura disappeared, I was always terrified, even while I was actively engaged in trying to find her. The first time I went with the Grandmothers to a Thursday afternoon march in the Plaza de Mayo, I was scared to death.

Two of the women saw this and surrounded me protectively, assuring me we'd be okay. I was horrified by the machine guns, the tanks, the sudden routings by the military. But slowly, in the activism itself, I began to transcend my fears. All that I hadn't done before because of my fear I could now do for love."

As I listen, I think about how the Mothers and Grandmothers were the first organizations to actively resist the culture of fear in Argentina. I remember as well that other individuals and groups eventually emerged to protest all aspects of the terrorist state's economic and social policies. At some point, in each of the Southern Cone dictatorships, people like Estela and Rosa found a collective voice to demand that the military relinquish its hold on the government and return to the barracks.

The Undoing of State Terror

It is difficult to pinpoint the precise moment when the tables turned on those whose arbitrary rule seemed absolute. In the three Southern Cone nations, various factors were at work by the early 1980s, moving them inexorably back to constitutional rule. International pressures, internal rifts among the armed forces, and the strength of an opposition bent on reasserting a democratic alternative were some. The specific political and cultural history of each country affected the tempo and character of the return to constitutional rule. While in Chile and Uruguay the transition to democracy was protracted and tightly controlled by the military leaders, in Argentina the military regime literally collapsed under the weight of its extraordinary corruption and humiliating defeat in a military confrontation with Great Britain over the long-disputed Malvinas/Falklands Islands.

The devastating results of neoliberalism, the free-market economic project sponsored by the armed forces, provided the important context for political change in all three nations. By the early 1980s, each country was characterized by high rates of unemployment, the reduction and impoverishment of the industrial working classes and their labor movement, the pauperization of the peasantry and rural working classes, the downward mobility of the middle classes, and the displacement of the industrial sector by the speculative finance sector within the ruling elite. By the time the military exited, the quality of life of the majority of people had painfully deteriorated. For example, in Argentina, by the end of the dictatorship, real wages were 50 percent of their pre-coup levels. Economic development, which had been touted as the purpose of the free-market economic policy, proved elusive. Although high interest rates had attracted foreign capital, it had gone directly to short-term deposits rather than fixed investment, resulting in a process of deindustrialization. The military accrued an astounding foreign debt that increased from nineteen billion to thirty-nine billion dollars in the three years before it was ousted from power, saddling future generations with repaying money that had gone into the speculators' pockets.

In Uruguay, during the military dictatorship the gross national product had begun rising at an impressive rate of 5 percent per year, but the devastating social cost was reflected in the high rates of emigration of the educated and skilled; a 28 percent decline in real salaries; an unprecedented concentration of wealth, while at the same time 240,000 children—nearly a tenth of the country's population—lived below the poverty line; and a growing pattern of foreign domination in the economy as reflected in the banking sector, where twenty of Uruguay's twenty-two private banks fell under foreign, multinational ownership. The military increased Uruguay's foreign debt from a half billion to five billion dollars, imposing on its citizens interest payments on money that had been transferred out of the country by domestic and foreign speculators.

Along the same lines, Chile's combination of neoliberal economic policy and repression of dissent ended its reputation for being one of Latin America's most equitable societies. Average wages in 1989 were 8 percent lower than they had been during the Allende years. The number of people living in poverty had risen from 20 to 40 percent of the population, while the wealthiest 20 percent increased their share of total consumption from 45 percent in 1969 to 60 percent in 1989. The dictatorship's cut in per capita social spending by a fifth during its rule only exacerbated the deprivation of the majority of Chileans.[3]

When protests against the economic and social impact of state terror emerged in each nation, the participants included the human rights communities, labor unions, democratic political parties, grass-roots community organizations, activist intellectuals, and individuals from all social sectors. Tato Pavlovsky recalls this transitional period well. He returned to Buenos Aires from exile in 1981 and realized that the consensus imposed by the culture of fear was beginning to be challenged. He felt more free to speak out and even began to publish articles critical of Argentina's authoritarian environment. "At the time I returned, it seemed as if there were two Argentinas. In one people manifested a fascist mentality, a kind of subjective complicity: 'there's nothing problematic happening here.' But there was also another Argentina, full of very courageous people who had stayed here. Many whom I had known happily welcomed me back, overjoyed to be together again, to struggle side by side, with an intense fervor to do something worthwhile." Tato and his friends were not alone.

Indeed, even the alliance of forces that had supported the military was straining under the weight of economic crisis, which was producing growing disaffection among hard-hit industrialists and middle-class professionals. The working class was mounting an increasingly militant protest movement, successfully organizing a number of general strikes from 1979 on. In 1981, one and a half million workers participated in a general strike in Buenos Aires, while fifty thousand white- and blue-collar workers took part in a demonstration demanding "Peace, Bread, and Work." The human rights issue was now being taken up by sectors beyond the human rights organizations and was being articulated by the Church, political parties, and the General Confederation of Labor. In October 1981, Argentine human rights activist Adolfo Pérez Esquivel was awarded the Nobel Peace Prize (Mothers of the Plaza de Mayo was also nominated), and as a result the military junta found it increasingly difficult to cover up its terroristic assault on the Argentine people. Popular sectors mobilized to protest higher local taxes; the destitute organized Neighbors' Commissions to occupy vacant lots and to establish new communities; and housewives rebelled against the high cost of living by beginning the Buenos Aires Housewives' Movement, which organized Thursday shopping boycotts. The "war against prices" was soon mirrored in similar movements around the country.

In the face of mounting opposition, the junta initiated a dialogue on a transition to constitutional government. Its ill-fated attempt to rally nationalistic support behind its war with the British over the long-contested Malvinas Islands proved to be its undoing. An ignominious defeat on the battlefield and the senseless death of hundreds of Argentine youths exposed the armed forces' inability to implement effectively any military strategy other than the repression of their own people. Seeing the writing on the wall, the military acceded to democratic elections, and on October 30, 1983, eminent human rights activist Raul Alfonsín was elected president by the Argentine people. He began his presidency by announcing the organization of an unprecedented government investigation into the human rights violations of the three military juntas that had ruled Argentina since 1976.

In Uruguay, the opposition to the generals was launched in 1981 with the establishment of a Montevideo branch of the human rights organization of Argentine Nobel Peace Prize recipient Pérez Esquivel. Its director, Jesuit priest Luis Pérez Aguirre, went to work on behalf of the victims of torture and poverty, and his group's unusual tactics, including hunger strikes, drew attention from a still-timid opposition press. More open defiance was demonstrated when housewives in Montevideo organized a *cacerola*, smashing their pots and pans together and chanting their protest in their darkened backyards against the lamentable state of affairs in their country. As Marcelo Viñar's friend, imprisoned playwright Mauricio Rosencof, put it when he referred to the Uruguayan people's growing ability to resist the military government,

"None of us, however alone we may be, is ever really alone. And in the most extreme situations, we are saved by our human condition, the cornerstone of which is not a particular ideology but rather a sense of solidarity: the strength of character which prevents us from transferring the weight of the crosses we bear to the shoulders of our brothers and sisters. That notion is common to Christians, Marxists, atheists, and Buddhists precisely because it lies at the heart of our shared humanity."[4]

In 1983, the solidarity to which Rosencof referred became apparent on November 27, Uruguay's traditional election day, when over three hundred thousand people gathered together in a central plaza in Montevideo to demand the ouster of the military from government. By January 1984, the union movement had resuscitated itself enough to carry off a general strike. Faced with a disastrous economy and growing public protest, the military began to consider a withdrawal strategy, one that would guarantee their continued influence after the return of constitutional government. Their behind-the-scenes negotiations with the major figures in Uruguay's two traditional parties made the military feel secure enough to permit presidential and legislative elections in November 1984. Their man, Colorado Party candidate Julio María Sanguinetti, won the presidency, but the fact that the progressive left coalition, the Frente Amplio, lost the Montevideo mayoralty—the second most important elective office in the country—by only a slim margin must have given them pause. When Sanguinetti took office the following March, his first act as Uruguay's president was to sign a bill giving amnesty to all remaining political prisoners. But several years later, in spite of widespread demands for the prosecution of the torturers, the ruling party proposed and passed a blanket amnesty for the military.

Chile's military dictatorship endured longer than its counterparts in Argentina and Uruguay, in part because in Chile almost two decades earlier Marxist parties had successfully been transformed from an opposition movement to the legitimately elected government. Dictator Pinochet was determined to eliminate the legacy of popular empowerment in Chile and any possibility that the country would ever repeat the challenge to free-market economics that the Allende period represented.

During the early years of extreme repression, a sector within the Catholic Church provided an important source of opposition to state terror. The Vicary of Solidarity (Vicaría de la Solidaridad) was organized to dispense medical, legal, and economic aid to victims of military repression. Under the auspices of the Vicary, Elizabeth Lira and other mental-health professionals were first able to offer psychological treatment to victims as well. During the late 1970s, the Vicary was joined by other human rights groups, such as the Association of Relatives of the Disappeared and the Chilean Human Rights

Organization, and by intellectuals and political parties of the opposition in publicly criticizing the dictatorship. In 1982, after several years during which human rights abuses declined, widespread unrest broke out among workers, students, middle-class professionals, housewives, and shantytown dwellers in response to a dramatic economic crisis that caused the formal unemployment rate to escalate to 36 percent (and an astounding 70 percent among youth). Eager to prevent the opposition from achieving organizational unity, the military implemented a state of siege and launched a new wave of repression.

Although the Pinochet regime continued intact, these collective struggles permitted thousands of people to emerge from their isolation and to share together their personal responses to years of living in the culture of fear. Elizabeth studied the salutary psychological effects of group experience on the individual capacity to resist authoritarian rule. In *Psicología de la amenaza política y del miedo* (The Psychology of Political Threat and Fear), a book she coauthored with María Isabel Castillo, Elizabeth writes that the "deprivatization" of feelings of terror facilitates the recuperation of subjectivity, by which she means the transition from passive victimization to individual autonomy and the ability to confront the private and social impact of the culture of fear. "Making visible what had been hidden and covert," she asserts, "meant that the Chilean people could collectively search for a solution."[5]

In fact, growing resistance to the military's hard line after a decade and a half provoked the Chilean right and the United States to worry that the conditions might be ripe for all-out revolution. By 1988, this concern, plus a flagging economy that desperately needed loans from the International Monetary Fund and World Bank, now more favorably disposed toward constitutional rather than authoritarian regimes, combined to pressure Pinochet to agree to a democratization process.[6] The first step was a plebiscite to determine whether the dictator would continue in power. The military government's "Yes" campaign proved to be no match for the spirited opposition, whose feverish campaigning culminated in a March of Happiness, which started from opposite ends of the country and included more than fifty mass meetings before its climax in a huge demonstration in the capital city of Santiago. The "No" campaign's most colorful innovation came the weekend before the election, when a yellow ribbon was tied around the entire city of Santiago and its four million inhabitants. The Chilean people responded in the plebiscite with a resounding "no" to Pinochet, which led one year later to the country's first democratic elections in sixteen years. On December 14, 1989, millions of Chileans chose the opposition's coalition candidate, Christian Democrat Patricio Aylwin, as their new president. When Aylwin was inaugurated as the chief executive in early 1990, he was obliged to share real political power in his country's fragile democracy with a parliament that was dominated by right-wing parties and that contained six senators appointed by Pinochet, who continued as commander-in-chief of an armed forces that would remain one of the major players in Chilean politics.

Liberation Psychology and Human Rights

In each of the three countries, successful democratic elections produced a momentary euphoria. But after the celebrations were over—the joy, the dancing in the streets, the mutual congratulations for a job well done—the people of the Southern Cone settled down to deal with the legacy of the terrorist state. A focal point of the struggle to heal the open wounds still festering with impotent rage and unresolved grief centered on the widespread wish to legally indict the torturers for their human rights abuses. But in each country, when the armed forces had begun to negotiate a return to democratic rule, they had made it amply clear that they would oppose any judicial investigation of their actions, which they maintained had been justified because their nations had been in a state of war. Now, in response to the outcry for human rights tribunals, the armed forces let it be known that the sabers would rattle from the barracks, threatening a return to the past, should civil society embark on such a foolhardy undertaking.

The conflict between those who advocated bringing the military to justice and those who wanted to leave the human rights issue behind was articulated as a confrontation between the advocates of forgetting about the past—*olvido*—and the proponents of remembering and understanding it—*memoria*. The proponents of liberation psychology became articulate critics of the dangers of individual and social amnesia. Along with a commitment to utilizing their psychological expertise to treat the individuals and families affected by state terror, they set about the task of elaborating a psychopolitical understanding of what had happened in the Southern Cone and what could be done about it. This elaboration took place during the years of the struggles against amnesty for the prior military rulers.

As Alfonsín assumed the presidency in Argentina, the Mothers and Grandmothers of the Plaza de Mayo and other human rights organizations demanded that a bicameral parliamentary commission be established to subpoena all military officers implicated in human rights abuses. But Alfonsín was concerned about a direct confrontation with the military and instead appointed the National Commission on Disappeared People (CONADEP), answerable to himself, which would be empowered to take voluntary testimonies from those affected by military human rights abuses. The Mothers and Grandmothers protested this approach, which they argued would "investigate the victims, not the criminals." CONADEP's work, which focused on the collection of thousands of declarations from those directly affected by state terror, had a paradoxical impact on Argentine society. Although the effort duplicated much of what had already been done by the human rights organizations, the Mothers and Grandmothers recognized its positive value. Its widely publicized, detailed, and agonizing testimonies brought the reality of state terror to those who had previously not known or had not wanted to know about it. Its findings were published as *Nunca más* (Never Again), which was the most widely read book by Argentines in 1984.

But the Mothers criticized CONADEP's analysis in *Nunca más* because of its portrayal of the disappearances in Argentina as the result of a conflict between two evils—*dos demonios*—the left and the right, a posture that essentially blamed the victims of state terror as well as its perpetrators. The Mothers also pointed out that although the horrors had been described, no solutions had been offered, a critique that was shared by Diana Kordon and Lucila Edelman. As the two members of the Equipo put it, the thousands of CONADEP public testimonies, detailing the abductions, the rapes, the tortures, were like "a horror show" in which "an excess of information was presented out of context, without an elaboration of the reasons for the repression or its goal." Thus, the information was not offered in a way that could help people understand the nature of what had occurred; they could only react emotionally or, at best, experience a catharsis. "In general," they argued, "the saturation of overwhelmingly disturbing information made it difficult for people to think about the issue; on the contrary, it provoked the psychic necessity to escape and 'think of other things.'" Diana and Lucila also criticized the mass media. During the Dirty War, the media had stereotyped the Mothers as hysterical and irrational women, dubbing them "the crazy women—*las locas*—of the Plaza de Mayo." Now they continued to psychologize the Mothers' struggle by accusing them of being overly emotional and making "extremist" demands for an accounting of the military that would threaten the newly established democracy. "Thus the victims of the repressive dictatorship," asserted Diana and Lucila, "yesterday's '*locas*,' later became the 'destabilizers' of the new constitutional government."[7]

Meanwhile, as the political struggle between the forces arrayed for and against prosecuting the military continued, the Argentine people were dealing with other aspects of the legacy of state terror. It was becoming clear that although participation in political movements against the military had had a regenerative effect that for a time returned to people a sense of agency and integrity, deep inside them lived the debilitating sequelae of the culture of fear. Wounds needed attending to, and the shattering of social bonds weighed heavily on them.

Many people were experiencing the complex emotional journey of return:

they came back from exile abroad, they emerged from internal exile (inxile), or they were released from prison. The reencounter of these three groups often generated a new kind of anguish. Each group expected a return to life as before. Such fantasies were dashed as they confronted the real changes in everybody and everything. But worse, the mutual hostility was palpable. Each group believed they had suffered the most or that the others had abandoned or betrayed them. Those who had stayed viewed with resentment those who had left, envious of their flight to safety and what they viewed as their self-serving accomplishments abroad. Those who had left were suspicious of those who had stayed, as if they must have colluded with the dictatorship in order to survive. Those who had been imprisoned were suspected of compromising themselves and their compañeros in order to still be alive when others were not. Marcelo and Maren Viñar noted the same phenomenon in Uruguay in their book *Fracturas de memoria.* "Between those who suffered torture and exile—interior and exterior," they wrote, "the dialogue has been difficult or impossible to resume, and instead of capitalizing on the rich diversity of experience, insults prevail, and difference is condemned. Our hypothesis . . . is that when extreme violence is endured, but not symbolized [elaborated consciously, making a psychological working-through possible], it results in the internalization of the aggressor's ways of operating, which reinforces the system of exclusion imposed by the dictatorship."[8]

For Juan Carlos Volnovich, the return was deeply painful because "we weren't the same; Argentina wasn't the same. Many of our friends weren't here, some because they were dead and others because they were in exile. Still others, with whom we'd shared our ideals and commitments, were no longer as we'd remembered them. Some had even taken up the Alfonsín position that the Dirty War had been caused by a confrontation between two demons, the guerrillas and the military, both with equal responsibility for the repression, and to us this represented a refusal to point the finger at the armed forces, the real culprits of state terror. I felt out of sorts. It was a very sad experience." This political disillusionment was compounded by the practical difficulties of repatriation, and Juan Carlos and Silvia, like thousands of other returnees, lived through a period of economic duress as they reconstituted their lives. They struggled with uncooperative bureaucracies to assure that their children could continue in school without losing credit for their education in exile. Meanwhile, Juan Carlos reactivated the network of colleagues who could help him reestablish a private practice. "I received invitations to give talks in hospitals and to supervise residents, and then I began to get referrals for my practice. I never joined any professional organizations or educational institutions because I preferred to keep myself apart and create my own space." Over time Juan Carlos acquired a high profile in the professional and academic communities and also became a familiar voice in the mass media, where he was repeatedly interviewed about the psychological impact of diverse social and political developments in the country.

New intellectual opportunities presented themselves as well when Juan Carlos and Silvia began to explore the feminist scholarship that was emerging within U.S. and European psychoanalysis. They revised their own psychoanalytic thinking through the new lens of gender, writing articles and organizing conferences to open a dialogue among their Argentine colleagues. Their growing feminist sensibilities also added a dimension to their political analysis, which permitted a new understanding of the failures of the revolutionary movements of the sixties and seventies. In addition to their assessment of the objective interests and psychology of the dominant classes who had embraced state terror to deal with their political opposition, Juan Carlos and Silvia were also interested in the role played by the left leaders themselves in their failure to sustain successfully the mass movement for change. Applying a feminist analysis, they saw that the strategic mistakes made by the mainly male left leaders were due in part to a psychology associated with traditional patriarchal values, whose contours often constrained their ability to develop political strategies based on a realistic evaluation of the existing power relations in their societies. Juan Carlos believed that although the left leaders had successfully mobilized a mass movement that challenged class and race oppression, they had uncritically and unconsciously reproduced among themselves elements of the authoritarian mentality associated with male chauvinism. Juan Carlos concluded that the leadership suffered from contradictions: while the leaders critiqued the political authoritarianism of the right wing and the military, they simultaneously manifested a psychological proclivity toward authoritarianism themselves, which led them to overemphasize the military aspects of the political struggle for change. "In so doing," he argues, "they weakened their struggle in many ways, not the least important of which was falling victim to the grandiose and omnipotent fantasy that they could take on a militarized state disposed to defend the status quo with a cruelty that knew no bounds." The male reluctance to tolerate feelings of weakness and vulnerability had led the leaders to deny their own and their followers' powerlessness in relation to their enemy, especially as systematic repression increased. This denial contributed to their inability to recognize their imminent defeat, and thus did not permit them to develop a defensive strategy to protect the movement; they thereby left hundreds of thousands of activists vulnerable and less prepared to safeguard themselves at the key moment of all-out military and paramilitary assault.

While such political assessments were an important part of the experience of return, in addition Juan Carlos sought a solution for his political alienation from the dominant discourse of the Argentine government through his activism in the human rights organizations. As part of the Mental Health Solidarity Movement, along with Julia Braun and Tato Pavlovsky, who treated the *afectados* of state terror, he began to work especially with children who were returning from exile. "We struggled together," says Juan Carlos, "they as patients and I as therapist, to elaborate the extremely painful phenomenon of repatriation."

Each of the protagonists of liberation psychology found ways to actualize a socially committed psychoanalysis in this new period, haunted as it was by the problem of the *desaparecidos*. Juan Carlos began to collaborate closely with the human rights work of Estela Carlotto and the Grandmothers of the Plaza de Mayo, which permitted him to retain a connection to the progressive ideals of previous times. Diana, Lucila, and Darío of the Equipo continued to treat families whose loved ones had been disappeared, working with the Mothers of the Plaza de Mayo as they had during the dictatorship. After the return to democracy, they also organized "reflection groups" of professionals, students, and mental-health workers as individuals expressed the need to elaborate collectively, in both a personal and intellectual way, the painful legacy of political repression and the complex implications of possible amnesty for the perpetrators. These groups, which the Equipo began to organize among other sectors of society as well, "permitted the psychological processing of traumatic situations that had a social origin in a more effective way than other modalities. . . . The group environment enables the participants to put into concrete words, articulated collectively, the different ways a social experience affects people subjectively and the personal manner in which each *afectado* negotiates the traumatic situation."[9] The three Equipo activists noted the following benefits of the groups' work in articulating the experience of trauma: the reduction of anxiety and an increased capacity to tolerate it; the lessening of guilt feelings, which are more frequent in families of *desaparecidos* than in other mourners; the strengthening of protective ego defenses; and the increase of self-esteem.

Julia Braun also found group psychotherapy an effective way for individuals and families to elaborate emotional problems whose origins were linked to the social trauma of the *desaparecidos*. Shortly after the return to constitutional rule, the Argentine Ministry of Health took the unprecedented step of establishing a special psychological service for the victims of military repression. Julia was appointed its director, the first time a psychoanalyst had assumed a leadership position within the ministry. No one could have been better suited for the position. In addition to her professional training Julia knew from her own experience—*en carne propia*—the anguish of having a loved one disappear. She organized therapy groups for the families of the *desaparecidos*, which focused on the special mourning required of persons affected by this perverse political policy. Julia also extended the psychological services of the Ministry of Health to the educational system. She aided school directors and teachers in making appropriate interventions with children who were manifesting psychological symptoms that were not only the cumulative response to the period of state terror but also a reaction to the rash of violence perpetrated by the right wing around the country as it tried to intimidate human rights activists in their efforts to seek accountability on the part of the military.

In 1985, Julia took part in the first conference organized by mental-health professionals in the Southern Cone to explore the meanings of state terror. Marcelo and Maren Viñar, who still lived in Paris, also participated in the meetings, which brought together psychoanalysts, psychologists, former-political prisoners, and colleagues from Europe for the purpose of thinking and talking together about the legacy of the culture of fear. When the conference concluded, Julia, Maren, and Marcelo, along with other colleagues, formed a work group that continued meeting for years to deal with various aspects of the psychological sequelae of social trauma.

During this period, Julia had the dubious privilege of learning the truth of what had happened to her son Gabriel. She was contacted one day by a judge, who offered her information that was subsequently confirmed by an ex-prisoner who had seen Gabriel during her own captivity. Julia discovered that Gabriel had been in the very police station where his father, Mariano, had initially gone to look for him the night he was abducted. Then he had been taken to a clandestine prison, where he was taunted for being a Jew and a subversive and subjected to terrible torture. He was later murdered along with two other prisoners in a way that was made to look as though they were juvenile delinquents who had been killed during an armed confrontation with the police. Like thousands of others, this political murder had gone through the theatrics of a police criminal investigation, followed by the burial of Gabriel and the two other victims in anonymous, unmarked graves. "Knowing the truth, even with its horrific details, gave me a certain amount of peace," says Julia. "Mothers of other *desaparecidos* called to tell me how lucky I was. My 'luck' was to know that they'd killed my son with machine guns. The mothers told me that they wished they were in my place. That's how important the truth—the knowing—is."

Estela Carlotto of the Grandmothers confirms Julia's assertion. "Knowing concretely is important. I have the terrible certainty of knowing about Laura's death. In my experience, the certainty that comes from having the body and being able to bury your loved one helps in the mourning process. It's impossible in the situation of the *desaparecidos*; many families leave a place set at the dinner table, celebrate the birthday, leave the clothes hanging in the closet. They are frozen." In Estela's case, her persistence paid off. Several years after Laura's disappearance she succeeded in locating her daughter's body. "But it was so disfigured, my husband didn't want me to see her. He said that it would be better for me to keep an intact image of her. I agreed, and I didn't view the body before she was buried." But in 1985 Estela had her daughter's body exhumed in order to disprove the military's story that she was a criminal who had been killed trying to escape from the police and to expose as false their assertion that she had not had a baby in captivity. The examination of the body demonstrated that Laura had been in a concentration camp, that she had been subjected to torture and had been shot at close range. It also proved that she had given birth to a baby before she met her death. "With the truth confirmed," says Estela, "my bereavement was possible. I saw her; I saw what remained. My mourning was now linked to reality. And I am still searching for my grandchild. Witnesses who saw Laura when she gave birth in a military hospital have told me the baby was a boy whom Laura named Guido after her father. But even if I find him someday," she adds, "I'll continue with the Grandmothers. This is a commitment for life."

In their concern for justice, the Mothers and Grandmothers took the position that the military should be prosecuted and then prevented from participating in politics altogether. This radical posture led them to criticize traditional Argentine political structures. When, on a trip to Europe, President Alfonsín publicly declared that he did not think the Mothers' political agenda coincided with the "national interest," the Mothers published a reply in their newspaper. "To this president, who claims to be democratic, it is necessary to explain . . . what the meaning of 'national' is to us. What is authentically national is a population that develops the wealth of this country for its own benefit; it is to receive an adequate wage, to have enough food, to have a home; it is to be able to educate our children, to have health protection, to improve our intellectual and technical capacity, to have our own culture and to have freedom of expression; it is to have armed forces to drive lorries, planes and boats that transport troops and materials to places of natural disaster, who work with the people in an efficient and rapid way; it is to have a police force that protects freedom and respects all citizens; it is to have impartial judges who guarantee justice; it is to have duties and rights that can be exercised freely; it is, simply, to have the right to life, but with dignity."[10] The Mothers were speaking for millions of their compatriots.

In April 1985, concerned about the widespread resistance to coming to terms with state terror, some of the members of the APA, including Julia, set about to study the psychological effects of political repression. They met for months and then wrote papers that were presented publicly at a symposium held in December of that year in Buenos Aires's most important cultural center.

The following year, a collection of the papers was published as *Argentina psicoanálisis represión política*. In the book's prologue, the editor wrote, "Psychoanalysis permits the patient to recover aspects of his life and his personality that have been repressed, denied, or dissociated. While what is 'overcome' in these ways is erased from one's memory, it always returns through symptoms, character problems, and inhibitions in love and work, which make one's life painful. In the same way, a people has a memory that is necessary to recover. The suppression of memory, the disinformation, the forgetting—all are enemies of individual and collective mental health. That which is forgotten makes itself present through repetition, which compromises the future and keeps people defenseless and in a state of desperation. Only the clarification of memory and knowledge of reality, however painful at the moment, permits us to recover those aspects of ourselves from which we have been alienated. It is urgent that we all take responsibility for the importance and value of the historical truth of what we as a people have suffered and its sequelae of horror, death, and deterioration. . . . The patient is only able to stop repeating his neurotic behavior by remembering, resignifying, and elaborating [the past]. We believe that a people should also remember and signify, so as not to repeat."[11] This argument on behalf of *memoria* became the battle cry of those who believed in the fundamental necessity of confronting and understanding the painful reality of the past so as to eliminate the chances of repeating it.

Closely connected to the effort on behalf of *memoria* was another issue that fueled the attempts to bring the military to trial. It had to do with the role of justice in society. The progressive psychoanalysts and psychologists in Argentina, along with their counterparts in Chile and Uruguay, agreed on the fundamental principle that without the rule of law citizens live together unprotected, defenseless, and in a permanent state of anxiety. They quoted Freud, who in *Civilization and Its Discontents* (written in 1929, after the First World War and on the eve of the rise of fascism) examined the origins of human social organization. "Human life in common is only made possible when a majority comes together which is stronger than any separate individual and which remains united against all separate individuals. The power of this community is then set up as 'right' in opposition to the power of the individual, which is condemned as 'brute force.' . . . The first requisite of civilization, therefore, is that of justice—that is, the assurance that a law once made will not be broken in favor of an individual. This implies nothing as to the ethical value of the law. The further course of cultural development seems to tend towards making the law no longer an expression of the will of a small community—a caste or a stratum of the population or a racial group—which, in its turn, behaves like a violent individual towards other, and perhaps more numerous, collections of people. The final outcome should be a rule of law to which all . . . have contributed by a sacrifice of their instincts, and which leaves no one . . . at the mercy of brute force."[12] The military dictatorships in all three Southern Cone countries, whose authoritarian discourse had ignored established law, had through brute force inflicted the arbitrary and brutal rule of a minority on the majority of citizens, thus countermanding what Freud had argued was one of the essential pillars of civilization.

This violation of the rule of law demanded an accounting. As Diana, Lucila, and Darío argued, formal judgment of the military's wrongdoing was a necessary prerequisite for the recovery from state terror. It was not a matter of vengeance; the human rights movement sought acknowledgment of the law, an admission that it had been violated, and some form of reparation. Only then was forgiveness possible, and only then could members of society feel they were protected. But the military did not seek pardon. They denied or justified their actions, and many civilians, frightened about the possible consequences of pursuing justice, believed that it was better to forget the past than to upset their fragile new democracies. They supported amnesty for the military. "Don't live in the past," they urged. "There has already been so much damage. Let us forget and move on to what lies in the future." Pérez Esquivel countered on behalf of remembering. "To recapture memory does not signify remaining in the past but the possibility of illuminating the present in order to construct critical consciousness and to recuperate values that sustain life, culture, and identity. It means that people stop being spectators and assume their role as protagonists of history."[13]

The confrontation continued. In Argentina, human rights organizations clamored for trials of all those military officers implicated in the disappearances, tortures, and murders described in *Nunca más*, but Alfonsín feared destabilization of the constitutional government by the armed forces. He finally sought a compromise: he would limit prosecutions to those members of the three juntas who were most responsible for human rights abuses. They, as well as members of the armed forces, security agencies, and prison guards who had carried out manifestly illegal acts, would be charged with criminal offenses as defined in the penal code in effect during military rule. They would be tried before military tribunals, whose sentences could be appealed before federal civil courts. This decision was widely interpreted as a concession to the military.

Outraged citizens claimed that the generals on trial would already be retired from the army and would thus retain virtually no power, so that in effect the middle-ranking officers—precisely those who would be the generals of the future—were receiving amnesties. From the point of view of the human rights groups, Alfonsín was promoting the very officers who had been accused of being the torturers in the testimonies they had collected. Because of their critical public stance, the outspoken human rights activists—including the Mothers and Grandmothers—continued to be targets of intimidation and harassment during this period.

In April 1985, when the Supreme Council of the Armed Forces had still not acted, the Federal Court determined an "unwarranted delay" and set the date for a civil trial, which was described as a court martial by civilians. The trial of nine junta members charged with 711 offenses, ranging from illegal detention to rape to murder, began in a volatile political environment that included a wave of bombings throughout Argentina. The government issued a call to defend democracy, and in Buenos Aires 250,000 people demonstrated in support of the trial. During the subsequent five months, the trial took place. Nearly one thousand witnesses came forth to testify with shocking detail about their extraordinary abuse at the hands of the torturers. A minimal number of guilty verdicts resulted. Although two generals were sentenced to life imprisonment, a third one to eighteen years, another to eight years, and a final one to four and a half years, the remaining junta members were acquitted on all charges.

To Alfonsín's credit, the convictions were a first in Latin American history. Never before had officers of a defeated military dictatorship been tried and sentenced for their crimes. But the public was outraged, and Alfonsín was criticized for not carrying out a thoroughgoing reform of the military and dismantling the intelligence services, which proceeded in their work of controlling the population. As numerous charges continued to be brought against members of the armed forces by Argentine citizens, in December 1986 Alfonsín responded to pressure from the military by signing into law the *punto final* (final stop), which allowed prosecution only of those officers charged within sixty days of the effective date of the statute. Although several (unsuccessful) military revolts in April and May 1987 seemed to justify Alfonsín's defensive strategy toward the armed forces, whose shadow continued to darken Argentine politics, millions of Argentines were enraged at the *punto final*, which would leave thousands of perpetrators free. But Alfonsín persisted, and in May he sent to Congress the *obediencia debida* (due obedience) bill, which was passed by both houses in June. Now officers from lieutenant colonel on down were exempted from being tried, even those who had tortured and killed prisoners, because they had done so under orders. As the Mothers and Grandmothers pointed out, *obediencia debida* exempted Argentina's entire active-duty officer corps because all its members had only been lieutenant colonels during the Dirty War.

In mid-1989, Argentina's newly elected president, Peronist Carlos Menem, received the presidential sash several months ahead of schedule from Alfonsín, who rushed to hand over to his successor a country embattled by hyperinflation and a dissatisfied armed forces still seeking complete amnesty and moral vindication. During his first year in office, President Menem, the man who had campaigned as a populist on the side of the people, allied himself with the powerful in society. Menem expanded the neoliberal free-market solution to his country's economic woes, including the sale of state-owned enterprises to mainly foreign-owned private corporations, which continued to exacerbate the gap between the haves and the have-nots. He also delivered a blow to those struggling on behalf of human rights by definitively closing the Dirty War with a blanket amnesty (*Impunidad*) for the military. The ideal of justice, which had been affirmed by the prosecution and imprisonment of some junta officers, was smashed when Menem's *Impunidad* pardoned them. Impunity came down on the side of social amnesia, which would have not only juridical but cultural and moral consequences as well.

In Uruguay, citizens struggled for several years to obtain legal indictments of military and political personnel whom they accused of participating in torture, kidnapping, disappearances, extortion, rape, and murder. But in spite of their persistent demands, on December 22, 1986, the Uruguayan Chamber of Deputies passed an amnesty bill, promptly signed by President Sanguinetti, to prevent the prosecution of any individuals accused of human rights violations committed from 1973 to 1985. "What is more just," asked President Sanguinetti in support of the law, "to consolidate the peace of the country where human rights are guaranteed today, or to seek retroactive values? I believe human rights trials would have been incompatible with peace and institutional stability." Foreign Minister Enrique Iglesias added, "No country can live permanently facing the past, in conflict with its army. Amnesty is an act of faith." And in a true act of faith (denial), he added, "We are betting the future on the army's historic tradition of noninterventionism and professionalism."[14] "Betting" was perhaps an unconscious reference to the increasing diversion of government funds from social programs, including education and health services, to the military, which had increased its share of the national budget from only 14 percent in the 1950s to more than 40 percent by the mid-1980s.

One Uruguayan activist opposed to amnesty for the military put it this way: "You can't pardon someone who's convinced he has behaved well. Someone asks for a pardon [after] having repented. I don't care whether anyone is incarcerated, as long as he confesses, repents, and *then* is pardoned."[15] And, on the basis of this sentiment, the Uruguayan people fought the amnesty law in bitter debates and street demonstrations, culminating in 1987 in the establishment of the National Commission for a Referendum, which tried to challenge the amnesty legally. The commission set about gathering signatures for a referendum to overturn the amnesty law, and in spite of every conceivable impediment created by the government and the media the commission's dramatic efforts resulted in the collection of more than the excessive number

of signatures required. Celebrations in the streets of Montevideo reflected the
people's sense that this success represented a victory for truth. Then the Electoral Court stalled for over a year in an intentionally tedious process of vali-
dating all the signatures.

Meanwhile, Uruguayans adjusted to the end of the military dictatorship.
Like the Argentines and Chileans, they, too, had to deal with a reencounter:
people came back from exile, they were released from prison, and they emerged
from internal exile. They now lived in the same society with those who had
actively colluded with the military and with many others who had passively
submitted to the authoritarian state. Each of these sectors had seen the culture of fear through a different lens, and they viewed one another with profound distrust. Together they constituted a fractured society. As Marcelo and
Maren have written, "In response to the experience of terror, Uruguayan society is split into two irreconcilable camps. For some, life simply continued,
and the terror was a detail in the course of history; for others, it was a con-
vulsion that broke the continuity of their destinies, obliging them to form scar
tissue over wounds that were irreparable. We propose that this horror and violence have imposed a fragmentation of memory and of collective identity,
whose dissociative mechanism corrodes and corrupts the social bond. The traumatic and violent origin of this fragmentation is the very reason it persists;
that is to say, while the cause is gone, its effects persist in the rupture of interpersonal understanding and alliances that tie people together and sustain
social bonds."[16] According to the Viñars, the intrapsychic and interpersonal
conflicts thus generated required a reparative process, one that was impeded
by amnesty. Like Argentines and Chileans, Uruguayans were living with the
torturers among them—traveling in the same subways, eating in the same restaurants, enjoying the same concerts. They inhabited an environment whose
physical reminders of terror—the public buildings, the factories, the private
mansions where people had been tortured and murdered—were inescapable.
Yet they were asked to forget about the past.

But those who would not forget, who supported the importance of *memoria* and of justice, did not give up. And, finally, the National Commission
for a Referendum won the right to hold a plebiscite on repealing the amnesty
law. Following an intensive campaign by both its supporters and the opposition, the plebiscite took place on April 16, 1989. The culture of fear was evi-
dent in its outcome: it was defeated nationwide by a margin of 57 to 43
percent. However, the fractures to which Marcelo and Maren refer were manifest in the significant percentage of Uruguayans who, in spite of intimidation
by the military and their allies, spoke out against amnesty. In Montevideo,
where the largest percentage of people in the country reside, 55 percent voted
in favor of repealing the law. And even in the interior of the country, where
bullying from the armed forces and cajoling by the civilian opposition was

strongest, over 40 percent voted to do so. These people, for whom prosecution of the torturers was a prerequisite for social reparation, were now living in a society whose "impunity" would compromise their ability to deal with the psychological sequelae of the culture of fear.

In Chile, events took a different route but toward the same destination. Shortly after his inauguration, President Aylwin named the eight-member Commission on Truth and Reconciliation, which included human rights activists and their sympathizers as well as conservative jurists and educators, two of whom had been members of Pinochet's government in the 1970s. Empowered to investigate the most serious violations of human rights that occurred during the last years of the military regime, the commission was allowed to recommend possible reparations to those affected by human rights abuses but not to engage in any judicial proceeding. In response to the creation of the commission, Pinochet instructed the army to issue a communiqué defending its actions and a warning that "irresponsible treatment" of these matters could lead to "reactions or regressive consequences" on the part of the military. The commission's 1,300-page report was published in March 1991. In addition to analyzing in detail more than two thousand deaths at the hands of the military, the commission's strong critique was also directed at the civilian judiciary, which it claimed had provided the perpetrators of repression with assurances that they would not be prosecuted for their criminal acts.

As in Argentina and Uruguay, during the struggle over amnesty Chileans lived through the complex adjustment to the return of democratic government. Here, too, social trauma had created a legacy of deep wounds that affected every domain of life. As Elizabeth Lira notes, "The difficult unraveling of dictatorship is never a return to the democracy imagined but to another democracy that has incorporated the conflictual structural and institutional aspects of the regime that proceeds it." The internalization of fear and fragmented social bonds compromised the ability of the Chilean people to fight successfully against the campaign for amnesty waged by the military and its allies. For many citizens, the possibility that the recently won constitutional government would be threatened in a confrontation with the right, which dominated the Congress and was allied with the armed forces, seemed too big a price to pay for justice. And the military demanded amnesty. Indeed, they vocally protested the report of the Commission on Truth and Reconciliation, stubbornly insisting that their actions had been legitimate because Chile had been in a state of war after the coup. They also argued that they were exempt from any consequences whatsoever because of the amnesty law that had been instituted in 1978 by a prescient Pinochet. When the left argued for a repeal of the 1978 amnesty law, Pinochet made it abundantly clear that he would resist legal proceedings involving any of his army officers.

However, even in the face of the military's intransigence, many Chileans stood firm against amnesty. In an emotional public pronouncement, Aylwin supported the commission's proposals for monetary and moral compensation to the victims and for a human rights public defender and judicial reforms. Public opinion polls showed that Aylwin's approval rating was high—more than 70 percent—indicating that the Chilean people were strongly opposed to Pinochet's stance. But in spite of the majority feeling in the country that the military should be tried and judged, the right favored "turning the page" on the question of human rights altogether, a sentiment that carried the conservative-dominated Senate. Thus, in Chile, no one in the armed forces was prosecuted for human rights violations that occurred during the dark years of military dictatorship.

Referring to the impact of amnesty, Elizabeth asserts that the internalized fear remains, independent of the existence of the threat that engendered it. She sees this fear operating in many of her patients in whom "it maintains itself as a latent phenomenon, which is restimulated any time an individual experiences personal problems and social or political situations that are evocative of previous threatening experiences. And any situation that represents change is feared more intensely than objectively warranted because it's likely to bear the weight of the terrors that have been denied or dissociated rather than worked through." The Commission on Truth and Reconciliation's investigation of the military's human rights violations was followed by a reparation law for the families of the victims. Although the reparations helped to resolve concrete problems in these families' daily lives, they have been viewed as insufficient given the social and juridical impunity enjoyed by the armed forces. As Elizabeth argues, "Because the culprits were not sanctioned for their criminal deeds, there are ethical and subjective sequelae that remain unresolvable. Amnesty highlights the irreparable nature of the crimes that were committed and at the same time it underscores the persistence of their impact on social relations."

Impunity and Social Violence

In all three countries of the Southern Cone, impunity has facilitated the psychological defenses of repression, denial, and dissociation in citizens who have been obliged to adjust to the new political situation which, while nominally democratic, nonetheless constitutes a permanent state of latent threat. The conditions necessary to facilitate a mourning process for the many losses caused by state terror were undermined by impunity, and thus a genuine working-through of social trauma was compromised.

Moreover, as our protagonists argue, the effects of impunity infuse all domains of life and are manifested in the intensification of social violence. Diana and Lucila believe that impunity legitimizes the generalized violation of the rights of others. "Impunity is reflected in criminal economic behavior—the corruption of government and corporate executives—and the murders—especially of our youth—carried out or covered up by the police, the army, or groups protected by the powers that be. . . . [When] crime is sanctioned, justice and law do not function to provide a moral climate, symbolic reparation, and social cohesion. Thus, in conditions of impunity, there has been a modification in habits, in definitions of what is permissible and what is forbidden, what is legal and what is illicit, to which the members of society universally respond. These habits and definitions have been internalized over time. . . . In the past fifteen years, we can attest to the fact that there has been a profound change in the fundamental norms of society."[17]

Julia agrees that life in her country today reflects patterns that were developed during the military dictatorship. "Impunity is manifested not only in a higher degree of corruption but in the open flaunting of it," she says, "and I relate this to the rupture of traditional restraints. Now anyone can do anything and get away with it. Before the powerful did what they wanted with other human beings. While they used to kill with machine guns, now they do the same thing but with laws and decrees. Political decadence and individualism are omnipresent. For instance, can you imagine that in this country, with its traditions of working-class consciousness, today a union leader can give a speech in which he tells workers, 'Whoever works is an ass because no one makes money working!'? He isn't offering a critical discourse, mind you, it's an identification with corruption. And it represents the level of social decomposition that results from living through the Dirty War, when they killed people as if they were ants and then were pardoned. There is a profound legacy of violation of the law, which was committed against the body before and is now committed against the mind."

From Elizabeth's point of view, similar conditions obtain in Chile. She speaks of the internalization of impunity, which reinforces traditionally overt and covert forms of authoritarianism in politics and in daily life. She gives the example of the impunity of male violence. In the private sphere of the family, men's abuse of their wives and children has been traditionally justified by custom and law, and now it is further legitimized by the impunity of political violence. Impunity, argues Elizabeth, has also imposed a pervasive conservatism in the mentality of the Chilean people. Like her colleagues in the other Southern Cone countries, she perceives that as years go by, the struggle for human rights has become associated with the past and is viewed by many as a danger to the political stability they are convinced is necessary for the survival of democracy. The discourse about justice, reparation, or impunity, they believe, is linked to the previous era of military dictatorship, with its political fear, violence, and repression. "So impunity in this context assures that the legacy of terror remains in the social and juridical structures. We see this phenomenon manifested in the limited forms of activism and in the narrowing of the political and social issues about which it is possible to think. There's a fear of change and an overestimation of stability and consensus, as if they themselves were substantive political goals. Impunity appears, dissociated from its original source, in the social fragmentation and in the suspicion with which each individual regards the other. It's there in the difficulty of contemplating a political project that is different from the contemporary model of limited democracy. And it's present in the inability to identify with the individuals and groups who challenge the present consensus in order to confront the traumatic experience of state terror."

The Viñars have given much thought to the legacy of social fragmentation reinforced by impunity. They believe the fractures in Uruguayan society about which they have written are reflected in the various strategies chosen by mental-health professionals to treat torture victims. During a 1991 conference of Latin American psychologists and psychoanalysts that took place in Santiago, Chile, organized by Elizabeth's institute, ILAS (Latin American Institute of Mental Health and Human Rights), Marcelo criticized the tendency in Latin America, Europe, and the United States to establish specialized centers for the treatment of torture victims and other *afectados* of state terror. He argued that this treatment approach tends to reinforce the social fragmentation that is a serious problem in his society. Repatriation brought him back to a Uruguay that suffers from a climate of suspicion in everyday life. Social bonds, he claimed, have been shattered because of the stereotyped assumptions people maintain of each other in relation to who they were and what they did during the years of dictatorship. Although the ABC system of segregation imposed on Uruguayan citizens by the military no longer exists, Marcelo pointed out, the attitudes that separate people do, sustaining the sense that each is a potential enemy of the other. This social split is complicated by the fragmentation of memory from which everyone suffers. "My sense is that our psychotherapeutic function is to circulate that which the dictatorship did not permit to circulate. If there's anything I've understood from this experience, it is what makes it possible to lose one's fear, to lose the fragmented memory that today makes up the collective mind, in order for a collective voice and a collective vision to emerge." Marcelo told his colleagues, "I strongly oppose the segregation of torture victims within specialized treatment centers. . . . I believe that the tortured should be treated in the regular health system of our countries. The assumption that we can treat victims more effectively with specialists means that we create a system of segregation and exclusion that reinforces exactly what we want to prevent." He agreed with the ILAS perspective in Chile, which is also critical of dividing the population into those who were directly affected by state terror and those who were not, or those who are committed to the human rights struggles and those who are indifferent. "As long as this split is maintained," he asserted, "the privatized and consumer society has won the battle of the last twenty years, and it will continue victorious. This is a political struggle. However, our specific approach with regard to how we treat the psychological effects of terror can contribute, even in a small way, to the larger political struggle that has to do with the transmission of values of solidarity and a fraternal community."[18]

The proponents of liberation psychology have consistently placed themselves on the side of *memoria* and of the need to develop a critical discourse about the historical role played by state terror in the Southern Cone. From their perspective, state terror was the handmaiden that assured the maturation of neoliberalism in Latin America, which has succeeded in increasing profits and consumerism for an elite international capitalist class while expanding poverty, marginalization, and social violence for the majority of Latin Americans. Elizabeth expresses it this way, "The massive and serious violation of the right to life and personal integrity [by state terror] tended to cover up its coexistence with the violation of social-economic rights. Political repression was able to generate diverse forms of subjugation that prepared people to accept unemployment, superexploitation, and the lack of basic necessities (health, housing, education). It smashed any manifestation of social resistance until it seemed as if the majority had resigned themselves to the loss of rights and hope."[19]

This view of the historical role of state terror is shared by all of our protagonists and by many of their compañeros in the human rights movement. Hebe de Bonafini, president of the Mothers of the Plaza de Mayo, echoes this view when she says, "The torture, the murders, the genocide were for one thing only: to apply an economic plan that would bring misery to the majority of the people. . . . Economic repression is the strongest form of repression. . . . There are so many recessions. Wages and salaries aren't enough to live on. There is unemployment. There is hunger. . . . We still have the same problems that our children were fighting to change."[20]

The Victims of Democracy

"I don't think we're living in a democracy," Rosa Roisinblit, who is the vice-president of the Grandmothers, tells me. "Maybe we're no longer under the military, but to my mind we live in a constitutional dictatorship. When the government says it has to reduce the pensions of the elderly in order to lower the foreign debt, I say that's ridiculous! It's a testimony to the lack of real economic democracy."

Rosa's comment refers to the fact that political democracy has overseen the steepest decline in social and economic democracy in recent memory. In fact, the 1980s were dubbed "The Lost Decade" because they produced the highest number of poor people in a single decade in Latin American history. Despite the change from military to constitutional regimes during the 1980s, the mammoth debt crisis and a continentwide 10 percent decline in the standard of living condemned 44 percent of the region's population to live below the official poverty line. The new democratic regimes throughout Latin America found themselves held hostage by the terms imposed by the International Monetary Fund and the World Bank. In exchange for renegotiating outstanding loans, the International Monetary Fund demanded that governments implement "structural readjustment" policies, including austerity measures, that facilitated the full implementation of the neoliberal economic model. This Faustian bargain between the powerful international lending agencies and Latin American democratic states included the deregulation of the economy, the liberalization of trade, the dismantling of the public sector through privatization of state-owned enterprises and the elimination of the social "safety net," and the predominance in the economy of the financial sector over production and commerce. Thus the state has abandoned its role as the agent of social development and equitable distribution and instead has supported the redistribution of the wealth upward.

Wherever social movements arose to challenge this model, as in Nicaragua, El Salvador, Guatemala, and Haiti, they became targets of the Doctrine of National Security. The United States and its elite allies in Central America and the Caribbean employed the strategy of Low Intensity Conflict, a variant of state terror, to liquidate opposition to neoliberalism and its economic agenda.[21] Throughout the eighties, in her work as the co-coordinator of the Internationalist Team, Mimi Langer actively opposed this policy and helped to treat the psychic trauma caused by the U.S.-sponsored Contra economic, military, and psychological war against the people of Nicaragua.

All our protagonists believe that neoliberal economics and conservative politics are the twin factors responsible for the exacerbation of the psychological and social problems of contemporary Latin America. Juan Carlos comments that the few who rule this *fin-de-siècle* world "have created an unprecedented degree of perfection in the technology of information and death and an equally unprecedented capacity to manipulate and suppress the vast majority of the world's peoples." And, as Tato argues, "in this sense, impunity has taken on new meanings." Impunity is manifested in the irresponsible policies of the transnational corporations, whose uncontrolled investments in Latin

America raise exports but leave in their wake land that is drying out and sinking and workers who are sick from the large-scale use of insecticides and chemical fertilizers that are prohibited in the United States and Europe. Over two hundred pesticides on the World Health Organization's black list are used with impunity in Uruguay, which now has one of the highest cancer rates of any country in the world. In Chile, the free market impunity has resulted in ever-escalating unemployment, which pushes 40 percent of the work force into the dirty, dangerous, and unregulated environment of the informal economy. The rapacious export-based economy in Chile results in deforested hills, fished-out shorelines, and chemical-ridden fields in the country's fruit belt. The indiscriminate use of fertilizers has been linked to alarming rates of birth defects in children of farm workers.[22]

In Argentina, impunity has been manifested in a variety of ways, including the manner in which the president and congress have extended the implementation of neoliberalism. They demolished the country's traditional welfare capitalism through a privatization policy, selling off nationally owned enterprises to foreign transnational corporations and severely downsizing employment and social services in the public sector. The neoliberal model encouraged ever-expanding consumerism among the elites and upper-middle classes at the same time that it devastated the purchasing power of millions. By the early nineties, luxury malls thrived in bourgeois neighborhoods, while 33 percent of the population was driven below the poverty line. Since then, the unemployment rate has risen to an unprecedented 20 percent. Another manifestation of impunity has been the ongoing abuse of authority by the police, who continue to act with free reign: in a two-year period—1988 to 1990—police officers committed over one-third of the homicides in the Greater Buenos Aires area. They have also made Argentine youth the new enemy, targeting them at rock concerts and on the streets, especially in working-class neighborhoods, for arbitrary detention and murder.

In this era of neoliberal impunity, children have suffered especially. Education levels throughout Latin America have declined, and in Argentina and Uruguay, where literacy levels once rivaled those of the developed countries, illiteracy is reappearing at an alarming rate. Moreover, the impunity of the market, reflected in the widespread elimination of traditional social protections, has resulted in a breakdown of the family. More and more children are forced to contribute to family income or to fend for themselves on the streets. As traditional structures like the family, Church, and schools no longer protect and nurture, millions of children are forced to survive in alternative structures of authority and community—often illicit—that make them the victims of drug lords, pimps, and right-wing death squads. They become the targets, as well, of rising numbers of vigilantes, whose lawless form of crime prevention is aimed at "social cleansing." The vigilantes kill with impunity in the urban slums and squatter settlements. Their self-declared "war against the disposable people" is aimed not only at children but at the homeless, gang members, and addicts, and it also extends to prostitutes, gays, and political activists.

In Nicaragua, the electoral victory of opposition candidate Violeta Chamorro in 1990 was part of the overall goal of reintegrating the country into the neoliberal political model and of dismantling the Sandinista social projects. By the mid-1990s, free-market economic policies were exacerbating the social and economic crises that had been provoked earlier by the Contra war. As Nicaragua's debt to the International Monetary Fund and other international lending agencies expands and its markets open up as a result of new free-trade strategies, its tiny elite sector has increased access to consumer goods, while the rest of its population experiences rising unemployment, lowered nutritional levels, less access to decent housing, education, and medical care, and expanding social violence, which includes an escalation in drug use and juvenile delinquency.[23]

"I live with a circumstantial pessimism," says Diana. And no wonder. She and the other proponents of liberation psychology note the psychological responses among people to the deterioration in their lives. As a Uruguayan colleague describes life in the nineties, "Whereas during the dictatorship our motto was 'Everyone against them,' now it is 'Everyone against everyone else.'"[24] In Argentina, public culture, with its traditional values of a just and cooperative society, has been replaced by the growing influence of the mass media, whose morals and aesthetics are driven by a market "survival of the fittest" that encourages an ethic of individualism and noncooperation. This social fragmentation is linked to profound changes in economic life. In Uruguay, as elsewhere in the Southern Cone, more and more people work alone as owners of small, marginal businesses, as temporary wage earners, or as itinerant vendors. In such conditions, they have little contact with other workers or neighbors and enjoy only limited time with their families. More women are forced into the wage-labor system, where they toil in the lowest-paid, least-organized sectors of the economy. In Chile, where strong traditions of community life show signs of disintegration, the psychological deterioration is notable. Between 1970 and 1991, suicides increased threefold and alcoholism quadrupled. Family breakdowns are multiplying, and crime rates are soaring. Over half of all visits to the country's public-health system, for example, involve psychological ailments, mainly depression.

This dramatic impact of neoliberalism on Latin America moved the Grandmothers of the Plaza de Mayo to ask the participants in their 1992 conference to address the need to redefine the human rights struggle. One speaker, Atilio Borón, vice-rector of the University of Buenos Aires, received an enthusiastic response from his audience when he told them, "The Grandmothers are right when they say that we need to develop a new agenda for human rights in response to the new world of neoliberalism that is so disastrously affecting all of our lives. We are basically speaking here of the right to life, liberty, and the pursuit of happiness. There are many ways to undercut these rights, one of them being state terror. But a much more subtle one, perhaps even more efficient, is economic terrorism. In this conference we are concerned with the relationship, identity, and restitution of the disappeared children of the Dirty War, and it is unacceptable to think of forgetting about them . . . .But how many other children must we restitute as a result of the neoliberal economic model? A recent UNICEF study of Argentina has shown that the most numerous group among the poor are children from five to fourteen years of age. This scandal is repeated throughout Latin America. We must restitute them as well: children who have no medical attention, children who have no basic care, children who lack education and who live in subhuman conditions, children who live in the streets, abandoned children, children who are assassinated by death squads and drug lords. This is a new form of torture, a new form of disappearance. The new *desaparecidos* of the 1990s are the poor, and the majority of them are children. These are the victims of democracy."[25]

The "economic terrorism" of neoliberalism, administered by democratic states, has been facilitated by another important development: the emergence of a unipolar world. The fall of the Soviet bloc has, for the historical moment, seemed to obliterate any alternative to world capitalism. Although the authoritarianism and centralized command economy of the Soviets were less than appealing to many on the left throughout Latin America, nonetheless the mere existence of the Soviet bloc and thus of a bipolar world had served as a deterrent to all-out economic, military, and political aggression by the United States in Latin America. The Soviet demise eliminated this function, as well as the existence of an alternative—and the idea of an alternative—to capitalism. The triumph of capitalism has been interpreted in the United States as the historic victory of a superior system and has been presented by conservative intellectuals as the "end of history," by which is meant the victory of a system that is the final and crowning achievement in the long evolution of human social organization. South of the border, however, the new unipolar world is viewed by many not as an achievement but as a defeat in the struggle to build a system characterized by equity and social justice. The problem facing the contemporary world, from the point of view of dissident Latin Americans, is that we now live in a singular international system—global capitalism—that draws human beings inexorably into a profoundly exploitative social order that appears at this historical period to be invincible.

The fall of the Berlin Wall in 1989 coincided in the Southern Cone with another significant phenomenon: the demise of the political movements that had been mobilized to challenge the military dictatorships. People withdrew from political activism, disillusioned with the quality of society and culture that replaced state terror. When the traditional political parties they had enthusiastically voted into power merely implemented conservative political principles to facilitate neoliberal economic practice, citizens seemed to lose interest in the old ways of participating in the political process. A withdrawal from politics both reflected and reproduced a cynical alienation in the popular classes that has been noted by our protagonists.

Tato addresses this aspect of the crisis when he comments, "I think it's like a boxer who's lost the fight in a knock-out. . . . 'Really existing socialism' failed, and that has favored the free-market economic model because there is no alternative. It's disillusioning, this lack of an alternative, the lack of hope that there is something else besides capitalism, besides the consumer culture. But I believe that Soviet-style socialism failed, not socialism in and of itself. I'm not an economist, but to me it seems that capitalism is driving a significant percentage of the population to disaster, certainly here in Latin America, but even in the United States. From my perspective, we are getting close to a global crisis, and, as intellectuals, we have a choice: we can either put our heads in the sand or get involved in every way possible, to raise the issues of a new morality, a new ethic, a new future."

Tato is not alone in his view that a new morality—indeed, a new politics—is demanded by the contemporary crisis. In this regard, the collapse of Soviet-style socialism has had a paradoxical effect on Latin America. While it eliminated a bipolar world, it simultaneously opened up the possibility for the emergence of new forms of radical thinking and practice. It is clear that the wish for a life of dignity, justice, and liberty did not fall with the Berlin Wall. Some of the victims of neoliberalism are rising up as its critics, turning themselves from objects of history into its social subjects. Amidst the widespread alienation of Latin Americans from politics sprouts a new radical praxis, one that is more local and more democratic and that involves civil society in new ways. Since the late 1980s, new grass-roots movements have developed, not only among organized labor but in other sectors as well. The contemporary left is undergoing a rebirth based on a reassessment of traditional ways of doing politics. The left is rethinking traditional Marxist notions about class, which often suffered previously from crude economic determinism, and is also rejecting the classic Marxist assumption that the industrial working class is the chief motor of revolutionary change. Increasingly, Marxist visions have amplified to include a new appreciation for the class, race, and gender identities that motivate people to build political movements. The old idea of a revolutionary vanguard party that determines analysis and strategy for its followers has given way to a new emphasis on grass-roots democracy within local struggles. When, for example, the Mexican revolutionaries, the Zapatistas, negotiate with the Mexican military, before agreeing to any accord, they return to their villages for discussions with their grass-roots base, whose democratic vote then determines the Zapatistas' positions.[26]

Moreover, there is a growing recognition that even though the current struggles are responses to the deterioration of life under global capitalism, they are multifaceted and often organize people around issues of individual freedoms, living conditions, and environmental concerns. Movements that address class oppression, moreover, are often fought in terms of gender, gay, and ethnic rights. Women are becoming visible players, not only in new feminist groups sprouting up throughout the continent but increasingly as leaders in political parties, labor unions, neighborhood organizations, and the ecology movement. Indeed, it is often argued that the increased activism of women has spurred the renewed commitment to democratic process and grass-roots involvement.

Electoral politics are once again the site of activism but now with a new emphasis on mobilizing civil society. New coalitions have been successful in elections in Uruguay and Argentina. In 1989, the Frente Amplio elected a Socialist as mayor of Montevideo and has been reinventing local government, stressing decentralized services and grass-roots participation. Since the late eighties, in Argentina, the center-left Frente Grande has emerged as an important third national force, winning the election of Julia's friend, outspoken human rights activist Graciela Fernández Meijide, to the National Congress. An even newer left coalition, Frepaso, elected Graciela as one of the members of a newly constituted assembly that is empowered to work out the historic creation of the city of Buenos Aires as an autonomous province. As Julia puts it, "Graciela is at the present moment the most prestigious political figure in Argentina, and her stature is without a doubt linked to her activism in the human rights movement."

However, as our protagonists are the first to point out, although these movements indicate people's capacity to counter the devastating effects of state terror, impunity, and neoliberalism, their constricted and sporadic success reveals the demoralization that continues to haunt society in general. Even while engaged in radical political struggles, many activists all too often manifest a psychological conservatism that is expressed in a wish for stability and a fear of confrontation with authority, as described by Elizabeth. They are also likely to reflect the social fragmentation of which the Viñars speak, making the solidarity they politically prize difficult to sustain psychologically. And as Julia and the members of the Equipo argue, the attitudes and values of impunity that operate at every level of society are frequently internalized by the individuals who politically oppose them, weakening the only organized source of resistance to their destructive effects. All too often activists forget about the long-range goal of social transformation in the struggle to meet immediate, specific objectives. Moreover, they have difficulty sustaining the optimism required to deal with the demoralization, competitiveness, and opportunism that inevitably emerge in oppositional movements and weaken the struggle for a decent society. Thus, the muted achievements of these new movements reflect not only the power of the entrenched political and economic interests against which they struggle but the limitations of the activists themselves.[27]

The legacy of state terror is kept alive in other ways as well, ready to be reactivated in the public psyche. Such is the case with the impact of the public confessions made by torturers in Chile and Argentina. In July 1995, disturbing memories of the culture of fear of Pinochet's dictatorship were stimulated for Chileans when Osvaldo Romo, a carpenter and former agent of the Directorate of National Intelligence (DINA), spoke publicly about how he had tortured political prisoners, often to death, during the military regime. Romo showed no remorse for his crimes; on the contrary, he claimed that DINA's biggest error had been not killing all its torture victims. "I wouldn't leave a parakeet alive," the torturer declared.[28] His publicized remarks not only reawakened anxieties, terrors, hatreds, and bitter feelings of impotence among Chileans but reminded them that because of impunity, hundreds of torturers were still free, living and working among them.

Romo's public declarations came on the heels of the confession in Argentina several months earlier by former navy lieutenant commander Adolfo Francisco Scilingo, who disclosed his participation in the murder of suspected "subversives" during the Dirty War. Scilingo, who had been in charge of a notorious center for the detention and torture of political prisoners in Buenos Aires, chilled the Argentine public by describing how political prisoners had been stripped naked, drugged, and hauled unconscious onto airplanes to be flown over the South Atlantic and thrown out to meet their deaths in the freezing ocean waters. Scilingo described his participation in these "death flights," during which, as he reported, he had seen photographs of the Nazi death camps in his mind's eye as he pushed the bodies of his victims into the darkened night sky. Almost two decades after the Dirty War, Scilingo filed a complaint in the federal court charging the head of the navy with illegally covering up "the methods that superiors ordered used in the Navy Mechanics School for detaining, interrogating, and eliminating the enemy during the war against subversion."[29] He argued that, given the amnesty laws, there was no sense in hiding the facts and moreover, because he and other military officers had merely been following orders from above, it was only fitting that his superior officers should share the terrible guilt from which he is now suffering.

The human rights movement in Argentina welcomed his confession because, for the first time, the perpetrators had publicly acknowledged the truth of the crimes of which they were accused by their victims. It also stimulated a debate about the previously unexamined role of the Catholic Church during the Dirty War, forcing the hierarchy to acknowledge that it had been complicit through silence and, in all too many instances, actual collaboration with the repression. In response to the renewed discussion about state terror, which reawakened for millions the trauma associated with the *desaparecidos*, a prominent human rights lawyer, Emilio Mignone, whose own daughter had been abducted in 1976 and taken to the Navy Mechanics School before she disappeared forever, said, "What do I feel? That what Scilingo says is enormously useful, because he has broken the barrier of silence. I believe he serves the struggle to bring out the truth about all this." In fact, Scilingo's confession forced a shift in the military's position, which heretofore held that they had been guilty only of "occasional excesses." The army chief of staff now was obliged to declare on national television that "it's time to assume the responsibility and no longer deny the horrors of the past." He went on to clarify that the army had "employed illegitimate methods, including the suppression of life [sic], to obtain information." The Scilingo scandal broke during a heated national election, provoking the ire of President Menem, who asserted that it was "rubbing salt in old wounds." But the Mothers of the Plaza de Mayo responded with outrage. "Let them go to hell with their repentance," declared their president, Hebe de Bonafini. "We will continue struggling so that some day we may see them in jail." Bonafini's militant declaration is typical of the Mothers and Grandmothers of the Plaza de Mayo, whose voices rise above the din of compromise and adaptation to an unacceptable status quo, in which economic exploitation, social injustice, political repression, and psychological alienation continue to characterize the capitalist enterprise in Latin America.

Liberation Psychology: What's Left?

Like the Mothers and Grandmothers, the proponents of liberation psychology continue to forge their political analyses and social activism on the basis of their understanding of the intensifying exploitative relations and social- and psychopathology that are endemic throughout Latin America. They believe that the mode of analysis they have developed since the late 1960s—namely, Marxist psychoanalysis—is as relevant today as it was more than two and a half decades ago. They point to the increasing contradictions emerging throughout the world as a result of globalization, a process made possible by the new technology that permits the capitalist class to raise profits by producing different components of manufactured goods in the lowest-cost countries in Asia, Africa, and Latin America. As globalization enriches an international elite, it simultaneously lowers the standard of living and the expectations of working people, not only in Latin America, Asia, and Africa, but in the United States and Europe as well, and misery, fearfulness, and social violence are the universal byproducts.

For the protagonists of this book, Marxism remains an essential tool for analyzing the central features of the capitalist system because it can account for both its vitality and its anarchy. They take this position in the face of the prevailing mood of postmodernism, which is skeptical of theories composed of universal categories and conceptions of absolute truth. Many postmodernists eschew Marxism and orthodox psychoanalysis, regarding them as relics of essentializing worldviews that miss the fundamental subjectivity and relativity of reality. The postmodern impulse, which pervades scholarly research and popular culture alike, stresses the need to expose the assumptions within all systems of thought and to reject the tendencies of all theoretical models to construct exclusive bipolar categories (bourgeoisie/working class, male/female, white/black, oppressor/oppressed) because conceptualizaing the world in this way overlooks the shared and overlapping attributes that move fluidly back and forth between such categories. Postmodernism focuses on knowing the social context that determines any individual narrative of reality and encourages a critical awareness of the kaleidoscope of perspectives and points of view that together constitute the multiplicity of human experience.

Each of our protagonists is an intellectual who has read and digested postmodernist political, social, and psychological theory. From their perspective, its critical essence is a direct outgrowth of the traditions of Marx and Freud: Marxism because of its insistence that modes of production, class relations, and dominant ideologies affect the nature of mental life and psychological experience of individuals, and Freudianism because of its assertion that the apparent unity and knowability of the human mind is an illusion hiding the essential discontinuity and multiplicity of the self that lies below the surface. And although our protagonists embrace the postmodernist insistence on the need to deconstruct all assumptions in the process of analyzing any object of study, they argue that in contemporary—postmodern—capitalism, class, race, and gender relations continue to be governed by general laws or patterns that can be known, understood, and struggled against. For them, the specificities of contemporary—postmodern—social pathology and psychopathology can be understood through Marxist psychoanalysis, a mode of analysis that is, as well, an emancipatory practice.

"It's what's happening in your country as well as in Latin America," Juan Carlos tells me, "that make Marxism in many ways as relevant today as it was in the past. I say this despite the apparent vitality of global capitalism and the failures of both 'really existing' socialism and the revolutionary movements of the previous era. You know, Marx recognized in his *Contribution to the Critique of Political Economy* that in his era a revolutionary change in capitalism was impossible because, as a mode of production, it was still immature. He argued that no social formation disappears before all its productive forces are fully developed. I think he anticipated what we see today through the globalization of neoliberalism: the intersystemic contradictions between capitalism and socialism, which evolved throughout the twentieth century, from the Russian Revolution in 1917 to the fall of the Berlin Wall in 1989, have collapsed, and in its place we are experiencing the intrasystemic contradictions in the crisis of late capitalism. For the first time in history, capitalism fulfills the basic assumption of Marxism. I mean to say that for the first time capitalism constitutes an autonomous and mature entity whose determinants, tensions and conflicts—insoluble contradictions—reside within the system itself. In the twenty-first century, capitalism will guarantee one constant reality: more than three-quarters of humanity will live in extreme misery."

But, Juan Carlos suggests, Marx was mistaken in his belief that the working class would inevitably develop a revolutionary, anticapitalist consciousness to become the moving force behind revolution. Marx could not foresee this stage of capitalism, in which the middle and popular classes would identify with the political conservatism that is the ideological component of economic neoliberalism. "Marx's radical theory included the human subject, who, from his perspective, was determined by objective historical processes. But today the lack of critical consciousness among so many imposes on us the need to creatively deepen our understanding not only of historical processes but of the history of each subject [human being], whose complex unconscious workings need to be analyzed in order to be known. Freud deepens our exploration into the historicity of each subject, and so it is psychoanalysis that can teach us who we are at this historical juncture and how each of us is limited and restricted, in ways we are not conscious of, by internal and external forces. For me, in spite of all the seductive qualities of postmodernist thinking, it is the new scholarship in contemporary Marxism and psychoanalysis that has the best chance to help us understand the world we live in and how—call me old-fashioned—to change it by assuming our position as the subjects of our own history."

This perspective is shared by each of the proponents of liberation psychology. And although they do not necessarily agree among themselves on particular issues, they all continue to express an attitude of engagement toward life. This stance sustains in each of them a psychological and physical vitality, unmarred by age or their traumatic histories. They all share a capacity to find joy with family and friends, to work productively, and to participate how and where they can with others interested in building community and invigorating the struggle for social justice.

Marcelo and Maren continue to work with patients who are struggling with the ongoing sequelae of state terror and to write as they learn more about the impact of the culture of fear. In 1995, Marcelo, as president of the Uruguayan Psychoanalytic Association, attended an international conference in Dachau, "The Concentration Camp and the Carefree World," which dealt with social trauma in Germany and its impact on historical memory. In his paper, "Memory and the Future," he spoke about this problem for the Southern Cone. On his return from Germany, he visited me in Los Angeles, and during an afternoon on the beach, he explained how in Dachau colleagues from all over the world spoke about the fact that several generations of Germans lived in *olvido* (amnesia) before the youth of today finally developed the capacity to search for the truth—*memoria*—of what had happened during the Nazi era.

Elizabeth continues to treat the *afectados* of the culture of fear and has studied the special complications of working with trauma survivors who have endured their pain in silence for years before they seek professional help. They must slowly recover the dissociated aspects of the experience in order to elaborate it. She has organized conferences addressing the psychological legacy of state terror and has written about the psychological impact on mental-health professionals whose work with torture survivors requires special attention to their own conscious and unconscious responses because of their vulnerability to vicarious traumatization.[30] Aware of the importance of the arts in articulating the experience of state terror and impunity, Elizabeth contributed to the film production of renowned Chilean writer Ariel Dorfman's *Death and the Maiden*; she taught Sigourney Weaver about the psychological response to torture and impunity so that Weaver could play the main character, a torture victim who must deal with her intense emotional reactions to an encounter with her torturer in postdictatorship Chile.

Diana, Darío, and Lucila also continue their work with *afectados*. They have published a book, *La impunidad*, which describes their psychotherapeutic experiences and analyzes the impact of impunity on Argentine culture. As mentioned before, they also produced a longitudinal study that reveals the relatively positive impact of human rights activism on the mental health of participants; the study indicates that women who participated in the Mothers of the Plaza de Mayo have lower rates of fatal diseases and longer life expectancy than individuals—women and men—who did not participate politically in response to state terror. In spite of the difficulties of their work, these three activists in the Equipo reflect a spirited enthusiasm and sense of community that are the direct benefits of their political activism. "I live with a . . . fundamental historical optimism," says Diana. "I believe that sooner or later . . . we will build a better world for our children."

Julia continues to work with colleagues to develop a psychoanalytic conceptualization of contemporary social violence in Argentina. When a terrorist bomb blew up the Jewish center in downtown Buenos Aires in August 1994, killing one hundred people and wounding hundreds more, suddenly there was a new kind of *desaparecidos*, people who were buried beneath the rubble for almost a week. Traumatic memories of state terror were restimulated, and anxious and paranoid states of mind were reactivated. "I remember many of the psychoanalysts asked what they could do in such a crisis, and we reminded them that Freud wrote about how in critical moments an analyst can listen and contain terrible anxieties. Because of the experience gained during the past decade in our work with the victims of state terror, many of us from the different psychoanalytic institutes went the same day the bomb exploded to offer psychological aid. The APA called me and a colleague to supervise the teams of analysts who were organized to provide therapeutic interventions." Julia pauses and then laughingly tells me, "Many of the candidates felt unprepared to deal with the situation because they believed that psychoanalysis is a different therapeutic mode than crisis intervention. But we told them that as psychoanalysts we have the necessary tools to treat these people, even if we don't have a course at the APA on 'What to Do If a Bomb Explodes'! We wound up doing some very good work." In 1996, when Julia's younger son, Bernardo, who lives and works in the San Francisco area, returned from a visit to his mother in Buenos Aires, he gave me a copy of the paper Julia presented on March 24 of that year at one of the many colloquia and mass mobilizations commemorating the twentieth anniversary of the military coup. Titled "Humanizing Death," the paper stressed the continued importance of working through the ongoing impact on the collective psyche of institutionalized violence. Julia also sent me a copy of a public statement, signed by herself and other analysts, announcing their withdrawal from the APA and the formation of a new psychoanalytic institute whose efforts will be devoted to developing a curriculum and therapeutic work more consistent with the values and principles that have guided Julia's and her colleagues' life and work.

Tato continues his psychotherapeutic work as the director of his Institute of Psychoanalytic Group Psychodrama, where he offers a two-year training program for group leaders. The students are social workers, teachers, and community organizers and, besides Argentines, include Spaniards, Swedes, and Italians. He has even trained a woman active in the human rights movement in the United States. In addition, Tato remains one of Argentina's most confrontational and controversial voices in the theater. Much of his work is informed by his interest in subjective experience in authoritarian societies. He argues that psychic reality is more complex than even psychoanalysts understand, and he often diverges from his psychoanalytic colleagues' views.

For example, Tato is skeptical of the position of most psychoanalysts who work with the Grandmothers in the restitution of their disappeared grandchildren. Their psychological understanding leads them to argue that the torturers cannot provide authentic love to the children they have stolen from their victims. They contend that because these children were given to families who were complicit in the kidnapping and murder of the biological parents, the parent-child relationship was built on an immoral and illegal foundation; basically the parents viewed these children as the bad seeds of their subversive parents and felt they were graciously saving and rearing the children as good Christian citizens. Love under such circumstances, these psychoanalysts say, is filled with perversity. Tato believes, on the contrary, that although these people may be torturers, they can also be good parents and love these children. "The real perversity is the reality of this contradiction." Furthermore, he observes, restitution is more complicated than many socially committed psychoanalysts would like to believe. "We are obliged to explain how it is that in the few instances when the relocated children of *desaparecidos* do not wish to leave their 'appropriators' and return to their biological relatives, public opinion allies with the children and the families that have raised them, even when the families are known to have been directly connected with the military regimes." Tato's plays attempt to capture such contradictory complexities of the human condition. His controversial *Paso de dos* (*Pas de deux*) fascinated Argentine audiences in 1990. The play, which featured Tato and his wife, Susie, dramatizes the sadomasochistic relationship between a torturer and his ex-victim, suggesting that the question of domination in such a relationship is not clear-cut. The play attempts to illuminate the authoritarian discourse on violence and sexuality, and offers no easy answers about love and hate, domination and submission.[31]

Juan Carlos has focused his human rights activities on collaboration with the Grandmothers of the Plaza de Mayo. "I am practical and an optimist, and they are the only human rights group with the potential to actually solve a concrete problem. The other human rights work has to be done, to be sure; the torture and disappearances still have to be denounced, and the *afectados* helped. I do participate in this, of course, but it's my work with the Grandmothers that I find most appealing. The children they search for exist; they can be found, and they can be restituted. It's the only work that wasn't declared null and void by the *punto final, obediencia debida,* and *impunidad* laws. The only thing the government did not decriminalize was the stealing of babies. We have the paradoxical situation that if a member of the military were proven to have disappeared, tortured, and murdered someone, he could not be prosecuted, but if he stole a child, and he's caught, he can be imprisoned. The main thing is that these children exist; they are living with the murderers of their parents and have been robbed of their identity. This situation has nothing to do with adoption, which is constituted out of love; here we are talking about a robbery based on assassination." When the Grandmothers succeed in locating a missing grandchild, Juan Carlos, along with other mental-health professionals, provides informal or formal psychotherapeutic interventions to help the children and their biological families through the psychological turmoil and period of adjustment related to restitution.

In addition, Juan Carlos continues his customary frenetic pace, writing papers, analyzing aspects of cultural and social crises for the media, and organizing conferences. His weekly e-mail notes, typically descriptive and entertaining, keep me apprised of his and his colleagues' activities. In answer to my question about how he assesses his life since his return from Cuba, he wrote me, "Since 1985, we've survived, and, despite the moments that have been very difficult, it hasn't gone badly for us. I've tried at each historical juncture to live and act in concert with my ideals and to make decisions that do not betray them, even during the difficult moments of having to put them away in the freezer for awhile. For me, they're not so frozen, simply waiting to be activated again. Each time that a movement appears, like the Zapatistas in Chiapas, even with their contradictions, it awakens in Silvia and me an enthusiasm, a conviction about the correctness of our ideals."

Our protagonists all agree that it is a difficult moment to be living in, one in which it is tempting to become dispirited. But throughout this project, threading in and out of our discussions together, has been the memory of Mimi Langer, who provides each of us with a model of how to live one's life in the bad as well as the good times. It seems fitting for me to give Mimi the last word, for she captures so well the conviction of us all that what we do with our lives has meaning, for ourselves and for the future.

Shortly before her death, Mimi said, "What do you do about your 'being in the world and for what,' as the Existentialists would say, if you cannot find something to outlive you? For me and for many others, it is to be—and I'm not attempting to define this analytically—on the side of history: you are born at a determined historical moment, you are part of what existed beforehand, and you live out your cycle, either with history or against it. At one point it is your turn to die, but if you have lived on the side of history, then you will die with the feeling that you will remain part of it, that you will exist beyond your personal life and that you will have contributed to the future, to however small a degree."[32] Mimi lived and died in accord with this principle. She is, indeed, *presente*, a part of the history that continues to be made on the side of human emancipation.

For the rest of the proponents of liberation psychology, living on the side of history means something quite specific. As mental-health professionals, they treat patients in an effort to help them resolve the ongoing effects of social trauma and to work through unconscious barriers to emotional growth and the capacity for critical thought and action. As socially engaged individuals, they align themselves with movements that struggle to transform society. Their fundamental historical optimism enables them to hold out the belief that, sooner or later, a world of peace and social justice will prevail for our children and our children's children.

Epilogue

A Liberation Psychology
for the United States

Dear philosophers,
Dear progressive sociologists,
Dear social psychologists:
don't screw around so much with alienation
here where what's most screwed up
is the alien nation.

—ROQUE DALTON, "Cartita,"
in *Poémas clandestinos* (1982)

IN APRIL 1992, I returned from the Grandmothers conference in Buenos Aires, still preoccupied with the many human rights issues that had been raised by the participants. One of the memories that stood out was the shocked reaction of the audience to my presentation, in which, as the conference organizers had requested, I had described the growing social violence in the United States and some of the factors responsible for it. A woman in the audience suggested that the metropolis-periphery dichotomy, used to explain the historic appropriation of wealth and privilege by the developed capitalist world, was apparently becoming outmoded. "It seems as though the new trends associated with globalization subject us all in similar ways to the disastrous effects of neoliberalism," she argued. "Not only is the world no longer divided along the West/East cleavage, but the North/South distinctions are disappearing as well." On my return, in short order her assertion would be confirmed and my description of social violence would pale in light of the dramatic events that unfolded in Los Angeles.

The city exploded in a rage-filled uprising sparked by the acquittal of four white police officers whose brutal beating of African American Rodney King had been broadcast worldwide. Like thousands of Angelenos lucky enough to live just outside the area of turmoil, I watched the civil unrest on television; aerial shots revealed a checkerboard pattern of neighborhoods going up in flames, violent clashes between different ethnic groups, and the sacking of stores by the desperate poor who appropriated diapers, milk, and canned goods alongside adults and youth who dragged videos and televisions through smashed store windows. While this turmoil was being interpreted as a response to the racist judicial system in the United States, I thought that if it were happening in Latin America, the underlying economic and social deprivation sparking the anger would lead people to interpret it as a riot against the International Monetary Fund. And while this challenge to law and order was certainly an expression of animosity toward authority, it also revealed an identification with the impunity of those U.S. economic and political leaders whose power and wealth come not from respecting the law but from breaking it and reaping the rewards.

The Los Angeles civil unrest powerfully showed the growing similarities between the social and economic realities of Latin Americans and of increasing numbers of people in the United States. As the social fabric deteriorates, there is a concomitant rise in frustration, apprehension, fear, and hatred among people in all classes and ethnic groups. How do we understand the underlying causes of such widespread distress and conflict and the increasing proclivities of people to express them in self-destructive and destructive ways? How does the present environment—external reality—compromise the psychic capacity to sustain an internal sense of safety, empowerment, optimism, and connection to self and others? To repeat Mimi Langer's observation, "Each of us is wonderful, but also a bit mad. Each loving, but also perverse. We are all heroes, but also cowards. And we need to accept rather than deny this so we can learn how to deal with conflict and fear." How do contemporary economic, political, and cultural forces impinge on people's ability to negotiate this internal dialectic that Mimi described?

Neoliberalism: Downsizing the American Dream

The edifice of late consumer capitalism displays serious cracks in its foundation, frustrating the strivings for the good life that it has stimulated in its citizens. Neoliberal free-market economics and globalization are "disappearing" the privileges traditionally enjoyed by working people in the developed capitalist world. Corporate downsizing, capital flight, deindustrialization, the shift from productive to speculative investment, and the elimination of the protective functions of the state are all dramatically affecting the middle and working classes, the unemployed, and the chronically poor. Like their Latin American counterparts, growing numbers of families in the United States are caught up in the maelstrom of shrinking opportunities, lowered standards of living, and the fears and insecurities associated with an unpredictable future.

Long-term trends over the past several decades reveal a shocking pattern not seen since the days immediately prior to the Great Depression. The United States now leads all other advanced industrial societies in inequality: by the early 1990s, the wealthiest 1 percent of the population owned 40 percent of the wealth, and its total net income was the same as the total net income of the poorest 40 percent of the population, nearly one-fourth of whom now earn less in real terms than the 1968 minimum wage. In the richest industrialized country in the world, a society of have-mores and have-lesses is being created.[1]

Many factors are responsible for these long-term trends, including the technological revolution, which decreases the need for human labor. But a major culprit is the state's support of free-trade economic policies, which open the world's economies to U.S.-based, multinational corporate investment; the rising profits of these corporations worldwide are accompanied by downward trends in U.S. employment, wages, job security, and benefits for workers and in increased bankruptcies for small businesses. Corporate restructuring in the United States has resulted in the loss of 2.6 million jobs since 1979. And by the mid-1990s—a period of so-called economic recovery—the manufacturing sector, the highest-paying, most secure sector of the economy, had shrunk from the 1960s level of 33 percent of the total workforce to 17 percent. Workers are being reemployed in the services, the fastest-growing sector of the economy, noted for its low wages and nonunionized jobs. By mid-decade, about one-third of displaced wage and salary workers in the manufacturing sector who found alternative employment suffered earnings losses of 20 percent or more.

Where do the manufacturing jobs go? Offshore, which is to say, to the superexploitable—mainly women and children—labor forces in Asia and Latin America. Honduras, for example, has been host to many corporations that have closed down plants in the United States to take advantage of this Central American country's low-cost labor, tax incentives, and lack of health and safety laws and environmental restrictions. As for Haiti, the "pearl of the Caribbean," it is the ninth largest offshore assembler of U.S. goods in the world. The island nation's minimum wage of three dollars a day results in huge profits for U.S. corporate investors while the death of a Haitian child occurs every five minutes from malnutrition, dehydration, or diarrhea. The products manufactured abroad are then imported into the United States, where the government's reduction and elimination of tariffs guarantee sales in the domestic market at a competitive price. This policy results in disaster for U.S. workers whose jobs have been exported and in bankruptcies for small businesses whose activities, previously linked to corporate production in the United States, have been eliminated.

Government and corporate policies are creating a new pattern of poverty in the United States. While in the past poverty was associated with female-headed families, today over 40 percent of the poor live in two-parent families. As wages have slipped downward in the past several decades, the poverty rate has doubled for young married-couple families. In this wealthy country, one in five children lives in poverty. And poverty has a different context than it had in the past. In previous periods economic downturns and reduced opportunities occurred within a generally optimistic climate of long-term productivity and growth. Historically, people in the United States, especially in economically troubled times, could rely on a strong reformist impulse that limited the destructive effects of laissez-faire capitalism. Laws were passed that improved wages, working conditions, and quality of products, and protected workers and small businesses alike from the detrimental impact of monopolistic corporate giants. But in today's political climate the state is responsive to corporate lobbies that seek to dismantle the framework put in place during the past century. The downsizing—devolution—of the state and its regulatory functions, along with the emphasis on free trade, is presented to the public as a strategy for getting rid of big government. But rather than being a move toward noninterference in economic activity, it is an active intervention that favors some economic interests over others.

In the United States today, short-term economic ups and downs are part of a long-term downward trend. For the first time in the country's history the next generation will have less opportunity and a lower standard of living and will experience more social violence than their parents. Although people in every part of the country exert great effort to make meaning out of their work, to build loving bonds among family and friends, and to strengthen their community ties, the hurdles to these aspirations loom larger all the time. More people live in fear of losing their jobs, of not being able to pay for their children's education, of not being able to care for their aging parents, and of losing everything they have spent a lifetime creating. The vast majority who experience these fears are individuals and families who keep doggedly on track, although the road is getting rougher. Their work ethic and family values are threatened not by their personal moral deterioration but by a system that is wiping out decent jobs, driving down wages, and eliminating social policies that once supported rather than sabotaged the American family. Too often people blame themselves for their failure to achieve what they think they ought to, an unfortunate undermining of the self that is reinforced by the discourse of the government and mass media, whose denial of reality is reflected in overly optimistic assessments of present and future conditions.

Alan Greenspan, the chairman of the Federal Reserve Board, commented in June 1996 that he was puzzled about the pervasive job insecurity in the United States, in the face of an economic recovery that had been going on for five years. He pondered why so many workers doubt they can make ends meet in an economy that is expanding.[2] But are peoples' fears unfounded? What do working families have to look forward to as neoliberal free-trade policies alter the economy? The government and many economic advisors argue that even though manufacturing jobs are being lost to foreign workers, the forecast is positive because these jobs will be replaced with new, better-paying, high-tech jobs for highly educated and trained U.S. workers. The Department of Labor, however, offers a different assessment of the situation.[3] Among the twenty occupations expected to generate the greatest job growth, only one could be considered high-tech: systems analysis. But this is an exception to the rule because high-paying jobs will become scarcer, especially for women. Projected employment opportunities in order of the increase in number of positions are projected as follows: cashiers, janitors and cleaners, retail sales clerks, waiters and waitresses, registered nurses, general managers, top executives, home-health aides, guards, and nursing aides. In six of these ten occupations workers today earn wages that put them in the category of the working poor. No wonder, then, that U.S. citizens live with an overriding pessimism about their own and their children's futures.

As throughout Latin America, the social welfare functions of the U.S. government are being eliminated through devolutionary policies. At the same time that governmental and corporate economic strategies have diminished the number of well-paying jobs, the social programs that have helped those in need since the New Deal are being radically downsized or eliminated. Now these groups—children born in poverty, young mothers who need interim help, the unemployed who are victims of unregulated corporate activities, the disabled and chronically ill, and legal immigrants seeking a better life—are abandoned. Millions more will live with poverty, hunger, illness, homelessness, and desperation. Increased social violence is likely to be the outcome, in poor and wealthy neighborhoods alike. The abandonment of the poor is most apparent in the ghettos—the "inner cities"—a clear example of the government's "third worldization" of sectors of the population whose fate is indistinguishable from that of millions of people in the so-called Third World of Latin America, Africa, and Asia.

Impunity and Social Violence

As in Latin America, an environment of impunity operates in the United States at the highest echelons: Wall Street speculators, corporate raiders, and savings and loan criminals steal with few consequences. Presidents, Cabinet members, the Pentagon, the Congress, and the CIA lie and cover up their illegitimate actions with little substantive accountability to the public. All set an example that is difficult to resist: in this culture, the law is made to be broken. Opportunism and self-interested behavior are being emulated by people in all social and ethnic groups.

Such impunity encourages cynicism and self-interested behavior. The traditional cultural values of deferred gratification and hard work have receded in importance and are less likely than previously to be modeled by the rich and powerful. Immediate narcissistic gratification has been fostered by consumer culture and is encouraged by the powerful mass media—especially film, television, the music industry, and advertising. Perhaps the addiction to constant stimulation encouraged by consumerism and the new entertainment technology predisposes people to seek the stimulation of drugs in their flight from deadening and defeating economic, social, and psychological realities. Youth—especially those who suffer class and racial discrimination—believe this society is not invested in their generation and increasingly respond with their own angry alienation and rebellion.

Violence has become more a part of people's lives and consciousness in many ways. It is an aspect of their actual experience or is incorporated into their psychic reality in response to the pervasive violence portrayed by mass-mediated culture. For example, by the time the average child leaves elementary school, he or she will have seen eight thousand murders and more than one hundred thousand acts of violence on television. But children's exposure to violence in the real world is also dramatically increasing: in a study of first and second graders in Washington, D.C., 31 percent declared that they had witnessed shootings and 39 percent reported that they had seen dead bodies. In 1993 alone, approximately three million children nationwide were reported as suspected victims of child abuse and neglect, and an estimated 1,299 of them died as a result. Adults, as well, are exposed to increased targeted and random violence: it is conservatively estimated that between 21 and 30 percent of all women have been beaten by a partner, and between 1992 and 1993, more than two million people in this country were victims of physical attacks at the workplace.[4]

This environment of violence expands the customary legitimate parameters for the expression of frustration, anxiety, and aggression—emotions that are intensifying for many people in direct relationship to the growing insecurity of their lives. Because the complex economic and social causes of this insecurity are often difficult to understand, simplistic explanations that rely on scapegoating become a prominent feature of group behavior. The racism, sexism, and xenophobia that are deeply embedded in the culture help define the particular scapegoats, who then become the targets of cruel and hateful attacks. Because of their ethnicity, gender, or nationality, specific groups come to be endowed with all the destructive impulses that have been unconsciously split off from the self and one's identificatory group. They are then experienced as dangerous and persecutory and thus become (ideologically legitimated) targets of aggression. The rise in interethnic violence, wife battering, rape, child abuse, and juvenile gang warfare is related to people's subjective experience of anxiety as conditions in the United States become more objectively unstable. So, too, is the growing acceptance of state-sanctioned violence, such as soaring rates of imprisonment, police brutality and corruption, the reinstatement of the death penalty, and aggressive policies abroad. Although scapegoating offers the illusion of empowerment, in fact the displacement of fear and aggression onto scapegoats operates to divide people against themselves and to strengthen, at least in the short run, the economic and social system that inflicts their pain.

Foreign policy is an arena rife with examples of U.S. government impunity, which affects citizens' lives in ways that are not visible to most of us. For example, the government slashes or withholds tax dollars going to domestic social programs—job retraining, aid to small businesses, preventative medical projects, low-cost housing, schools, parks, and libraries. At the same time, a massive amount of taxpayers' money is used in foreign-aid programs that are destructive and not even designed essentially to provide aid to the people of foreign countries. For example, the U.S. government supplies credits to many countries which are, in turn, required to spend them on U.S. corporate products; this is not foreign aid but a tax-supported subsidy to U.S. businesses. Even worse, U.S. government loans, credits, and subsidies go to authoritarian governments all over the world, which purchase military equipment from U.S. arms manufactures in order to maintain authoritarian "law and order" in their own countries, even as their citizens are demanding economic equity and social justice.

U.S. policy in Latin America has consistently supported governments that employ military solutions to social problems. U.S. support is practiced with an arrogant impunity: while the United States publicly criticizes repressive governments, behind the scenes it finances, trains, and arms them. This U.S. policy in Central America, which during the 1980s contributed to the murder of hundreds of thousands of citizens by authoritarian regimes in the region, prompted exiled Guatemalan journalist Julio Godoy to ruefully declare, "One is tempted to believe that some people in the White House worship Aztec gods—with the offering of Central American blood."[5]

More recently, Mexico has become a U.S. government and corporate focus, especially since the North American Free Trade Agreement (NAFTA) went into effect on January 1, 1994, tying the two economies together in a neoliberal partnership that was intended to improve life for workers and consumers on both sides of the border. In the southern state of Chiapas, the Zapatista revolutionary organization exploded on the political scene the same day to protest the economic and social conditions in their country that they claimed NAFTA would only exacerbate. Several years later, as economists in the United States were confirming that NAFTA had caused a net loss of jobs for U.S. workers, the Zapatistas' prediction with respect to Mexico was validated in the dramatic economic and social crisis that ensued in that country. The Mexican economy has been caught in an unstoppable downward spiral: the standard of living of working people has plummeted, the middle class has been decimated, revolutionary movements have arisen to challenge the government and the military. The U.S. government protects U.S. corporate interests in Mexico with the money of American citizens: it rescued the Mexican government from a currency crisis in early 1995 by loaning U.S. taxpayers' dollars to halt the withdrawal of foreign investment from Mexican stocks. And as more political unrest emerges in Mexico, human rights organizations in the country are adding their voices to others who question the new cooperation between the Mexican and U.S. militaries; they fear these forces are repressing political dissidents under the guise of a military offensive against drug trafficking.[6]

A shocking example of how U.S. foreign policy can be injurious to people in the United States as well as those in other countries may be seen in the role of the CIA in the Contra war against Nicaragua. Newspaper reports in 1996 have alleged that, in order to finance the Contras, the CIA may have been involved in introducing crack cocaine to black youth gangs in Los Angeles. A Nicaraguan employee of the U.S. Drug Enforcement Administration is said to have confessed that he and his cohorts sold Colombian cocaine in South-Central Los Angeles, where street-level drug users invented a way to make the expensive powder into nuggets that could be smoked—crack—and sold in smaller, less expensive quantities. The profits earned by the gangs permitted them to buy the Uzis that turned the inner cities—first in Los Angeles and then elsewhere across the country—into battlefields.[7]

If true, this situation clearly reveals the simultaneous destructive effects on U.S. citizens and citizens of other countries of the government's ability to act illegally and with impunity. In this case, a single criminal strategy addicted thousands of African Americans to a deadly drug and spread gang wars that devastated their communities while it raised millions of dollars to train and equip a mercenary army that carried out an illegal and immoral war against the civilian population of Nicaragua. And although the CIA denies the allegations, thousands of citizens believe the CIA is guilty. They argue that the U.S. government, by either design or passive acquiescence, facilitated the devastation of black communities. They are outraged. Their conviction is a reflection not only of the actual role the CIA often plays, here and abroad, but of the cynicism many citizens feel toward their government.[8]

Democracy as Victim

It may be easier to see the similarities in the economic and social turbulence that characterize Latin America and the United States than to imagine that there are political parallels as well. After all, Latin America's history of authoritarian politics is distinct from the consistent and deeply rooted democratic traditions of the United States. But are there fissures in the edifice of U.S. democracy? Might it be that authoritarian trends whose symptoms are difficult to perceive are emerging in this country?

Let us listen again to Marcelo Viñar's description of living in democratic Uruguay before the advent of authoritarian rule. "The process of political change and the capacity to subjectively absorb and understand this change operate at distinctly different rates. . . . It's as if I continued to believe in democracy when I was living in a country that was already totalitarian. I believe that it is characteristic of the period of transition between democracy and dictatorship that people function by denying reality." Do Marcelo's words resonate in light of contemporary political realities in this country? Although it has been generally assumed that the United States is a uniquely democratic society and culture, there is increasing concern that we are sliding slowly and invisibly toward political authoritarianism with a democratic mask.

Academics, investigative journalists, and political commentators raise unsettling questions as they describe the current reality of politics in the United States. Here are some issues they point to:

- In general it is the wealthy or those with ties to the wealthy who can run for national office.
- The heavily funded Political Action Committees have the greatest opportunities to affect policy decisions by the Congress and the President.
- Information is increasingly controlled as media mergers concentrate ownership in several large conglomerates whose economic interests affect the kinds of information and analysis available to the public in the broadcast and print media.
- The two-party system actually represents a narrow spectrum of ideology and policy, and the hegemonic power of the two parties makes the emergence of a genuine, grass-roots alternative party nearly impossible.
- There is a rightward drift of legitimate political discourse.[9]

The leadership of both the Democratic and the Republican party continues to move to the right. And many national Republican leaders and their grass-roots followers engage in hatemongering that scapegoats specific sectors of society—women, gays, minorities, immigrants, unions—whom they view as responsible for the moral and material decline of the country. Their protofascism is reflected in the politics of neo-Nazi skinheads, Aryan nationalists, Christian fundamentalists, armed militias, and is manifested in the anti-immigration and anti-abortion movements, attacks on gay rights, and attempts to eliminate affirmative action. Their ideology and psychology aggravate an already polarized society.

Meanwhile, the progressive movement is disorganized and demoralized. People who identify with the liberal tradition of the Democratic Party are alienated by its rightward drift. But some reluctantly continue to support the Democrats, arguing that they are the lesser of two evils with respect to the extremist sectors of the Republican Party. Others, who feel more alienated, opt out of voting altogether or choose to follow their conscience by voting for progressive political parties like the Greens, which remain completely marginal to the national political process. As for the poor, the young, the overworked, the unemployed, and the homeless, many are cynical about politics and are convinced that voting will not make a difference in the degree of their social and economic disenfranchisement.

But when those who feel least represented by the government—who tend to be the poorest, least educated, most marginal sectors of the society—withdraw from the democratic process, electoral politics fall into the hands of the upper class, who are bent on maintaining their privilege, and the middle classes, who are frightened of losing more than has already slipped away from them. Because the middle classes subscribe to the two-party system, their vote, whether Democratic or Republican, winds up endorsing the status quo. Those for whom there is less economic democracy are thus also the victims of the kind of political democracy that oversees this stage of late capitalism.

Moreover, as philosopher Karl Popper once observed, "'It can't happen here' is always wrong: a dictatorship can happen anywhere."[10] The groundwork is being laid for the institutionalization of arbitrary rule, which could be activated by any government with authoritarian proclivities. The "Antiterrorism and Effective Death Penalty Act of 1996" challenges the constitutional balance between government power and personal freedoms. Although ostensibly aimed at the perpetrators of terrorist acts, the law gives the government unprecedented authority to infringe on the civil rights of citizens and noncitizens alike. For example, the law reintroduces from the McCarthy era the concept of guilt by association: at the discretion of the Secretary of State, any foreign group may be designated a "threat to national security" and "terrorist," a judgment that cannot be challenged. And citizens and noncitizens who belong to organizations that provide money or goods to the designated "terrorist" group or any of its affiliates, even for legal or humanitarian purposes, can be prosecuted for criminal acts. If this law had been in effect when the

African National Congress was struggling against apartheid in South Africa, anyone raising money for its political or humanitarian activities would have faced criminal charges if the Secretary of State had deemed it a terrorist group. Likewise, at the discretion of the Secretary of State, anyone active in humanitarian organizations, like Medical Aid to El Salvador or Pastors for Peace, may be subject to criminal charges.

Some sections of the law are not limited to terrorism. For example, in violation of First Amendment rights, the law has removed a legal provision that had explicitly limited the ability of the FBI to investigate individuals because of their views or affiliation. Another section has removed the right previously guaranteed to alleged criminals, some of whom are on death row, which permitted them to appeal to the federal courts to investigate possible violations of their constitutional rights during their trials in state courts. With respect to immigrants, the law empowers the Immigration and Naturalization Service to declare that an immigrant has entered the country without a visa and to deport him or her without proving deportability to a judge.[11]

The critics of the antiterrorism law argue that there is no indication that it makes the United States more secure from terrorist attack. In fact, suggest some, it may very well drive further underground those who represent a threat to citizens' safety. Furthermore, they argue that, in the long run, its clear violation of established principles of freedom of association and due process are more of a threat to citizens' rights than terrorist bombs. The legal framework is in place for potential arbitrary rule to be implemented by present and future governments. As the state becomes less able to sustain the basic social contract with its citizens, U.S. law now permits the imposition of repressive measures that nurture rather than contain violence.[12]

Throughout the United States many individuals are aware of the shifts—even the less visible ones—in our political culture, and some engage in a host of different struggles on behalf of social justice, economic equity, and authentic democracy. Unfortunately, at the present moment their critical voices are but a whisper amid the inchoate suffering of so many people. As U.S. citizens become more anxious and insecure, the media manipulates them by focusing on sensationalist stories aimed at exacerbating real and imagined fears. Consequently, the world seems ever more threatening. In response, people seem ever more willing to give up their civil rights in exchange for a paternalistic state that promises to protect them from danger. It is easy to understand how in such a climate the 1996 Antiterrorism Act readily passed into law. The irony is that the danger comes less from terrorist acts than from the terrifying economic and social conditions endemic to the neoliberal framework of late capitalism.

But the situation is even more complex because in the face of corporate globalization national rights are slowly entering the domain of international organizations whose authority transcends that of the nation-state. U.S. membership in the General Agreement on Tariffs and Trade (GATT) and NAFTA, for example, will have a deleterious effect on civic democracy. These organizations facilitate unregulated flows of capital among countries, providing new rights for foreign investors without requiring new responsibilities to the peoples and environments affected. Groups that have struggled successfully for laws to improve the working conditions of rural and industrial workers, protect workers' and consumers' health from dangerous pesticides, and save poor neighborhoods from unsafe toxic dumps will be increasingly obliged to fight on behalf of these and related issues by appealing to appropriate committees of GATT and NAFTA rather than the U.S. Congress. In this case globalization requires local organizers to engage in lengthy and time-consuming appeals to bureaucracies composed of individuals who may not be citizens of their country and who may not have any awareness of localized conditions. This process diminishes the functioning of civic democracy not only in the United States but in all member countries.

Growing internationalism, of which GATT and NAFTA are but two organizational manifestations, is characterized by a contradictory trend. National borders are being erased to permit the flow of capital, technology, and goods, but they are being drawn with bold lines to impede the mobility of human beings, especially working people and the poor who are forced to cross borders in search of work. While the U.S. government supports the type of internationalism that privileges corporate mobility and profits, it sabotages the type of internationalism aimed at generalizing policies of peace, social justice, and human rights. For example, on December 10, 1948, the General Assembly of the United Nations adopted the Universal Declaration of Human Rights, which was proclaimed as a common standard of achievement for all nations and all peoples, regardless of race, color, sex, language, religion, and political or other opinion. The Declaration includes in its definition of human rights:

- the right to life, liberty, and security of person
- the right to equal protection before the law
- the right to equality in marriage
- the right to freedom of thought, religion, peaceful assembly, and association
- the right to social security
- the right to work in just and favorable conditions
- the right to protection from unemployment
- the right to equal pay for equal work

- the right to just and favorable remuneration for an existence worthy of human dignity, with supplementation, if necessary, by other means of social protection
- the right to rest and leisure, including holidays with pay
- the right to a standard of living adequate for health and well-being of oneself and one's family
- the right to education

The United States has never signed this declaration.[13] Moreover, the United States has refused to abide by an International Court of Justice ruling that it owes Nicaragua seventeen billion dollars in reparations for illegal armed aggression against a sovereign state that resulted in deaths and injuries of Nicaraguan citizens and massive destruction to property. People throughout the world believe that international agencies such as these are needed so that a universal set of political principles and laws guaranteeing civil liberties and human rights can be guaranteed to all people in the world. Recently the International Criminal Court initiated trials of the perpetrators of genocidal policies in Rwanda and Bosnia, but they will be successful only if those who masterminded the policies are brought to trial. And this can happen only if the nations that harbor these individuals permit them to be extradited. Many statesmen and legal specialists, including former U.S. Attorney General Ramsey Clark, believe that the International Criminal Court shows great promise as an international body that can challenge the impunity enjoyed by perpetrators of crimes against humanity. But, as Clark soberly warns, "Those who wield power naturally oppose international law because such law would impose limits on the use of power and require peaceful resolution of disputes. Power prefers to have its way."[14]

An internationalism oriented toward improving human rights also comes as a result of people-to-people activism in many groups, such as Amnesty International and Americas Watch. Their efforts are directed at exposing the politically repressive policies of governments who violate the human rights of their citizens through abduction, imprisonment, torture, and murder. The public campaigns of these groups often save lives of innocent victims. Other kinds of human rights movements concentrate on cross-border cooperative struggles of workers. One dramatic case is the battle waged in a Coca-Cola bottling plant by Guatemalan workers organizing for better working conditions, livable wages, and union recognition. Their innovative strategies were strengthened by the solidarity shown by the American Friends Service Committee staff in Central America, the New York-based Interfaith Center on Corporate Responsibility, the Geneva-based International Food and Allied Workers Secretariat, the Guatemalan Labor Education Project, and a host of

Guatemalan labor organizations. Together they fought successfully through let-ter-writing campaigns and a boycott of Coca-Cola in twenty countries and won union recognition and better wages.[15] More recently, an educational cam-paign has been undertaken on behalf of Indonesian workers—mostly women and children—who are paid $2.30 a day for working in a Nike plant. They are prevented by Nike from organizing a union or securing an independent oversight investigation of the horrendous working conditions and low wages at the multibillion-dollar corporation. The San Francisco–based Global Ex-change is promoting the Indonesian workers' struggle by mobilizing U.S. la-borers and consumers to pressure Nike to engage in responsible corporate behavior. International campaigns like these, which bring people together in an effort to improve the conditions of the most exploited and repressed work-ing people in the world cannot help but ultimately improve the conditions of us all.[16] Indeed, those who echo the refrain "think globally, act locally" rep-resent another form of globalization that perhaps can challenge the inequi-table structures of neoliberal capitalism.

A Liberation Psychology: What's Possible?

Do mental-health professionals have something to contribute to social struggles at this historical juncture? Could a liberation psychology emerge in the United States to address the connection between unconscious mental pro-cesses and socioeconomic forces that determine the crises facing humankind in the present era? Is it possible that a socially engaged psychology can take its place alongside the struggles for a humane social order?

The psychological burden of living in these times oppresses us all, evi-dence of which mental-health professionals see every day in their clinical prac-tices. Moreover, like their patients, they are psychologically subjected to the deterioration of social and economic structures and its impact on their work lives. They are witness to how the state and corporate elites collude in an abandonment of responsibility toward the physical well-being and psychologi-cal health of U.S. citizens. In neoliberal capitalism, work, housing, education, and health care are not human rights and neither is mental-health care.

In the former Soviet Union, mental-health professionals were used by the state to maintain its coercive control over its citizens. Psychiatrists often helped defuse potential threats to the state by diagnosing dissidents as mentally in-sane and medicating or incarcerating them (or both). Although this close re-lationship of the mental-health profession and the state is usually associated with authoritarian regimes—whether they are military dictatorships in the Southern Cone or centralized, single-party dictatorships like the ex–Soviet Union—there are disquieting hints of similar patterns in the United States.

In the United States, psychology—regardless of theoretical orientation—has historically functioned uncritically as a mode of adapting the individual to societal norms. This tradition is cemented in developments in health care that are characterized by patterns of impunity and free-market economics. Managed care has been designed by corporate elites to organize health care on the basis of maximizing profits and minimizing costs, rather than providing services. Finance capital determines whether an individual has the right to medical treatment, surgical intervention, hospitalization, or mental-health care. Medical decisions are increasingly driven by cost-cutting objectives rather than patient need. For mental-health care, short-term therapy and psychotropic drugs are the treatments of choice. Mental-health clinicians in the managed-care networks are bound by the limited parameters imposed on them. They become—often reluctant—accomplices in an increasingly dehumanized system of mental-health care. Moreover, as insurance companies reduce the number of sessions for which they are willing to pay, private practitioners often find themselves having to design their interventions to be brief, symptom-oriented, and superficial. Psychoanalytically oriented mental-health professionals are out of sync with the cost-effective objectives of the managed-care system: they are not interested in managing their patients, but in helping them understand the underlying dynamics of their conflicts and symptoms so that they might work through the impediments to psychological growth and the achievement of critical thought.

How can psychoanalytic theory and practice—a complex and profound conceptualization of the human mind and a labor-intensive clinical-treatment modality—make a contribution to the current crisis in mental health? How does a profession considered by most to be elitist because it is an expensive and time-consuming endeavor align itself with progressive struggles for social change? Is there any reason to think that a U.S. version of liberation psychology can develop? Trends within psychoanalytic theory suggest encouraging possibilities: first, the emergence among individual psychoanalysts, psychologists, and other mental-health professionals of an interest in moving beyond a theory of individual mental functioning or of dyadic relations (parent/child, patient/analyst) to consider the role played by culture in unconscious mental functioning; and, second, evidence of the conviction that a socially conscious psychoanalysis has a contribution to make to the struggles against authoritarian discourse and practice in this country.

Psychoanalysis has been affected over the past several decades in the United States by the theoretical and clinical exploration of trauma—initially in the work with Vietnam veterans and in the analysis of the subjugation of women. Both areas highlighted the important impact of external reality as well as unconscious fantasy on psychological experience. Studies of trauma in relation to war, wife battering, and child abuse, for example, reintroduced an exploration of the interaction between traumatagenic social experience and the unconscious meanings made of it. The feminist insistence on the social construction of gender and its internalization in the unconscious mind has affected psychoanalytic understandings of mothering, sexuality, and creativity. Because of the groundbreaking work of feminist psychoanalysts, there is a deepening theoretical and clinical appreciation of the impact of patriarchal culture in the formation of sexual and gender identity and unconscious conflict.[17]

Some feminists have argued that an analysis of the ways patriarchal culture shapes women's emotional lives is essential to the effective treatment of women patients and that therapists must interpret their patients' conflicts as an expression of the confluence of intrapsychic, interpersonal, and cultural experience. For example, feminist psychoanalytic writers have offered an astute integration of cultural critique with psychological theory in their work on eating problems in women. They contextualize their psychoanalytic interpretation of how women negotiate the fundamental human activity of eating and their feelings about food and body size within a critical feminist theory of the internalization of culture. Increasing numbers of psychoanalytically informed mental-health professionals argue that the culture and its impact on psychic reality must be brought into the psychotherapeutic endeavor so that patients understand the social context of their psychic pain.[18] Moreover, the feminist perspective in psychoanalysis and psychology has often been identified with a conviction that the study of psychological trauma—whether it be of young men in war or of battered wives or of abused children—is not possible without the support of political movements that legitimate an alliance between investigators and patients and that challenge the customary social barriers of silence and denial. "In the absence of strong political movements for human rights," argues feminist psychiatrist Judith Herman, "the active process of bearing witness inevitably gives way to the active process of forgetting. Repression, dissociation, and denial are phenomena of social as well as individual consciousness."[19]

There is also an expanding interest in the application of psychoanalytic theory to the social, cultural, and political aspects of human experience, with the goal of illuminating the convergence of unconscious mental functioning and class, race, and gender relations of domination and subordination. There are the beginnings of a psychosocial critical analysis of U.S. culture and the role psychotherapy has played in constructing a self completely adapted to consumer society. Concerns are being articulated about the interface between the politics of hatred and psychological alienation. Increasing numbers of psychotherapists argue that neutrality in the therapeutic enterprise is not possible. They are interested in accepting the challenge to participate in movements whose goal is to develop a society in which the sense of well-being and worth of individuals and nations will not be based on disowned projections that inevitably stimulate hatred and fear and thus aggression toward others.[20]

Another psychoanalytic perspective argues for a psychoanalytic theory that accounts for differences in race, gender, culture, and social class. It postulates that psychoanalysis has much to offer in the current crisis in mental-health care, including a critique of the dehumanizing approach to human suffering represented by managed care. There is growing encouragement for psychoanalysts to take an activist stance that goes beyond direct treatment, and there is a sense that even with managed care psychoanalysts could become important resources as consultants and supervisors whose depth of analysis can transmit important insights to professionals working in other treatment modalities. Psychoanalysis is viewed in light of the significant contribution it can make to treatment interventions with patient populations in low-income and minority communities. As a theory of the mind, psychoanalysis is increasingly being viewed as an important resource in providing understandings of race, culture, and class so that respect rather than animosity might come to characterize our multicultural society.[21]

There are also perspectives within psychoanalysis in the United States that explicitly explore the relationship between Marx and Freud and examine contemporary society through a psychoanalytic-Marxist lens. Refusing to reduce psychoanalysis to a conformist psychology and Marxism to Stalinist orthodoxy, writers and practitioners in this tradition elaborate an interpretation of the emancipatory trends in both modes of thought and illuminate the intersection between psychology and the social world. A psychoanalytic-Marxist interpretation is offered of racism and of the threat of a neofascist movement in the United States. In this tradition, the psychoanalytic enterprise is infused with an understanding of class, gender, race, and ecology, and sees itself as an integral part of transformational social movements.[22]

Hopefully, the voices that represent these perspectives and the others who echo their message will be strong enough to mobilize a progressive movement within psychoanalysis and psychology in the United States. Such a movement could enhance the struggle against the social trauma created by impunity and neoliberalism in this country and contribute to an alternative social vision for the future. The mental-health profession is gradually taking up the task of understanding the interrelationship between alienated personal existence and alienated social relations, between individual anomie and social oppression, and between individual mental health and collective empowerment. It may be that a chorus will emerge to call for a "preferential option for the poor" and to proclaim that psychotherapeutic neutrality—as well political neutrality—is impossible, especially in the polarizing social conditions of the United States.

LIKE OUR COMPAÑEROS in Latin America, progressives in the United States agree that it is a difficult moment to be living in. When I feel discouraged, I remember a poster that hung on my wall in the sixties, when I was a graduate student studying history and struggling for social change. It was a large photograph of Mary Harris Jones—Mother Jones—the fiery organizer of the United Mine Workers in the early 1900s. A woman full of vitality and dedication, she would travel the country from mine to mine, and when workers were shot down in their confrontations with their greedy and violent bosses, she would rally the miners and their families to stay in the good fight. "Don't mourn—organize!" she would passionately challenge. Mother Jones was right, of course: workers had to organize in order to empower themselves in the battle with the ruling class. But now I imagine saying to this heroine of U.S. history that we need to mourn in order to organize, that we need to be able to tolerate the pain and grieve as we go. Mourning is an aspect of what Latin Americans mean by *memoria:* the willingness to remember, to know, to understand, and to grieve all that is painful and unjust about our human condition. And then to act on behalf of repairing it: to mourn—*and* organize!

Throughout the United States today, people fight on different fronts for human rights. They struggle for decent working and living conditions, psychological well-being, respect for diversity, ecological sanity, and toward a social vision that challenges the neoliberal capitalist economic model, whose industrial base and consumerist values now threaten the earth's delicate ecosystems. These activists are a valuable link to the tradition of radical politics in the United States. They are, as well, fighting on the side of history for a peaceful and just future. We need a liberation psychology that can align itself with this fight to assure its emancipatory potential.

Notes

Introduction

1. Marie Langer, *Motherhood and Sexuality*, trans. Nancy Caro Hollander. (New York: Guilford Press, 1992).
2. Quoted in Duncan Green, *Faces of Latin America* (London: Latin America Bureau, 1991), 175. For a summary of the radicalization of the progressive sector of the Church, see Green's chapter 11, "Thy Kingdom Come: The Church"; for a compelling study of the origins of liberation theology, see Penny Lernoux, *Cry of the People* (London: Penguin Books, 1982).
3. For the relationship between Marxism and the Catholic religion in Latin America from the 1960s on, see the discussion by Sheldon B. Liss, *Marxist Thought in Latin America* (Berkeley: University of California Press, 1984), 282–286.
4. See, for example, a collection of English translations of Martin-Baró's articles edited by Adrianne Aron and Shawn Corne in Ignacio Martin-Baró, *Writings for a Liberation Psychology* (Cambridge, Mass.: Harvard University Press, 1994). In a prescient moment, Martin-Baró once commented to a North American colleague, "In your country, it's publish or perish. In ours, it's publish *and* perish" (2). And, indeed, because of his critical psychological perspectives, his encouragement of his colleagues to develop a new, socially engaged epistemology and praxis, and his stature as Central America's most important social psychologist, Martin-Baró represented a threat to existing class relations and the brutal domination of the military in El Salvador. On November 16, 1989, along with the rector of San Salvador's Universidad Centroamericana, José Simeón Cañas, four of their Jesuit brothers, and their housekeeper and her adolescent daughter, Martin-Baró was assassinated by the U.S.-trained troops of the elite Atlacatl Battalion.

Chapter 1

1. Eduardo Galeano, *Open Veins of Latin America: Five Centuries of the Pillage of a Continent* (New York: Monthly Review Press, 1973), is a brilliant and passionate analysis of continued existence of colonial patterns, especially the dominant role played by the developed capitalist countries in the exploitation of Latin American natural resources.

2. Many authors have written about the persistence of economic, social, and political colonial institutions in the independence period. See, for example, E. Bradford Burns, *Latin America: A Concise Interpretive History* (Englewood Cliffs, N.J.: Prentice-Hall, 1990), especially chapters 2 and 3; also see Stanley J. Stein and Barbara H. Stein, *The Colonial Heritage of Latin America* (New York: Oxford University Press, 1970). The 1969 Gillo Pontecorvo feature film *Burn* is a powerful depiction of British imperialism in a fictional Caribbean island called Quemada; Marlon Brando as the brilliant and opportunistic British agent gives us a carefully constructed cinematic history lesson on the shift from colonial to neocolonial patterns in Latin America.

3. For the history of women in Latin America, see, for example, June Nash and Helen Safa, *Women and Change in Latin America* (New York: Bergin & Garvey, 1985); Latin American and Caribbean Women's Collective, *Slaves of Slaves: The Challenge of Latin American Women* (London: Zed Press, 1977); Audrey Bronstein, *The Triple Struggle: Latin American Peasant Women* (Birmingham, U.K.: WOW Campaigns, 1982); Pat Ellis, ed., *Women of the Caribbean* (London: Zed Books, 1986); Carmen Diana Deere and Magdalena León, *Rural Women and State Policy* (Boulder, Colo.: Westview Press, 1987); Jane Jaquette, ed., *The Women's Movement in Latin America, Feminism, and the Transition to Democracy* (Boston: Unwin, 1989); Elizabeth Jelin, ed., *Women and Social Change in Latin America* (London: Zed Books, 1990); Nancy Hollander, "Women Workers and the Class Struggle: The Case of Argentina," *Latin American Perspectives* 12 and13, nos. 1 and 2 (1977): 180–193. See bibliographies in these books and articles for sources in Spanish and Portuguese on women in Latin America.

4. The U.S. interventionist policies of the 1980s stimulated much academic interest in the region's social and political conflicts, which resulted in the publication throughout the decade of many important studies. For an especially lively depiction of U.S. intervention from the late nineteenth century on in Central America and the Caribbean, see George Black, *The Good Neighbor: How the United States Wrote the History of Central America and the Caribbean* (New York: Pantheon Books, 1988); also see Walter LaFeber, *Inevitable Revolutions: The United States in Central America* (New York: Norton, 1983), and Noam Chomsky, *Turning the Tide: U.S. Intervention in Central America and the Struggle for Peace* (Boston: South End Press, 1985). For a critical view of U.S. interventionism in Mexico and its impact on the United States, see Howard Zinn, *A People's History of the United States* (New York: Harper Perennial, 1990).

5. Discussions within the State Department and the Commerce Department in the postwar era revealed that U.S. policymakers and their colleagues in the private sector understood all too clearly the nature of the threat to the United States. While the U.S. government framed its policies to the public in terms of cold war rhetoric, insiders spoke to one another in exclusively economic terms about the nationalist threat in Latin America to U.S. financial and investment expansionism in the region. Documents published by the Commerce Department are especially revealing and are available in government publications archives in university libraries.

6. For background on the State Department–CIA organization of the 1954 coup in Guatemala and the brutal military rule that flourished in subsequent decades, see Richard H. Immerman, *The CIA in Guatemala: The Foreign Policy of Intervention* (Austin: University of Texas Press, 1982), and Stephen Schlesinger and Stephen Kinzer, *Bitter Fruit. The Untold Story of the American Coup in Guatemala* (Garden City, N.Y.: Doubleday, 1983).

7. See, for example, Peter Wyden, *Bay of Pigs: The Untold Story* (New York: Touchstone Books, 1980). For background on relations between the United States and

Cuba before and after the revolution, see Philip Foner, *A History of Cuba and Its Relations with the U.S.*, 2 vols. (New York: International Publishing, 1962, 1963); Leo Huberman and Paul M. Sweezy, *Cuba: Anatomy of a Revolution* (New York: Monthly Review Press, 1961); Sandor Halebsky and John M. Kirk, eds., *Cuba in Transition: Crisis and Transformation* (Boulder, Colo.: Westview Press, 1992), and their *Transformation and Struggle: Cuba Faces the 1990s* (New York: Praeger, 1990)

8. John J. Johnson's *Political Change in Latin America: The Emergence of the Middle Sectors in Latin America* (Stanford, Calif.: Stanford University Press, 1958) is the classic academic source in English for this point of view.

9. Jorge G. Castañeda's *Utopia Unarmed: The Latin American Left after the Cold War* (New York: Vintage Books, 1994) offers an analysis of the central role that Marxism has played philosophically and politically in Latin America since the nineteenth century, a critical evaluation of the armed struggles in the 1960s and 1970s, and an indictment of the current conditions that make Marxism still a viable theory of Latin American economic underdevelopment and political turmoil. For an approach that analyzes the conditions that sparked armed struggle as well as an assessment of its various strategies and tactics, which the author argues are still aspects of political struggles in today's Latin America, see Daniel Pereyra, *Del Moncada a Chiapas: Historia de la lucha armada en América Latina* (Madrid: Los Libros de la Catarata, 1994); for analyses of the contemporary strategies of progressive and left struggles in contemporary Latin America, also see North American Congress on Latin America, *Report on the Americas (The Latin American Left: A Painful Rebirth)* 25, no. 5 (May 1992): 13–45; *(Introduction to Hope: The Left in Local Politics)*, 29, no. 1 (July/August 1995): 14–44.

10. For an elaboration of dependency theory, see Fernando Henrique Cardoso and Enzo Faletto, *Dependency and Development in Latin America* (Berkeley and Los Angeles: University of California Press, 1979); André Gundar Frank, *Lumpenbourgeoisie, Lumpendevelopment: Dependence, Class, and Politics in Latin America* (New York: Monthly Review Press, 1974); Joseph Collins, *What Difference Could a Revolution Make? Food and Farming in the New Nicaragua* (San Francisco: Institute for Food and Development Policy, 1986).

11. An analysis of authoritarian regimes in the Southern Cone as a response to popular demands may be found in Guillermo A. O'Donnell, *Modernization and Bureaucratic-Authoritarianism: Studies in South American Politics* (Berkeley: Institute of International Studies, University of California, 1973), and his "Reflections on the Patterns of Change in the Bureaucratic-Authoritarian State," *Latin American Research Review* 12, no. 1 (winter 1978): 33–38; see also David Collier, ed., *The New Authoritarianism in Latin America* (Princeton, N.J.: Princeton University Press, 1979), and Guillermo O'Donnell, Philippe C. Schmitter, and Laurence Whitehead, eds., *Transitions from Authoritarian Rule* (Baltimore, Md.: Johns Hopkins University Press, 1986).

12. Background on the history of Uruguay may be found in Martin Weinstein, *Uruguay: Democracy at the Crossroads* (Boulder, Colo.: Westview Press, 1988), Russell H. Fitzgibbon, *Uruguay, Portrait of a Democracy* (New Brunswick, N.J.: Rutgers University Press, 1954); Edy Kaufman, *Uruguay in Transition: From Civilian to Military Rule* (New Brunswick, N.J.: Transaction Books, 1979).

13. Background on Chile may be found in Ian Roxborough et al., *Chile: The State and Revolution* (New York: Holmes & Meier, 1977); Regis Debray, *The Chilean Revolution Conversations with Allende* (New York: Pantheon Books, 1971); Paul W. Drake, *Socialism and Populism in Chile, 1932–1952* (Urbana: University of Illinois Press, 1978).

14. For information on the Allende years and the U.S. role in the Chilean coup, see Dale L. Johnson, ed., *The Chilean Road to Socialism* (New York: Anchor Books,

1973); "Chile: Blood on the Peaceful Road," *Latin American Perspectives* 12 (summer 1974); Federico Gil, Ricardo Lagos, and Henry Landsberger, eds., *Chile at the Turning Point: Lessons of the Socialist Years, 1970–1973* (Philadelphia: Institute for the Study of Human Issues, 1979); Pamela Constable and Arturo Valenzuela, *A Nation of Enemies: Chile under Pinochet* (New York: Norton, 1991); North American Congress on Latin America, "Chile: Beyond the Darkest Decade," and "Pinochet's Plebiscite: Choice with No Options," *NACLA Report on the Americas* 15, no 5, and 22, no 2 (September/October 1983 and March/April 1988).

15. For background on Argentina, see Juan E. Corradi, *The Fitful Republic: Economy, Society, and Politics in Argentina* (Boulder, Colo.: Westview Press, 1985); Donald Hodges, *Argentina 1943–1976: The National Revolution and Resistance* (Albuquerque: University of New Mexico Press, 1976); Carlos H. Waisman, *Reversal of Development in Argentina* (Princeton, N.J.: Princeton University Press, 1988).

16. For the historical significance of Peronism, see Frederick C. Turner and José Enrique Miguens, eds., *Juan Perón and the Reshaping of Argentina* (Pittsburgh Pa.: University of Pittsburgh Press, 1983); Nicholas Fraser and Marysa Navarro, *Eva Perón* (New York: Norton, 1980); Joseph Page, *Perón: A Biography* (New York: Random House, 1983); Nancy C. Hollander, "Si Evita Viviera . . . ," *Latin American Perspectives* 1, no. 3 (1974): 42–57. The stage play *Evita*, whose brilliant music captures something of the angst and drama of this period in Argentine history, does so by depicting Argentine politics from a conservative, Eurocentric, and misogynist perspective.

17. This period is described by Hodges, *Argentina 1943–1976*, and his "Argentina: The Protracted Struggle," *NACLA Report on the Americas* 7, no. 7 (September 1973).

18. Quoted in Ervin Staub, *The Roots of Evil: The Origins of Genocide and Other Group Violence* (Cambridge, U.K.: Cambridge University Press, 1989).

19. For a brilliant and complex analysis of remarks like this and their ideological and unconscious symbolic meanings (from a Lacanian psychoanalytic perspective), see Frank Graziano, *Divine Violence: Spectacle, Psychosexuality, & Radical Christianity in the Argentine "Dirty War"* (Boulder, Colo.: Westview Press, 1992).

Chapter 2

1. For more detailed information, see Nancy Hollander, "Buenos Aires: Latin Mecca of Psychoanalysis," *Social Research* 57, no. 4 (winter 1990): 889–919.

2. *Porteño* refers to the port city of Buenos Aires or one of its residents

3. This and subsequent information about the formative years of psychoanalysis in Buenos Aires was gathered through interviews with first- and second-generation Argentine psychoanalysts, including, in addition to Marie Langer over a number of years, Arnaldo Rascovsky, Jorge Mom, and Mauricio Abadi in Buenos Aires during August 1990. Also see the APA's official history—Asociación Psicoanalítica Argentina, *APA, 1942–1982* (Buenos Aires, 1982)—and Jorge Balán, *Cuéntame tu vida: Una biografía colective del psicoanálisis argentino* (Buenos Aires: Planeta Espejo de la Argentina, 1991).

4. Marie Langer, "Psicoanálisis y/o revolución social," in Marie Langer, ed., *Cuestionamos I* (Buenos Aires: Gránica Editor, 1971), 262–263.

5. Author interview with the past president of the APA, Buenos Aires, August 1990.

6. *Transference* is a psychoanalytic term that refers to the patient's projection onto the analyst of thoughts and feelings associated with primary people in the formative period of the patient's life; *abuse of the transference* refers to an analyst's taking advantage of the patient's dependence, occasionally through an erotic flirtation or even seduction. Langer was consistently critical of any manifestation of such behavior on the part of any analyst. Several colleagues claimed, however, that her

critique was somewhat hypocritical because her charismatic personality, intentional or not, wound up having the same impact on the candidates; because she was such a fascinating person, the candidates wished to become her analysands or supervisees. Her critics argued that this situation could be seen as a kind of indirect transference abuse.

7. See my introduction in Langer, *Motherhood and Sexuality*, 12–14.

8. Author interviews with Julia Braun and Argentine psychoanalyst Edmundo Zimmerman, Buenos Aires, August 1990.

9. Author interviews with Chilean psychologists María Isabel Castillo and Juana Kovalsky, Santiago, October 1995.

10. For more details of this tumultuous period, see Hodges, *Argentina, 1943–1976*, and Corradi, *The Fitful Republic*.

11. The dissident Argentines' criticism in the 1960s of the psychoanalyst as a neutral participant or a blank screen was one that would be treated at length and in a variety of ways in the psychoanalytic literature on countertransference that emerged during the next several decades in that country as well as in the United States and Europe; since the mid-1980s, the relational and intersubjective orientations within U.S. psychoanalysis have come to view the psychoanalytic process as a two-person enterprise in which the social world—culture—intervenes and is manifested. For the contemporary development of these ideas, see Steve A. Mitchell, *Relational Concepts in Psychoanalysis* (New York: Basic Books, 1993), and Neil Altman, *The Analyst in the Inner City* (Hillsdale, N.J.: Analytic Press, 1995). Also see *Psychoanalytic Dialogues*, a journal that features conversations among psychoanalysts about contemporary trends in the field.

12. C. Bigliani, L. Bigliani, and L. Esmerado Capdouze, "Dependencia y autonomía en la formación psicoanalítica," in Langer, *Cuestionamos I*.

13. *Señor Galindez* has been performed in theaters in the United States, where it has been received with interest and where audiences have had the opportunity to discuss with Tato the provocative questions the play raises with respect to what makes a torturer.

14. Langer, "Psicoanálisis y/o revolución social," 268.

15. Author interview with Antonio Barrutia, Buenos Aires, August 1990.

16. These two volumes, published by Gránica Editor (Buenos Aires) in 1971 and 1973, included contributions from many of the participants in the social movement within the profession; they raised significant issues regarding the relationship between psychoanalysis and ideology, politics, and violence.

17. For discussions on this perspective, see Marie Langer, *From Vienna to Managua*, trans. Margaret Hooks (London: Free Association Books, 1989); Altman, *The Analyst in the Inner City*; C. F. Alford, *Melanie Klein and Critical Social Theory* (New Haven, Conn.: Yale University Press, 1989); Women's Therapy Centre Institute, *Eating Problems: A Feminist Psychoanalytic Treatment Model* (New York: Basic Books, 1994); Michael Ruskin, *The Good Society and the Inner World: Psychoanalysis, Politics and Culture* (London: Verso, 1991).

18. When I lived in Buenos Aires in the late 1960s and early 1970s, I participated in the emerging "second-wave" women's movement and, together with Gabriela Cristeller, founded the UFA, a center that offered women a lending library of feminist literature from around the world, lecture series about the history of women and the women's movements in other countries, and the opportunity to participate in consciousness-raising groups. Participants in UFA, as well as in a number of other feminist groups that grew up in that period, were middle-class and upper-middle-class professionals and students, individuals from the arts, and those with activist experience in progressive and left movements. The movement also attracted working-class women with long histories of union militantism. During this period,

my friend Juanita Pereyra, whom I mention in the Introduction as the owner of the café-bar El Portalon in Madrid, was a member of a feminist collective that translated and published contemporary North American and European feminist literature.

19. See Hollander, "Women Workers and the Class Struggle" and "Si Evita Vivi-era . . . "; see also Fraser and Navarro, *Eva Perón*.

20. Marie Langer et al., "Psychoanalysis, Class Struggle and Mental Health," unpublished paper.

21. Quoted in Amnesty International, USA, *"Disappearances: A Workbook* (New York: Amnesty International USA Publications, 1982).

Chapter 3

1. See the report of the Senate Select Committee, headed by then-Senator Frank Church, that documented the U.S. conspiracy; the committee discovered, for example, that from 1969 to the day of the coup, the CIA generously gave financial support to anyone or any group that could be useful in bringing down the Allende government. As a former Chilean diplomat put it, "This meant that this CIA undertaking, first known as Track I and then as Track II, included everything— . . . cloak-and-dagger operations, involving the murder of generals and civilians, the strangulation of [the] Chilean economy and subversion of its legally elected government"; quoted in Samuel Chavkin, *The Murder of Chile* (New York: Everest House, 1982), 40. See also Lois Hecht Oppenheim, *Politics in Chile: Democracy, Authoritarianism, and the Search for Development* (Boulder, Colo.: Westview Press, 1993), and *La tragedia chilena: Testimonios* (Buenos Aires: Merayo Editor, 1973). For a history of the dictatorship that focuses on the personality, thought, and role of Augusto Pinochet, see Mary Helen Spooner, *Soldiers in a Narrow Land: The Pinochet Regime in Chile* (Berkeley, Los Angeles, London: University of California Press, 1994).

2. See Michael Klare and Nancy Stein, *Armas y poder en América Latina* (Mexico City: Era, 1978); D. F. Fleming, *The Cold War and Its Origins, 1917–1960*, 2 vols. (Garden City, N.Y.: Doubleday, 1961). Between 1950 and 1975, the following number of officers were trained in the United States or at U.S. bases in Panama: Argentina: 2,766 of a total 3,676 officer corps; Chile: 2,811 of a total 6,328 officer corps; and Uruguay: 1,120 of a total 2,537 officer corps: Timothy P. Wickham-Crowley, *Guerrillas and Revolution in Latin America* (Princeton, N.J.: Princeton University Press, 1992), 79.

For an analysis of the role of the United States in the creation of the ideology and strategy of state terror, see Alexander George, ed., *Western State Terrorism* (New York: Polity Press, 1991): Edward S. Herman and Gerry O'Sullivan in their chapter, "'Terrorism' as Ideology and Cultural History," provide statistics that compare killings by state and nonstate terrorists in numbers and orders of magnitude and conclude that "the services of the terrorism industry have been very much needed in the West to cover over its own activities and crimes. During the past forty years the Western states—including South Africa and Israel as well as the great powers—have had to employ intimidation on a very large scale to maintain access, control, and privileged positions in the Third World, in the face of the nationalist and popular upheavals of the 'post-colonial' era. This has been a primary terrorism, in two senses: First, it has involved far more extensive killing and other forms of coercion than the 'terrorism' focused upon in the West, . . . and second, it represents the efforts by the powerful to preserve undemocratic privileges and structures from the threat of encroachment and control by popular organizations and mass movements" (40–43). Also see chapters by Noam Chomsky, "International Terrorism: Image and Reality"; Richard Falk, "Terrorist Foundations of Recent US Foreign Policy"; and Michael McClintock, "American Doctrine and Counterinsurgent State Terror."

3. As Argentine General Ramón J. Camps explained, "France and the United States were the great proponents of the antisubversive doctrine. They organized centers, particularly in the United States, to teach the anti-subversive principles. They sent advisors, instructors. They sent out an extraordinary quantity of literature." Quoted in the report of the Argentine National Commission on the Disappeared, *Nunca más* (New York: Farrar, Straus & Giroux, 1986), 442.

4. See Eduardo Luis Duhalde, *El estado terrorista argentino* (Buenos Aires: Argos Vergara, 1983); Samuel Chavkin, *Storm over Chile: The Junta under Siege* (Chicago: Hill, 1989); Patricia Weiss Fagen, "Repression and State Security," in Juan E. Corradi, Patricia Weiss Fagen, and Manuel Antonio Garretón, eds., *Fear at the Edge: State Terror and Resistance in Latin America* (Berkeley and Los Angeles: University of California Press, 1992).

5. *Nunca más*, 444.

6. *Nunca más* contains information about U.S. involvement in Argentina during the Dirty War.

7. Quoted in Jo Fisher, *Mothers of the Disappeared* (Boston: South End Press, 1989), 14.

8. Donald C. Hodges, *Argentina's "Dirty War": An Intellectual Biography* (Austin: University of Texas Press, 1991), see especially chapters 5 and 6.

9. Discussion of this and similar statements depicting the military's worldview may be found in Graziano's *Divine Violence*, 107–146, and Hodges's *Argentina's "Dirty War*," 172–194.

10. Quoted in Patricia Weiss Fagen, "Repression and State Security," in Corradi, Fagen, and Garretón, *Fear at the Edge*, 43.

11. Cited in Rudolph Binion, *Hitler among the Germans* (New York: Elsevier, 1976), 1 and 24, respectively.

12. Quoted in Richard H. Immerman, *The CIA in Guatemala: The Foreign Policy of Intervention* (Austin: University of Texas Press, 1982), 113 and 117, respectively.

13. Quoted in Daniel Frontalini and María Ciati, *El mito de la guerra sucia* (Buenos Aires: CELS, 1984), 21.

14. Quoted in Graziano, *Divine Violence*, 111. For an elaborate discussion of this ideology, see Marcial Castro Castillo, *Fuerzas armadas: Etica y represión* (Buenos Aires: Editorial Nuevo Orden, 1979).

15. For a theoretical analysis of the relationship between gendered social arrangements in patriarchal capitalism and the impact on women of the terrorist state in Latin America, see Nancy C. Hollander, "The Gendering of Human Rights: Women and the Terrorist State in Latin America," *Feminist Studies* 22, no. 1 (spring 1996): 41–80. For a detailed analysis and description of the various psychological and physical tortures applied to women, see Ximena Bunster, "Surviving beyond Fear: Women and Torture in Latin America," in Marjorie Agosín, ed., *Surviving beyond Fear: Women, Children & Human rights in Latin America* (Fredonia, N.Y.: White Pine Press, 1993).

16. See Graziano, *Divine Violence*, and Hodges, *Argentina's "Dirty War."* Also see Cynthia Brown, *With Friends Like These* (New York: Pantheon Books, 1985); Salvador Ferla, *El drama político de la Argentina contemporánea* (Buenos Aires, 1985); Frontalini and Ciati, *El mito de la guerra sucia*; Alan Rouquié, ed., *Poder militar y sociedad política en la Argentina*, 2 vols. (Buenos Aires: Emecé, 1983). See also Amnesty International, *Torture in the Eighties* (London: Amnesty International Publications, 1984), especially 143–180. For reports and analyses of the practice and psychological and physical impact of torture worldwide, see the quarterly

publication of the Rehabilitation and Research Centre for Torture Victims, *Torture: Quarterly Journal on Rehabilitation of Torture Victims and Prevention of Torture*.

17. Jacobo Timmerman, *Prisoner without a Name, Cell without a Number* (New York: Vintage Books, 1982), 148.

18. See the analysis of this military cooperation among Southern Cone countries in *Nunca más*, 254–272.

19. Radio interview with author, May 1988, Los Angeles.

20. This information is included in detail in repeated testimonies in *Nunca más*.

21. Graziano, *Divine Violence*, 133.

22. Pamela Constable and Arturo Valenzuela, *A Nation of Enemies: Chile under Pinochet* (New York: Norton, 1991), 94.

23. Graziano, *Divine Violence*, 66.

24. Oscar Abudara et al., *Argentina psicoanálisis represión política* (Buenos Aires: Ediciones Kargieman), 24–25.

25. Timmerman, *Prisoner without a Name, Cell without a Number*, 125.

26. See Nancy C. Hollander, "Psychoanalysis and State Terror," *American Journal of Psychoanalysis* 52, no. 3 (September 1992): 273–289; Robert Godwin, "On the Deep Structure of Conservative Ideology," *Journal of Psychohistory* 20, no 3 (winter 1993): 289–304; Fernando Bendfeldt-Zachrisson, "Torture as Intensive Repression in Latin America: The Psychology of Its Methods and Practice," *International Journal of Health Services* 18, no. 2 (1988): 201–310.

27. See John Simpson and Jana Bennett, *The Disappeared and the Mothers of the Plaza* (New York: St. Martin's Press, 1985), 54.

28. Quoted in Elaine Scarry, *The Body in Pain: The Making and Unmaking of the World* (New York: Oxford University Press, 1985), 58.

29. Scarry, *The Body in Pain*, 122.

30. Servicio Paz y Justicia, *Uruguay: Nunca más: Human Rights Violations, 1972–1985*, trans. Elizabeth Hampsten (Philadelphia: Temple University Press, 1992).

Chapter 4

1. Among mental-health professionals in the United States who deal with the impact of ongoing trauma, such as child abuse and wife battering, there is a similar dialogue with respect to how to conceptualize the nature of trauma when it is imposed by external reality; see for example, Judith Lewis Herman, *Trauma and Recovery: The Aftermath of Violence—From Domestic Abuse to Political Terror* (New York: Basic Books, 1992); Laura S. Brown, "One Feminist Perspective," *American Imago* 48 (spring 1991): 119–33; R. J. Lifton, *Home from the War: Vietnam Veterans: Neither Victims nor Executioners* (New York: Simon & Schuster, 1973); J. M. Davies and M. G. Frawley, *Treating the Adult Survivor of Childhood Sexual Abuse* (New York: Basic Books, 1994).

2. Although she is stressing the ongoing nature of social trauma, Julia Braun would agree with the current literature on sexual abuse or wife battering, for example, which indicates the ongoing and repetitive nature of trauma within this private context.

3. Uruguayan sociologist Carina Perelli, quoted in Lawrence Weschler, *A Miracle, a Universe: Settling Accounts with Torturers* (New York : Penguin Books, 1990), 89; also see Perelli's analysis in "Youth, Politics, and Dictatorship in Uruguay," in Corradi, Fagen, and Garretón, *Fear at the Edge*; Elizabeth Lira, ed., *Psicología y violencia política en América Latina* (Santiago: ILAS, 1994); Elizabeth Lira and María Isabel Castillo, *Psicología de la amenaza política e del miedo* (Santiago, Chile: ILAS, 1991). For other sources on the dynamics of repression, see Saúl Sosnowski and

Louise B. Popkin, eds., *Repression, Exile, and Democracy: Uruguayan Culture* (Durham, N.C.: Duke University Press, 1993), and SPJ, *Uruguay: Nunca más.*

4. Moises Kijak and María Lucila Pelento, "Mourning in Certain Situations of Social Catastrophe," *International Review of Psycho-Analysis* 13, no. 4 (1986): 468. For additional sources on the impact on children of living in the culture of fear, see Marcelo M. Suarez-Orozco, "The Treatment of Children in the 'Dirty War': Ideology, State Terrorism and the Abuse of Children in Argentina," in Nancy Scheper-Hughes, ed., *Child Survival* (Dordrecht, Netherlands: Reidel, 1987), and Movimiento Solidario de Salud Mental, Familiares de Detenidos y Desaparecidos por Razones Políticas, *Terrorismo de estado: Efectos psicológicos en los niños* (Buenos Aires: Paidos, 1987).

5. For an analysis of the psychopolitical functions of public forms of punishment, see Michel Foucault, *Discipline and Punish: The Birth of the Prison*, trans. Alan Sheridan (New York: Vintage Books, 1979).

6. Graziano, *Divine Violence*, 73.

7. For a discussion of psychoanalytic thought regarding the notion of an environmental container (mother or social group or both) for intolerable and undigested or indigestible anxieties, see D. W. Winnicott, *The Maturational Processes and the Facilitating Environment* (New York: International Universities Press, 1965), and his *Playing and Reality* (New York: Basic Books, 1971), especially 111–118; W. R. Bion, *Experiences in Groups* (New York: Basic Books, 1959), and his *Second Thoughts* (New York: Aronson, 1967); Thomas H. Ogdon, *The Matrix of the Mind* (Northvale, N.J.: Aronson, 1986).

8. Quoted in Constable and Valenzuela, *A Nation of Enemies*, 165.

9. Maria L. Pelento and Julia Braun, "La desaparición: Su repercusión en el individuo y en la sociedad," *Revista de Psicoanálisis* 42 (1985): 1391–1397.

10. The testimony about Norberto Liwsky's horrendous abduction and torture is published in *Nunca más*, 20–26.

11. Timmerman, *Prisoner without a Name, Cell without a Number*, 31.

12. Marcelo Viñar, "Pedro o la demolición: Una mirada psicoanalítica sobre la tortura," in Marcelo Viñar and Maren Viñar, *Fracturas de memoria: Crónicas para una memoria por venir* (Montevideo, Uruguay: Ediciones Trilce, 1993), 40–41.

13. For discussions of this aspect of the experience of torture, see Bendfeldt-Zachrisson, "Torture as Intensive Repression in Latin America"; Seminario Internacional, *La tortura en América Latina, 2–5 diciembre 1985* (Buenos Aires: Codesedh, 1987).

14. See Mauricio Rosencof, *Memorias del Calabozo* (Nafarroa/Navarra, Uruguay: Txalaparta Editorial, 1993) for an evocative analysis of the experience of imprisonment, torture, and the capacity to maintain hope.

15. See Herman, *Trauma and Recovery*, especially Chapter 4, "Captivity," for a description of the similarities in the sadomasochistic relationships between the torturer and tortured and between the abuser and abused.

16. In *Fracturas de memoria* Marcelo describes in gruesome detail his torture in the chapter entitled "Un grito entre miles." It is interesting to note that in my interview with him, Marcelo did not describe the extent to which he had been tortured. For a profoundly moving exploration of the way that torture inflicts a sense of impotence and infantilization on prisoners through its attack on one's location in time and space and on one's control over basic biological functions, see Scarry's analysis in *The Body in Pain.*

17. Viñar and Viñar, *Fracturas de memoria*, 40–41.

18. Simon Wiesenthal maintained that Adolf Eichmann, the bureaucrat in charge of deporting millions of Jews to death camps, was simply the logical product of a system that would have expected any order to be implemented in similar fashion—for example, "if he had been ordered to kill all men whose name began with P or

B"; quoted in Hans Askenasy, *Are We All Nazis?* (Secaucus, N.J.: Stuart, 1978), 28. Other studies of Nazi commanders of concentration camps reveal them to have been administrators interested in doing a good job who became desensitized to the extreme human suffering they caused rather than perverse personalities deriving pleasure from their work; see, for example, G. M. Gilbert, *The Psychology of Dictatorship* (New York: Ronald Press, 1950), and Henry Dicks, *Licensed Mass Murder: A Socio-Psychological Study of Some SS Killers* (New York: Basic Books, 1972).

19. The books the friend loaned Elizabeth included *Cuestionamos I* and Hans Peter Gente, ed., *Marxismo, psicoanálisis y sexpol* (Buenos Aires: Gránica Editor, 1972); the Gente book was part of the publisher's Left Freudian Collection, a series edited by Marie Langer.

20. FASIC was a foundation within the Catholic Church involved in a variety of human rights activities during the dictatorship in Chile.

21. Their book is an exploration of the particular type of research and political commitment that typified their work with the Mothers: Diana R. Kordon and Lucila I. Edelman, eds., *Efectos psicológicos de la represión política* (Buenos Aires: Sudamérica Planeta, 1986).

22. The following is a brief list of articles and books on the movements of mothers throughout the continent: Fisher, *Mothers of the Disappeared*; Jo Fisher, *Out of the Shadows: Women, Resistance and Politics in South America* (London: Latin American Bureau, 1993); Agosín, *Surviving Beyond Fear;* Renny Golden, *The Hour of the Poor, the Hour of Women: Salvadoran Women Speak* (New York: Crossroad, 1991), especially Chapter 3; Jelin, *Women and Social Change in Latin America*; Jean Bethke Elshtain, "The Mothers of the Disappeared: Passion and Protest in Maternal Action," in Donna Bassin, Margeret Honey, and Meryle Mahrer Kaplan, eds., *Representations of Motherhood* (New Haven, Conn., and London: Yale University Press, 1992), 75–91; Morna McLeod, *GAM-Comadres: Un análsis comparativo* (Mexico City: Citgua, 1986); Marilyn Thomson, *Women of El Salvador: The Price of Freedom* (Philadelphia: Institute for the Study of Human Issues, 1986); Beatriz Manz, *Refugees of a Hidden War: The Aftermath of Counterinsurgency in Guatemala* (Albany, N.Y.: State University of New York Press, 1982); Rigoberta Menchú, *I Rigoberta Menchú*, trans. by Ann Wright (London and New York: Verso, 1992).

The first group in Latin America with the goal of locating disappeared family members emerged in Guatemala in 1967, following a wave of repression in that country a year earlier. A continentwide movement was founded in 1980, the Latin American Federation of Associations of Relatives of the Detained-Disappeared. At its first congress, held in 1981 in Costa Rica, it was estimated that during the prior two decades over ninety thousand people had been disappeared throughout the continent. The group meets annually so that member organizations can exchange information and strategies.

23. There seem to be gender differences in the psychological manner of responding to the impact of state terror; see Hollander, "The Gendering of Human Rights," 65–66; Seminario Internacional, *La tortura en América Latina*; Golden, *The Hour of the Poor, the Hour of Women*.

24. This term, which literally means "present," is used by Latin American progressives to indicate that a compañero or family member who has died in the struggle is still present in spirit and lives in the hearts and minds of the people who carry on the battle for justice and human rights.

25. Kordon and Edelman, *Efectos psicológicos de la represión política*, 63.

26. In their interviews with me in 1994, the members of the Equipo and Julia Braun all referred to a recently finished epidemiological study they coauthored, in which they found that women who were activists in the Mothers organization during or after the military dictatorship had lower rates of serious illness and longer life ex-

pectancy than the population at large in their age cohort, including both men and women.

Chapter 5

1. Author interviews with Mimi Langer and Nacho Maldonado, Mexico City and Nicaragua, various times, 1983–1987. The two also coauthored a manuscript about their experience in Mexico and Nicaragua, a copy of which Mimi gave me. It was never published.

2. For an exploration of the psychological meanings of the experience of exile from a psychoanalytic perspective, see León Grinberg and Rebeca Grinberg, *Psychoanalytic Perspectives on Migration and Exile* (New Haven, Conn., and London: Yale University Press), 1984. León Grinberg was an analysand of Mimi Langer's; his scholarly analysis is informed by his own personal experience of exile. He and his wife/colleague left Argentina in the late 1970s and have lived in Spain ever since. For a description of the impact of exile on Central American refugees, see María Cristina Bottinelli, Ignacio Maldonado, et al., *Psychological Impacts of Exile: Salvadoran and Guatemalan Families in Mexico* (Washington, D.C.: Hemispheric Migration Project, Center for Immigration Policy and Refugee Assistance, Georgetown University, 1990).

3. W. R. Bion, *Learning from Experience* (New York: Basic Book, 1962), and his "Attacks on Linking," *International Journal of Psycho-Analysis* 40 (1959): 308–315; D. W. Winnicott, "Primary Maternal Preoccupation," in *Through Paediatrics to Psycho-Analysis* (New York: Basic Books, 1975), 300–303.

4. Grinberg and Grinberg, *Psychoanalytic Perspectives on Migration and Exile*, 94.

5. Quoted in Viñar and Viñar, *Fracturas de memoria*, 87.

6. *El Día*, 5 June, 1977.

7. Many therapists who work with Holocaust survivors point out that the patient's awareness that the therapist repudiates the Nazi project or that the therapist has had some direct or indirect personal experience with the horrors of the Holocaust (or both) has a positive impact on the patient's capacity to trust the therapist and to develop a "therapeutic alliance." See, for example, Dinora Pines, "Working with Women Survivors of the Holocaust: Affective Experiences with Transference and Countertransference," *Revista de Psicoanálisis* 42, no. 4 (1985).

8. Viñar and Viñar, *Fracturas de memoria*, 60.

9. Viñar and Viñar, *Fracturas de memoria*, 60.

10. In November of that year, the elections took place and were certified by international observers as meaningful, clean, and competitive; in a contest with political parties to the right and the left of them, in which 75 percent of the registered voters cast ballots, the Sandinistas won 65 percent of the vote. The presidency and vice-presidency went to Sandinistas Daniel Ortega and Sergio Ramirez, respectively, and sixty-one of the ninety-six seats in the new National Assembly were won by the Sandinista Front; see Thomas W. Walker, ed., *Reagan versus the Sandinistas: The Undeclared War on Nicaragua* (Boulder, Colo., and London: Westview Press, 1987), Introduction.

11. The popular Church was involved with the Sandinista government; "between revolution and religion, there is no contradiction" was a popular slogan during the Revolution.

12. The Reagan administration attacked the Sandinista government, even breaking U.S. law to do so, not because it was a communist threat but because it represented a legitimate model for sovereignty and development in the Americas, much akin to the welfare capitalist model of the Scandinavian countries: a number of political parties functioned legally—the right wing was even financed by the "new

right" in the United States—and in the economy, by design, the private sector controlled at least 60 percent of industrial and agricultural production. For an analysis of the kind of politics and socioeconomic order the Sandinistas were developing, see E. Bradford Burns, *At War in Nicaragua: The Reagan Doctrine and the Politics of Nostalgia* (New York: Harper & Row, 1987); Thomas W. Walker, ed., *The Undeclared War on Nicaragua* (Boulder, Colo.: Westview Press, 1987); Richard Harris and Carlos M. Vilas, *Nicaragua: A Revolution under Siege* (London: Zed Books, 1985); Joel Kovel, *In Nicaragua* (London: Free Association Books, 1988).

13. To understand LIC, see Michael T. Klare and Peter Kornbluh, eds., *Low Intensity Warfare: Counterinsurgency, Proinsurgency, and Antiterrorism in the Eighties* (New York: Pantheon Books, 1988), especially Chapter 6, "Nicaragua: U.S. Proinsurgency Warfare against the Sandinistas," 136–157. According to a Defense Department official, the project in Nicaragua was to "keep some pressure on the Nicaraguan government, force them to use their economic resources for the military, and prevent them from solving their economic problems—and that's a plus"; quoted in George, *Western State Terrorism*, 19.

14. The Contras got training in psychological torture from the United States; an example was what they learned from a 1968 lessons book, "Armed Psyop," used at the Army Special Warfare School at Fort Bragg, North Carolina, which called for the use of selected violence against civilians, as reported in the *Washington Post*, 24 October 1984. According to Edgar Chamorro, who testified before the World Court on September 5, 1985, FDN (a Contra army) "would assemble all the residents in the town square and then proceed to kill—in full view of the others—all persons suspected of working for the Nicaraguan government." Also see the CIA training manual on psychological warfare, including torture: *The CIA's Nicaragua Manual: Psychological Operations in Guerrilla Warfare* (New York: Vintage Books, 1985). As a U.S.-trained and -supported anti-Sandinista counterinsurgency operative expressed his sentiments about work, "I love killing; I have been killing for the past seven years. There's nothing I like better. If I could, I'd kill several people a day"; quoted in Americas Watch, *Human Rights in Nicaragua: Reagan, Rhetoric and Reality* (New York, 1985). In Mimi's mind, U.S. policy in Nicaragua constituted a form of state terror perpetrated from abroad.

15. Mimi and I had lengthy discussions about this priority shift from the experience in Argentina, and this concise expression of it appears in Langer, *From Vienna to Managua*, 229.

16. In fact, Mimi did write the article about a year later and presented it as an invited paper to people in the arts and literature in Havana at Casa de las Américas. Her presentation was followed by a renewed interest in psychoanalysis on the part of the Cubans. Subsequently, Mimi and other colleagues organized the Latin American Congress of Marxist Psychology and Psychoanalysis (Encuentro Latinoamericano de Psicología Marxista y Psicoanálisis), which has met biannually since 1986 at the University of Havana, Department of Psychology. Mental-health professionals from all over Latin America and Europe, with some participation from U.S. colleagues, meet to discuss their ideas about the intersection between individual psychology and social structures. Mental-health and social issues are examined by those attending, all of whom share a progressive view of the world and a commitment to mental health and a politics of justice and equality.

17. I would later interview Dora María for my radio program. She made a complex critical assessment of the Sandinistas' struggle with male chauvinism to the effect that although they had initially supported women's equal rights and had launched an important AIDS-awareness campaign, their willingness to sustain women's issues as primary and their ability to support gay rights paled as other priorities emerged during the war against the Contras. Dora María and other Sandinistas

interested in feminist issues criticized the Sandinista leadership for its resistance to allowing women an equally prominent role in the organization. To see the shift in many women's views about how their gender interests were being represented by the Sandinistas, see Margaret Randall's two studies, separated by eleven years: *Sandino's Daughters: Testimonies of Nicaraguan Women in Struggle* (Vancouver and Toronto, Canada: New Star Books, 1981) and *Gathering Rage* (New York: Monthly Review Press, 1992). See also Randall's *Our Voices Our Lives: Stories of Women from Central America and the Caribbean* (Monroe, Maine: Common Courage, 1995), especially Chapter 4.

18. Mimi had told me this many times, and this concise version of her sentiment is quoted in Langer, *From Vienna to Managua*, 221.

19. N. Hikmet, *Antología poética* (Buenos Aires: Quetzal, 1968). I have translated this poem from the Spanish; I was unable to locate an English translation. However, Hikmet may be read in English; see, for example, *The Epic of Sheik Bedreddin and Other Poems* (New York: Crown Publishers, 1985).

20. Mimi died before the U.S. economic and military aggression against the Sandinistas succeeded in dislodging them from power. When the 1990 elections in Nicaragua took place, the U.S.-funded conservative candidate, Violeta Chamorro, won on the basis of a campaign that presented her as the only hope to stop the war with the Contras and the vehicle through which the United States would send much needed money instead of arms to her country. The Sandinistas honored the outcome of the elections, which brought to power a Chamorro-led coalition whose rule did not attract the promised U.S. dollars and whose policies have unraveled all the Sandinista social programs developed during the 1980s. The standard of living has declined for Nicaraguans, and social violence has escalated. The Sandinistas remain the best organized political force in the country and often ally themselves with the president in her struggles against the more reactionary elements in her ruling coalition.

Chapter 6

1. The conference commemorated the fifteenth anniversary of the Grandmothers of the Plaza de Mayo in April 1992. A book that includes the proceedings and presentations at the conference was subsequently published under the same title as the conference: Abuelas de Plaza de Mayo, *Filiación, identidad, restitución: 15 años de lucha de Abuelas de Plaza de Mayo* (Buenos Aires: El Bloque Editorial, 1995).

2. See especially Silvia Bleichmar, "Traumatismo: Apropiación—Restitución," in Abuelas de Plaza de Mayo, *Filiación, identidad, restitución*, 107–114. This perspective represents the most optimistic assessment of the ultimately benign effects of this human drama; some mental-health professionals are less sanguine about the impact on young people who learn they are the children of *desaparecidos*, and they are concerned about what happens to children and their biological families who do not seek professional help to negotiate the difficult emotional states produced by these painful circumstances. Because of the uniqueness of this situation, there is no knowledge about the long-term psychological effects on these young people, who must grapple with the knowledge that their biological parents were disappeared and probably tortured and murdered and that the people with whom they grew up and whom they called Mama and Papa were either direct collaborators or childless couples willing to close their eyes and not ask questions when the possibility of "adopting" a child presented itself. Some mental-health professionals have noted in these children symptoms associated with an inability to mourn and with guilt connected to having survived or to having (unknowingly) betrayed their parents by loving the family who brought them up (or both). There is a growing

literature in Spanish on this topic, but for a source in English that tells the moving story of the first restituted grandchild, see Marifran Carlson, "A Tragedy and a Miracle: Leonor Alonso and the Human Cost of State Terrorism in Argentina," in Agosín, *Surviving Beyond Fear*, 71–85.

3. The statistics throughout this section come from the following issues of *NACLA Report on the Americas*: 26, no. 3 (December 1992); 26, no. 4 (February 1993); 27, no. 3 (November/December 1993); 27, no. 6 (May/June 1994); 28, no. 1 (July/August, 1994); 28, no. 2 (September/October 1994); 29, no 6 (May/June 1996).

4. Mauricio Rosencof, "On Suffering, Song, and White Horses," in Sosnowski and Popkin, *Repression, Exile, and Democracy*, 131.

5. Lira and Castillo, *Psicología de la amenaza política y del miedo*, 239.

6. This shift in international financial support from authoritarian, right-wing governments to the constitutional regimes that would succeed them and institutionalize the essential aspects of their rule is too complex to detail here but is examined in Paul E. Sigmund, *The United States and Democracy in Chile* (Baltimore and London: Johns Hopkins University Press, 1993), 173.

7. Diana Kordon et al., *La impunidad: Una perspectiva psicosocial y clínica* (Buenos Aires: Editorial Sudamericana, 1995), 29–31.

8. Viñar and Viñar, *Fracturas de memoria*, 125. For an analysis of the differences in the experience of repatriation among Argentines and Uruguayans because of their respective governments' policies, see Lelio Mámora and Jorge Gurrieri, *Return to Rio de La Plata: Response to the Return of Exiles to Argentina and Uruguay* (Washington, D.C.: Center for Immigration Policy and Refugee Assistance, Georgetown University, 1988).

9. "Práctica social y proceso de elaboración," in Kordon et al., *La impunidad*, 189–94.

10. Editorial in the Mothers publication, *Madres de Plaza de Mayo*, no. 2 (January 1985), quoted in Fisher, *Mothers of the Disappeared*, 142–143.

11. Abudara et al., *Argentina psicoanálisis represión política*, 16. During the late 1980s and 1990s, other studies were published that analyzed various aspects of the psychological impact of state terror on individuals, children, and families. See, for example, Janine Puget and Rene Kaes, eds., *Violencia de estado y psicoanálisis* (Buenos Aires: Bibliotecas Universitarias Centro Editor de América Latina, 1991); *Revista de Psicoanálisis* (special issue entitled *Acerca del malestar en la cultura*), 42, no. 6 November/December 1985); Movimiento Solidario de Salud Mental, *Terrorismo de estado*. There is much literature on specific extraordinary events that marked the advance of the draconian policies of the military; see, for example, María Seonane and Héctor Ruiz Núñez, *La noche de los lápices* (Buenos Aires: Planeta Espejo de la Argentina, 1992). Many individuals whose children were disappeared published books about them and their experience under state terror; see Noemí Ulla-Hugo Echave, *Después de la noche: Diálogo con Graciela Fernández Meijide* (Buenos Aires: Editorial Contrapunto, 1986), and Matilde Herrera, *José* (Buenos Aires: Editorial Contrapunto, 1987). See also Julio E. Nosiglia, *Botín de guerra* (Buenos Aires: Cooperativa Tierra Fértil L Tada y Julio E. Nosiglia, 1985).

12. Quoted in Kordon et al., *La impunidad*, 74–75, and in Abudara et al., *Argentina psicoanálisis represión política*, 22–23; the English version is in Sigmund Freud, *Collected Works*, vol. 21 (London: Hogarth Press and Institute of Psycho-Analysis, 1927–1931), 1995.

13. Quoted in Kordon et al., *La impunidad*, 22.

14. *Los Angeles Times*, 30 March 1987, quoted in Weschler, *A Miracle, a Universe*, 194.

15. Weschler, *A Miracle, a Universe*, 198.

16. Viñar and Viñar, *Fracturas de memoria*, 125.

17. Kordon et al., *La impunidad*, 27.

18. In Lira, *Psicología y violencia política en América Latina*, 171–181.
19. Quoted in Viñar and Viñar, *Fracturas de memoria*, 14.
20. Quoted in Fisher, *Mothers of the Disappeared*, 145.
21. LIC begins with counterinsurgency and extends to economic, political, military, and psychological operations, both overt and covert. It represents a commitment by U.S. policymakers to employ force in its global attempts to suppress third-world revolutionary movements and governments; see Klare and Kornbluh, *Low Intensity Warfare*.
22. The specific data used in this description of the various indicators of impunity in the Southern Cone are from the following issues of North American Congress on Latin America, *Report on the Americas* 26, no. 3 (December 1992); 26, no. 4 (February 1993); 27, no. 3 (November/December 1993); 27, no. 6 (May/June 1994); 28, no. 1 (July/August, 1994); 28, no. 2 (September/October 1994); 29, no. 6 (May/June 1996). Also see Horacio Verbitsky, *La posguerra sucia: Un análisis de la transición* (Buenos Aires: Editorial Legasa, 1987), and Pablo Giussani, *Menem: Su lógica secreta* (Buenos Aires: Editorial Sudamericana, 1990).
23. For monthly reports and analyses of the situation in Nicaragua, see *Envío* (Universidad Centroamericana, Managua, Nicaragua).
24. Hugo Achugar, "Postdictatorship, Democracy, and Culture in the Uruguay of the Eighties," in Sosnowski and Popkin, *Repression, Exile, and Democracy*, 234.
25. In Abuelas de Plaza de Mayo, *Filiación, identidad, restitución*, 166–173.
26. See John Ross, *Rebellion from the Roots: Indian Uprising in Chiapas* (Monroe, Maine: Common Courage Press, 1995).
27. Information on the new social movements in Latin America can be found in North American Congress on Latin America, *Report on the Americas* 25, no. 5 (May 1992); 27, no. 2 (September/October 1993); 27, no. 4 (January/February 1994). I want to thank Juan Carlos Volnovich and my colleague Marjorie Bray, both of whom cautioned me not to idealize peoples' struggles and the role they play in changing history. Juan Carlos, for example, is cautious about the import of peoples' struggles in the elimination of the military dictatorships, arguing that although people did mobilize to oust them, the militaries had, in fact, fulfilled their historical function and could withdraw to the barracks with the conviction that the articulate opposition to the neoliberal project had been eliminated and that their civilian heirs to political power would continue their basic policies. Marjorie reminded me that although new social movements have, indeed, appeared, they have been fraught with problems that should not be ignored. I thank them both for their measured assessments—especially given that each identifies with these movements for social change—but in defense of my highlighting peoples' struggles, I quote renowned U.S. historian Howard Zinn, who writes in his preface to *The Twentieth Century: A People's History* (New York: Harper & Row, 1980), "If history is to be creative, to anticipate a possible future without denying the past, it should, I believe, emphasize new possibilities by disclosing those hidden episodes of the past when, even if in brief flashes, people showed their ability to resist, to join together, occasionally to win. I am supposing, or perhaps only hoping, that our future may be found in the past's fugitive moments of compassion rather than in its solid centuries of warfare" (xi).
28. Quoted in "First Argentina, Now Chile: A Nation Looks Back in Anger," *Los Angeles Times*, 3 June 1992.
29. Quotes in this paragraph and the next are from "Argentina: Chilling Reminder of 'Dirty War,' " *Los Angeles Times*, 13 March 1995.
30. Elizabeth has presented many papers on this subject at Latin American and international conferences. For an example of how this subject is approached in work with abuse survivors in the United States, see L. A. Pearlman and K. W. Saakvitne,

Trauma and the Therapist: Countertransference and Vicarious Traumatization in Psychotherapy with Incest Survivors (New York: Norton, 1995); also see Dinora Pines, "Working with Women Survivors of the Holocaust: Affective Experiences in Transference and Countertransference," *Revista Psicológica* 42, no. 4 (1985).

31. For a provocative feminist critique of Tato's play by a U.S. professor of Spanish and comparative literature, see Diana Taylor, "Spectacular Bodies: Gender, Terror, and Argentina's 'Dirty War,'" in Miriam Cooke and Angela Woollacott, eds., *Gendering War Talk* (Princeton, N.J.: Princeton University Press, 1993), 20–40.

32. Langer, *From Vienna to Managua*, 192.

Epilogue

1. For sources that contain these and the following statistics about the distribution of wealth in the contemporary United States, see Michael Levi, Bureau of Labor Statistics, internet: http://stats.bls.gov/eag.table.html, and Donald L. Bartlett and James B. Steele, series "Who Stole the Dream?"in the *Philadelphia Inquirer*, 15 September 1996, internet: http://www.phillynews.com/packages/america96/free/ NOFRAMES. For a more detailed analysis, see Donald L. Bartlett and James B. Steele, *America: What Went Wrong?* (Kansas City, Mo.: Andrews & McMeel, 1992). Also see Stephanie Coonz, *The Way We Never Were: American Families and the Nostalgia Trap* (New York: Basic Books, 1992), 272, also Chapter 11.

2. Bartlett and Steele, "Who Stole the Dream?" section entitled "The Burden of the Working Woman," 1.

3. Quoted from the 1996–1997 edition of the Department of Labor's biannual publication *The Occupational Outlook Handbook*, in Bartlett and Steele, "Who Stole the Dream?" Also see John Cavanagh et. al., eds., *Trading Freedom: How Free Trade Affects Our Lives, Work and Environment* (San Francisco: Institute for Food and Development Policy, 1992), and Doug Henwood, "Impeccable Logic: Trade, Development and Free Markets in the Clinton Era," in North American Congress on Latin America, *Report on the Americas, (Window of Opportunity)* 26, no. 5 (May 1993): 23–29. For an elaboration of the downside of the global economy for working people and what might be done, see William Greider, *One World, Ready or Not: The Manic Logic of Global Capitalism* (New York: Simon & Schuster, 1996) and Jerry Mander, ed., *The Case against the Global Economy: And for a Turn toward the Local* (San Francisco: Sierra Club Books, 1996).

4. For these and other statistics and an analysis of violence in the United States, see the National Mental Health Association, *Violence in America: A Community Mental Health Response*, internet: http//www.worldcorp.com/dc-onlinemnha/prvention/ previol.html.

5. Quoted in Noam Chomsky, "Introduction," in Jennifer Harbury, *Bridge of Courage* (Monroe, Maine: Common Courage Press, 1993), 2–3. For an analysis of the institutional sources of U.S. public complicity in aggressive U.S. foreign policy, see Douglas V. Porpora, *How Holocausts Happen: The United States in Central America* (Philadelphia: Temple University Press, 1990). Currently a struggle is being waged by citizens to close the School of the Americas in Fort Benning, Georgia, where many Latin American military men are trained in counterinsurgency methods. For an analysis of how taxpayers' dollars fund Washington lobbying by foreign governments that are violators of human rights, see Pamela Brogan, *The Torturers' Lobby: How Human Rights-Abusing Nations Are Represented in Washington* (Washington, D.C.: Center for Public Integrity, 1992). For an assessment of the changing role of U.S. corporate capital in Latin America and in the rest of the world in the face of rising competition from Japanese, German, and Taiwanese capital, see Liz Dore and John Weeks, "The Changing Faces of Imperialism," in North Ameri-

can Congress on Latin America, *Report on the Americas* (*Injustice for All: Crime and Impunity in Latin America*) 30, no. 2 (September/October 1996): 10–15.

6. See Ross, *Rebellion from the Roots*.

7. See the series of articles by Gary Webb in the *San Jose Mercury News*, 18, 19, and 20 August 1996. However, in 1997 these allegations are in dispute.

8. An extraordinary amount of documentation exists regarding the involvement of the CIA and other agencies of the United States government in drug operations that have funded military strategies in Asia, the Middle East, and Latin America. See Jonathan Marshall, Peter Dale Scott, and Jane Hunter, *The Iran-Contra Connection: Secret Teams and Covert Operations in the Reagan Era* (Boston: South End Press, 1987), and Celerino Castillo, *Powderburns: Cocaine, Contras & the Drug War* (Oakville, Ont.: Mosaic Press, 1994); also see the Academy Award winning documentary *The Panama Deception*. Jennifer Harbury, a U.S. attorney married to Guatemalan revolutionary Efrain Bamaca Velasquez, waged a courageous campaign to force the U.S. government to investigate the role of the CIA in her husband's torture-murder by the Guatemalan military as well as its involvement in the murder of one and the torture of another U.S. citizen in Guatemala. Although a presidential advisory panel ruled that there was no clear evidence of the CIA's involvement, Director John M. Deutch was obliged to order his staff to justify their missions in Latin America.

9. A number of studies critically analyze the impediments to authentic democracy in this country; see, for example, Noam Chomsky, *Deterring Democracy* (London and New York: Verso, 1991), and his *Letters from Lexington: Reflections on Propaganda* (Monroe, Maine: Common Courage Press, 1993); Michael Parenti, *Democracy for the Few* (New York: St. Martin's Press, 1995), his *Dirty Truths: Reflections on Politics, Media, Ideology, Conspiracy, Ethnic Life and Class Power* (San Francisco: City Lights Books, 1996), and his *Inventing Reality: The Politics of the Mass Media* (New York: St. Martin's Press, 1986); William Greider, *Who Will Tell the People: The Betrayal of American Democracy* (New York: Simon & Schuster, 1992). For an analysis of the growing concentration of capital in huge conglomerates and their control over the mass media, see *The Nation* (special issue on the media, *The National Entertainment State*), (June 3, 1996); the issue contains a four- page graph illustrating the centralization of power and thus of decision making about content and information in the mass media.

10. Quoted in Bertram Gross, *Friendly Fascism: The New Face of Power in America* (Boston: South End Press, 1980), 331.

11. See "Terrorizing the Constitution," *The Nation*, 25 March 1996, 11–15.

12. For an analysis of the restrictions on civil liberties inherent in the Antiterrorism and Effective Death Penalty Act, see the National Committee Against Repressive Legislation, *The Bill of Rights at Risk* (1996); for information, 3321 Twelfth St. NE, Washington, D.C. 20017.

13. The text of the Universal Declaration of Human Rights may be found on the internet: http://www.worldcorp.com.

14. See *On a Permanent International Criminal Court*, internet: http://www.web.apc.org, and *The World Court* (International Court of Justice at The Hague), internet: www.web.apc.org/pgs/pages/unicci.html, 3.

15. See North American Congress on Latin America, *Report on the Americas* (*Reinventing Solidarity*) 28, no. 5 (March/April 1995).

16. Global Exchange, *An Information Packet on Nike's Overseas Labor Practices and the Impact of Globalization* (1996); for information, 2017 Mission St. #303, San Francisco, Calif. 94110. For background, see Kevin Danaher, *Fifty Years Is Enough* (Boston: South End Press, 1994). Similar campaigns are being carried out against Oshkosh and other U.S. corporations that rely on low-cost labor in Central

American free-trade zones—areas created so that U.S. corporations can enjoy tax benefits, employ low-cost labor, and export their manufactured products tax-free into the United States. A campaign is being organized to press the U.S. Agency for International Development, which uses taxpayers' money to build free-trade zones, to ensure that workers' rights are respected. For information about grass-roots organizational activities and how to participate in actions that affect national policy, see the weekly publication *The Nation Alert*; internet: http://www. thenation.com. For a critique of U.S. policy toward Latin America and policy recommendations for a just and equitable alternative, see Lisa Haugaard, *Better Neighbors: A Blueprint for Just U.S. Relations with Latin America and the Caribbean* (Washington, D.C.: Latin America Working Group, 1996).

17. See, for example, Nancy J. Chodorow, *The Reproduction of Mothering* (Berkeley: University of California Press, 1978) and her *Feminism and Psychoanalytic Theory* (New Haven, Conn.: Yale University Press, 1989); Jessica Benjamin, *The Bonds of Love: Psychoanalysis, Feminism and the Problem of Domination* (New York: Pantheon Books, 1988), and her *Like Subjects, Love Objects: Essays on Recognition and Sexual Difference* (New Haven, Conn., and London: Yale University Press, 1995). Also see Dorothy Dinnerstein, *The Mermaid and the Minotaur: Sexual Arrangements and Human Malaise* (New York: Harper Colophon Books, 1963), and *Psychoanalytic Dialogues* (special issue on gender) 1, no. 3 (1991).

18. See, for example, Louise Eichenbaum and Susie Orbach, *Understanding Women: A Feminist Psychoanalytic Approach* (New York: Basic Books, 1983), and Women's Therapy Centre Institute, *Eating Problems* (New York: Basic Books, 1994).

19. Herman, *Trauma and Recovery*, 9

20. Philip Cushman offers a fascinating study of the historical emergence of the self as a cultural construct and persuasively argues that, as a social institution, psychotherapy in the United States reproduces many of the problems it intends to cure. In his *Constructing the Self, Constructing America: A Cultural History of Psychotherapy* (Reading, Mass.: Addison-Wesley, 1995), Cushman urges his colleagues to recognize "the remarkably intertwined nature of the cultural, moral, political and psychological in human beings. If our eyes are closed to all that, psychotherapy is nothing more than an effective tool of the status quo. But if we can open our eyes, or rather lift them and see more of what is possible, we will be able to move toward a critical, subversive, and perhaps even occasionally 'constructive' moral discourse" (356).

21. An articulate and persuasive argument concerning these and related themes may be found in Neil Altman's important work, *The Analyst in the Inner City: Race, Class, and Culture through a Psychoanalytic Lens* (Hillsdale, N.J., and London: Analytic Press, 1995).

22. See the classic study by Joel Kovel, *The Age of Desire: Case Histories of a Radical Psychoanalyst* (New York: Pantheon Books, 1981), and the groundbreaking study by Eugene Victor Wolfenstein, *Psychoanalytic-Marxism: Groundwork* (New York and London: Guilford Press, 1993). For a British vision of this integrative trend within psychoanalysis, see Michael Rustin, *The Good Society and the Inner World: Psychoanalysis, Politics and Culture* (London and New York: Verso, 1991). Also, the British journal *Free Associations: Psychoanalysis, Groups, Politics, Culture*, published in cooperation with Guilford Publications, addresses the interface between social and psychological reality.

Index

About the Author

Nancy Caro Hollander lived in Buenos Aires for extensive periods between 1969 and 1974, and has traveled widely in South and Central America. She is professor of history at California State University, Dominguez Hills, where she teaches Latin American history and women's studies. She is a clinical affiliate of the Psychoanalytic Center of California and is in private practice in Los Angeles.

Hollander has published articles on a variety of topics, including patriarchal capitalism and women in Latin America, the historical significance of Eva Perón, the psychological impact of political repression, the history of psychoanalysis in Argentina, and the life and work of Marie Langer. She translated Marie Langer's major work on women and wrote an extensive biographical essay; it was published in English as *Motherhood and Sexuality*. Hollander has also been active in community organizations that have educated the U.S. public about the political, economic, and social turbulence in Central America. From 1981 to 1996, she produced and hosted a biweekly, one-hour radio program on Pacifica Radio, in which she explored themes related to feminism, Latin American social and political struggles, and psychoanalysis.

Hollander lives in Los Angeles with her husband, Stephen Portuges, a psychologist and psychoanalyst, and her son, Rafael, a middle-school *aficionado* of soccer.